Digital Education

Palgrave Macmillan's Digital Education and Learning

Much has been written during the first decade of the new millennium about the potential of digital technologies to produce a transformation of education. Digital technologies are portrayed as tools that will enhance learner collaboration and motivation and develop new multimodal literacy skills. Accompanying this has been the move from understanding literacy on the cognitive level to an appreciation of the sociocultural forces shaping learner development. Responding to these claims, the **Digital Education and Learning Series** explores the pedagogical potential and realities of digital technologies in a wide range of disciplinary contexts across the educational spectrum both in and outside of class. Focusing on local and global perspectives, the series responds to the shifting landscape of education, the way digital technologies are being used in different educational and cultural contexts, and examines the differences that lie behind the generalizations of the digital age. Incorporating cutting-edge volumes with theoretical perspectives and case studies (single authored and edited collections), the series provides an accessible and valuable resource for academic researchers, teacher trainers, administrators and students interested in interdisciplinary studies of education and new and emerging technologies.

Series Editors:

Michael Thomas is Senior Lecturer at the University of Central Lancashire and Editor-in-Chief of the *International Journal of Virtual and Personal Learning Environments* (IJVPLE).

Marc Prensky is an internationally acclaimed speaker, writer, consultant, futurist, and visionary in the areas of education and learning. He is the author of *Teaching Digital Natives: Partnering for Real Learning* (2010).

James Paul Gee is Mary Lou Fulton Presidential Professor at Arizona State University. His most recent book is *Policy Brief: Getting Over the Slump: Innovation Strategies to Promote Children's Learning* (2008).

Digital Education
Edited by Michael Thomas

Digital Education

Opportunities for Social Collaboration

Edited by
Michael Thomas

DIGITAL EDUCATION
Copyright © Michael Thomas, 2011.

All rights reserved.

First published in 2011 by
PALGRAVE MACMILLAN®
in the United States—a division of St. Martin's Press LLC,
175 Fifth Avenue, New York, NY 10010.

Where this book is distributed in the UK, Europe and the rest of the world,
this is by Palgrave Macmillan, a division of Macmillan Publishers Limited,
registered in England, company number 785998, of Houndmills,
Basingstoke, Hampshire RG21 6XS.

Palgrave Macmillan is the global academic imprint of the above companies
and has companies and representatives throughout the world.

Palgrave® and Macmillan® are registered trademarks in the United States,
the United Kingdom, Europe and other countries.

ISBN: 978–0–230–11158–5

Library of Congress Cataloging-in-Publication Data

Digital education: opportunities for social collaboration / edited by
Michael Thomas.
    p. cm.
ISBN 978–0–230–11158–5 (hardback)
    1. Internet in education. 2. Online social networks. I. Thomas, Michael,
1969–

LB1044.87.D55 2011
371.33'467—dc22   2010035430

A catalogue record of the book is available from the British Library.

Design by Newgen Imaging Systems (P) Ltd., Chennai, India.

First edition: March 2011

10 9 8 7 6 5 4 3 2 1

Printed in the United States of America.

LIST OF PREVIOUS PUBLICATIONS

The Reception of Derrida: Translation and Transformation

Handbook of Research on Web 2.0 and Second Language Learning

Interactive Whiteboards for Education: Theory, Research and Practice (with Euline Cutrim Schmid)

Task-Based Language Learning and Teaching with Technology (with Hayo Reinders)

Contents

Illustrations

Figures

Tables

Foreword

In the 1980s and 1990s, many scholars were noting the revolutionary potential of new information and communication technologies for transforming human communication and production of knowledge. Yet, even by the turn of the millennium, only a fraction of the world's population had access to the Internet and fewer still were able to publish material online. One decade later, though, Internet access has quadrupled to reach more than a quarter of the world's people, and hundreds of millions around the world are using new Web 2.0 tools, such as wikis, blogs, microblogs, and social network sites, to connect, create, remix, and share. The "read-write" vision of Internet pioneers (i.e., that the Web would be a site not only for information retrieval but also for mass creativity and participation) is starting to come to fruition.

What then is the role of Web 2.0 in education? Much discussion of technology in education *understates* its potential by only considering how its use may or may not accelerate the achievement of extant learning goals. As Seth Godin wisely warns on *Seth's Blog*, "A car is not merely a faster horse. And email is not a faster fax...And Facebook is not an electronic rolodex." We need to "play a new game, not the older game but faster." At the same time, we are also in danger of *overstating* the potential of technology, by getting swept up in its ability to enthrall our students whether or not any positive results are achieved.

Digital Education introduces a healthy corrective to exaggerated techno-optimism or techno-pessimism. The thought-provoking edited collection represents one of the first serious attempts to examine how Web 2.0 may not only improve but also help transform education. Contributors to the book bring a wide range of social theory to the task, from realms of education, communication, cultural studies, and media studies. And they apply this theory to examining incipient efforts to deploy Web 2.0 tools in a broad range of formal educational settings, especially at the tertiary and adult level. Chapters from and about

Australia, Canada, Germany, Indonesia, South Africa, Spain, the UK, the United States, and Venezuela result in a diverse international discussion that is not common in educational research, and this breadth helps us to better understand the relationship of theory to practice.

Speaking from diverse countries and contexts, the authors challenge the simplistic notion that all twenty-first century students are "digital natives" who effortlessly learn with new technology, and instead illuminate the complexities of promoting digital literacies among today's learners. They show how students' access to, participation with, and fluency in the use of new technologies do not in themselves guarantee that any serious learning is taking place. Rather, as pointed out throughout and emphasized in the conclusion, the latter also requires educators or mentors to provide expert scaffolding, expert modeling, and expert critique. Examples abound in the book of how we might begin to do so.

Finally, although the contrasts between today's Web 2.0 and the first-generation Web are great, from a broad historical perspective they represent a continuation of older trends from plain text to multimedia, from static to dynamic content, from authorship by an educated elite to mass authorship, and from high costs of entry into the public sphere to low ones. The long trajectory of these changes and their significance for human development make it even more important that we critically evaluate their relationship to education. The contributions in this book represent an especially broad and thoughtful overview of where we have come on these issues and where we stand today.

MARK WARSCHAUER

CHAPTER 1

Digital Education: Opportunities, Challenges, and Responsibilities

Michael Thomas

Enter some classrooms today, and you will see that instructors have made great efforts to integrate digital technologies in order to enhance learners' access to information and collaborative activities. In others, the start of the class can be compared to boarding an airplane: learners are expected to sit down and immediately switch off all of their electronic devices.

This book is an attempt to address many of the important questions, contradictions, and opportunities related to digital education and to consider them from the perspective of different learning contexts and international researchers around the world. The chapters collected in this volume present numerous reasons to explore, in particular, the responsibilities educators must assume in the digital age. The first part of the book includes chapters mainly from a theoretical perspective, focusing in particular on digital literacy (chapter 2), existing research studies on Web 2.0 in education (chapter 3), adult education (chapter 4), educational networking (chapter 5), and a model for technology integration based on mentoring (chapter 6).

Five more chapters are included in the second part of the book, which address particular research-based or practical applications of digital technologies in more detail: virtual and personal learning environments (chapter 7), virtual worlds (chapter 8), Web 2.0 in an Asian context (chapter 9), social media (chapter 10), and social networking sites (chapter 11). In the final chapter, Stephen Bax presents a critical appraisal of many of the assumptions of digital education and looks forward to its future prospects.

Twenty years ago, first as an undergraduate and then a graduate student, I walked to the university library to search for books for my essays and dissertations. Generally, I saw books as a trustworthy and authoritative source of information. Today, students faced with a similar task intuitively head straight to their computers and open an Internet browser to access an online library before going to campus, if they cannot first read the article or book online. Indeed, a recent study of first-year students' online search habits in Australia (Judd & Kennedy, 2010) reported that they relied on Google and Wikipedia about 80 percent of the time. When asked further, however, to rank the Web sites they least trusted in terms of information accuracy, Google and Wikipedia were at the top of the list of sites identified.

The term "digital native," popularized by Marc Prensky in his 2001 essay, is now a decade old, and while even in 2010 it is the subject of major conferences, it has provoked vociferous critique from academics in recent years, suggesting that researchers are no longer willing to accept the taken-for-granted assumptions of the educational marketplace (see chapter 12). Similarly, Web 2.0 technologies burst onto the scene less than half a decade ago, and while a great deal of potential exists in areas such as virtual worlds, blogging, wikis, and podcasting, they are still used by a minority rather than a well-informed majority of instructors or learners (see chapter 3). Indeed, in a recent survey of 4,600 professors in the United States, the only technology instructors regularly used was a course management system (CMS) such as Blackboard, usually as little more than a repository for course documents and information. According to the *Chronicle of Higher Education*, "Only 13 percent of the professors surveyed said they used blogs in teaching; 12 percent had tried videoconferencing; and 13 percent gave interactive quizzes using 'clickers,' or TV-remotelike devices that let students respond and get feedback instantaneously" (Young, 2010, n.p.). Faced with such a sobering reality it is necessary to deconstruct terms such as "digital education," "digital literacies," and "Web 2.0" and to examine ways of applying them in a wider range of educational contexts as well as how to embed them in the curriculum, long after the vendors promoting them have left the scene (Ito et al., 2010).

The attempt to integrate new technologies is affected by a number of factors, and they have been strongly in evidence once again in the emergence of digital education: the speed at which educational technologies move in and out of fashion; the cost of acquiring and developing them;

the effort needed to train teachers to use them; and the time needed to adapt existing learning resources to new systems (see chapter 6). If we follow the logic of the airplane analogy introduced above, it is easy to see how technology, in particular digital technologies, can be used as a mechanism for *control* (see chapters 7 and 11). Digital, wireless, and mobile technologies can clearly also be a source of distraction in the classroom, whether in the form of mobile phones, handheld games machines, electronic dictionaries, or laptop computers. They can also be used by teachers to control learners and content or by administrators to control teachers with the aid of virtual learning environments (VLEs). At the same time, techno-enthusiasts would argue that digital technologies can be used to promote learner autonomy and creativity (see chapters 9 and 10).

The constant overload of information made possible by the Web has foregrounded the importance of learning how to *filter* information; this process is equally applicable to the hype surrounding digital education itself, and we need to distinguish what can be applied in education from the unhelpful revolutionary rhetoric. What is important, as even a cursory understanding of the history of educational technologies suggests (Cuban, 1986), is establishing the right balance between these opposing tendencies—drawing on the infectious enthusiasm while tempering it with a central role for instructors as more than mere facilitators who enable learning to take place (see chapter 12). As Weller (2009) has pointed out in this regard, we need to be aware of the centralization/decentralization dilemma that has underpinned much of the history of educational technology—the opportunity to balance the use of technology for controlling learners as well as for promoting autonomy, collaboration, and creativity; we might add, of course, that this has also been true of the history of education in general, from Plato to Web 2.0.

Indeed, in *The Republic* (1955), Plato sets out three main aspects of his philosophy that remain relevant for educators in the digital as well as any other age. First, educators must be truly engaged with the act of teaching as a moral duty. Second, educators must be highly knowledgeable in their subject areas but underline that learning stems from an active and dialogical process of questioning rather than mere knowledge transfer. Third, education should be seen as a lifelong endeavor and can best be understood in the wider context of the learning society.

While the iconic cover of *Time* magazine in January 2007 depicting a computer screen as a reflecting mirror announced the arrival of Web 2.0 technologies in the popular imagination, the reflecting mirror of user-generated content can also be seen as something of a narcissistic mirror—one in which educators and learners need to reestablish a balance between opportunities for self-expression, speaking the truth to power, and responsibility. In order to understand the possible futures of digital education, we must consider the past rather than risk repeating it. While this dictum has rarely been used in association with the application of technology to learning, it ought to remain uppermost in the minds of digital educators.

In *Oversold and Underused* (2001), Larry Cuban describes the introduction of a multimillion-dollar learning environment called the Stanford Center for Research, Development, and Teaching (SCRDT) at Stanford University in the late 1960s. Federal funds were used to build a "state-of-the-art" television studio consisting of cameras, videotape recorders, and monitors. In addition, a large-group instruction (LGI) room shaped like an amphitheater was built to accommodate 160 students. Beside each seat, a "student responder" was positioned consisting of a punch-button controller with the numerical digits 1–10, and the letters Y, N, and O inscribed on it. At the front of the room there was a stage with a large screen and a lectern for the teacher, and two large TV screens were suspended from the ceiling. For technical assistance, the teacher could draw on the technician who was seated in a glass-paneled room at the back of the amphitheater. Assistance ranged from increasing the sound to simultaneous interpretation and help with data projection. The student responders were aimed at allowing students to interact with the lecturer by replying to his/her questions—"do you understand?" "Am I speaking too quickly?"—or to multiple choice questions using the numerical scale. According to Cuban, the "data went directly to a mainframe computer, where students' responses were immediately compiled and displayed at a console on the professor's lectern. The lecturer was then able to adjust the pace and content of the presentation, based on feedback from this advanced interactive technology" (p. 100). By the early 1970s, however, the student consoles were already disconnected and had become merely "toys that students fiddled with during boring lectures"; the rest of the equipment was unused or had fallen into a state of disrepair. By the early 1980s, almost all of the original equipment had been removed, and the student responders "had become a harmless anachronism that an occasional professor could cite as an example of a passing technological fad." Significantly, by 2001, the room had become something of historical interest as an "archeological slice of a technological past," and was being used as a regular lecture hall, not significantly different from those from the previous century. Cuban's enquiries to Stanford faculty about the use of the facilities suggest that very "few professors had been involved in the design of the building or LGI" and that as "a result, only 2 of 35 professors in the School of Education had ever used the machinery back when it was operational" (p. 101). Over a short period of time, the original support staff for the facilities were made redundant as federal funding dried up. When the technology broke down, there was no one left to repair them, and equipment rapidly became out-of-date as newer machines came on the market.

Cuban's narrative presents in many respects a fascinating case study on the risks facing any attempt to integrate learning technologies and a counterweight to all the transformational rhetoric that has all too often accompanied Web 2.0 technologies in particular. In keeping this perspective in mind, as well as the real opportunities for increased social collaboration offered by emerging technologies (Davies & Merchant, 2009), it is hoped that this book will contribute to timely debates on the future of digital education in order that instructors, learners, and policymakers can learn from, rather than merely repeat, the mistakes of the past.

References

Cuban, L. (1986). *Teachers and machines: The classroom use of technology since 1920.* Teachers College, Columbia University: New York & London.

Cuban, L. (2001). *Oversold and underused: Computers in the classroom.* Cambridge, MA, & London: Harvard University Press.

Davies, J., & Merchant, G. (2009). *Web 2.0 for schools: Learning and social participation.* Frankfurt: Peter Lang.

Ito, M. et al. (2010). *Hanging out, messing around, and geeking out: Kids living and learning with new media.* Cambridge, MA: MIT Press.

Judd, T. S., & Kennedy G. E. (2010). Expediency-based practice? Medical students' reliance on Google and Wikipedia for biomedical inquiries. *British Journal of Educational Technology.* doi:10.1111

Plato (1955). *The republic.* London: Penguin.

Weller, M. (2009). The centralization dilemma in educational IT. *International Journal of Virtual and Personal Learning Environments, 1*(1), 1–9.

Young, J. R. (2010). Reaching the last technology holdouts at the front of the classroom. *Chronicle of Higher Education*, July 24, 2010. Retrieved July 24, 2010, from http://chronicle.com/article/Reaching-the-Last-Technology/123659/

PART I

Theoretical Perspectives

CHAPTER 2

Modified, Multiplied, and (Re-)mixed: Social Media and Digital Literacies

Mark Pegrum

Introduction

The way educators talk about "literacy" has changed. More and more often, we pluralize it or preface it with adjectives—or both. Actually, this is not entirely new. Literacy started to multiply decades ago, giving rise, for example, to visual literacy, media literacy, and, more lately, information literacy. Paul Gilster, who popularized the term "digital literacy," called it into service as a book title as far back as 1997 (Gilster, 1997). It is a process that led logically to the New London Group's (2000) promotion of "multiliteracies." And it is a process that has recently gained speed and urgency, thanks to the proliferation of digital tools and platforms like blogs, wikis, social sharing and social networking sites—in short, social media built "on the ideological and technological foundations of Web 2.0" and promoting "the creation and exchange of User Generated Content" (Kaplan & Haenlein, 2010, p. 61).

Yet it is no easy matter to deal with the explosion of contemporary modes of literacy driven by social media. In the new millennium, literacy is simultaneously more important and more complex than ever before. Long gone are the days when basic functional literacy was sufficient for everyday life. In networked, postindustrial societies, holding down a job, staying connected with friends, and keeping up with the latest information demands competence in a wide swathe of literacies, active as well as passive. And participation is not optional: Those who lack appropriate literacies barely exist in digital culture and are doomed to hover on the fringes of digital societies and digital economies.

But surely there is little danger of that happening to today's students? Surely the younger generation is dragging the rest of us, kicking and screaming, into the technological millennium? So the myth that has grown up around the "digital generation" would have us believe. Like many myths, it is built around a kernel of truth: Young people have a strong impetus to connect and socialize with their peers online, as adults increasingly bar them from traditional play spaces and hangouts like parks and malls (boyd, 2008; Watkins, 2009); they have plenty of time to develop expertise through tinkering with technology; and they do not have a pre-digital mind-set about how technology can or should be used. Unsurprisingly, researchers find that youth are heavy users of participatory digital technologies and that some young people have built up considerable know-how in this area (Ito et al., 2010). Early indications from an ongoing CIBER project suggest that young net users are increasingly "crowdsourcing" their knowledge (Krotoski, 2010), effectively drawing it from their online social networks, while new research by Accenture (2010) demonstrates that many young people are making extensive use of digital technologies, or expect to do so, in the workplace.

For all that, in the public imagination the "digital generation" has been unhelpfully mythologized in at least three ways. First, a growing body of research shows that factors like gender, race, language, geographic location, socioeconomic status, and education level complicate easy assumptions about young people's access to and use of technology (e.g., Australian Communications and Media Authority, 2008; Hargittai, 2010). The "digital generation," in other words, is far less homogenous than the term implies (e.g., Hague & Williamson, 2009; Livingstone, 2009). Second, just because kids are using technology for social and entertainment purposes, it does not mean they are acquiring the critical literacies necessary to use it for educational or professional purposes, or that they fully understand its affordances and pitfalls (The Committee of Inquiry into the Changing Learner Experience, 2009; Hague & Williamson, 2009). In short, many kids are "tech-comfy" but, with limited exceptions—notably a substantial minority who "geek out" (Ito et al., 2010) in remix culture, and whom we will come to later—they are not "tech-savvy" (Dudeney, 2009; Pegrum, 2009). Third, many adults are far more technologically accomplished than many kids and, indeed, remix culture, which is often seen as the hallmark of the younger generation, may be better viewed as a loose partnership between older and younger digerati (cf. Ito et al., 2010), with less digitally able youth acting mainly as a receptive audience and/or viral agents for its spread.

So we should not be duped by the sight of fingers flying across keypads or keyboards. If we fall for the "myth of the cyberkid" (Facer & Furlong cited in Livingstone, 2009, p. 70), we will fail to realize how patchy many young people's technological knowledge is. And, as a result, we will fail kids in their need to acquire digital literacies. If we want to ensure that the old digital divide does not simply reconfigure itself around literacy issues, we have to start addressing new literacies more systematically and more extensively in the classroom. While certainly not intended as a checklist of discrete literacies, this chapter maps out some of the key, often overlapping, areas we must consider in preparing students of all levels to make the most of their potential in a Web 2.0 world.

Focus on language

The Web is not (just) writing. The Web is not (just) a book. The Web is not (just) a library. Yet the Web is largely about writing, is partly a book, and is, among many other things, a library. *Print literacy* remains a core literacy, not just offline but also online, where a high level of competence in traditional skills—the ability to write eloquently, communicate clearly, and argue persuasively—is essential to hold your readers' attention in a Web article, present yourself authentically on a blog, or carry a point in a controversial Wikipedia entry. Although such skills are grounded in the print era, they can also be trained digitally. Students at lower levels can begin to develop a public identity on individual or class blogs, with those at higher levels maintaining interactive diaries, debating controversial topics in discussion forums, or building collaborative projects on a class wiki. Advanced students could post to public blogs, discussion boards, or wikis, with their work being assessed not only on its accuracy or coherence but on its appropriateness, persuasiveness, and overall contribution to the interactive digital context.

Although traditional print literacy skills remain important, language use online is changing in some ways. Netspeak, or textspeak—or indeed "txtspk"—is emerging as a new linguistic register that is perfectly suited to its context of rapid textual communication on the net or mobile phones. Rather than repressing its use, a codeswitching approach to *texting literacy* in the classroom would show students when and how to switch into and out of txtspk. In the case of language learners, this would help them access everyday usage, a little like studying idioms in

---

the target language. In the case of native speakers, it would allow them to make use of preexisting txtspk skills as appropriate, while raising their awareness of contextual issues like those flagged up by the English teacher in the following email exchange that took place with a final year secondary school student in Australia in mid-2009 (names have been changed). It is a classic example of an educator seizing a "teachable moment" to deliver contextualized input:

> hey Ms S, im not at school 2da. cn u mark my essay and ill fix it 4 thur. cheers Fred
>
> Fred,
> We have discussed this in class before. Consider your audience and the task. Try again.
> Miss S.
>
> Hi Ms. Smith,
> I am not at school today because I have dental and medical appointments,
> Please find attached a draft of my essay; I know you don't have much time but if you could please just take a quick look over it to see if my structure and links are good that would be really helpful!
> Thanks a lot,
> Fred

Punctuation is changing too. Hyperlinks, suggests Weinberger (2009a), can be seen as a new form of punctuation, one that, unlike most punctuation, tells us how to continue rather than where to stop. But the effects of hyperlinks go well beyond this. They often serve to indicate the main points of emphasis of a text and can shift, subtly or strongly, the weight of its arguments. They signal how open a text is, how interwoven it is with other texts around it and, depending on which sources have been linked to, they tell us something about its credibility and balance. Of course, hyperlinks can impact negatively on the narrative coherence of a reader's experience online—with each link giving the reader an opportunity to depart and, perhaps, not return—at the same time as they impact positively on a reader's autonomy. Students need to acquire *hypertext literacy* to analyze and evaluate such text, and, increasingly, they will need to learn how to punctuate their own digital writing with hyperlinks that amplify and bolster their messages.

Multiple literacies, or *multiliteracies*, as promoted by the New London Group (2000) and others, have a dual focus. On the one hand, "multiliteracies" can refer to the multiple languages and cultures with which we come into contact through new communication channels and media; literacy, after all, is not just about one's native language. On the other hand, "multiliteracies" can refer to the newly prominent literacies that occasionally supersede, but in most contexts complement, print literacy's modern(-ist) emphasis on letters and words: visual literacy, audio literacy, video literacy. Although these are unlikely to ever entirely eclipse print literacy, they will continue to gain in relative importance as the age of print recedes. Visual literacy, broadly defined, merits special consideration. With research showing that young net users are easily impressed by slick Web design (Livingstone, 2009, p. 74, p. 133), they are in need of guidance on how to interrogate visual elements. Visual literacy is also fundamental to reading the Web's proliferating tag clouds, not to mention its visual search displays, and it will be at the core of the ensemble of literacies all net users will need if—as in some predictions of the "geospatial Web" or "3D Internet"—the future Web grows to resemble a virtual world navigated by avatars. Multiliteracies can be usefully complemented by *media literacy* to promote a critical understanding of traditional media and advertising, which often work in multimodal formats with the accent on the visual. It is worth noting that multiliteracies will be crucial, too, at the point where the Web meets the world (O'Reilly & Battelle, 2009), giving us both the "Internet of things" (where physical objects are integrated into the net) and augmented reality (where Web-based information is overlaid on the "real" reality around us). It has even been suggested that the skills necessary to navigate this new informational universe powered by embedded, embodied devices will include *physical literacies* (Sandford, 2009, pp. 12–13). Certainly, we will all need multiple, enmeshed skills of perception and analysis.

But multiliteracies are not just passive skills. A person who can consume but not produce media, suggests Henry Jenkins, should not be considered literate (Lacasa, 2010). Students can sharpen their multiliteracy skills by using Web 2.0 tools like blogs or wikis to create multimedia documents; by not just listening to or watching but actively producing podcasts and vodcasts; by building multimedia narratives in digital storytelling formats; and, perhaps most productively of all, by engaging in a simplified version of what Jenkins (2008) calls "transmedia storytelling," where they would learn to express their developing ideas across multiple media. Thus, at different stages of a project, they might individually or collaboratively produce written (hyper-)texts, slideshows, or audio or video files. Language learners could introduce the target language(s) into the mix, learning to codeswitch between tongues at the same time as they learn to codeswitch between semiotic modes (Hampel & Hauck, 2006).

Naturally, multiliteracies must be underpinned by a certain level of *technological literacy*, that is, the ability to use common Web 2.0 and other software, and the ability to adapt to new software as it becomes available. Ideally, technological literacy should be complemented by a deeper level of *code literacy* (i.e., the ability to read and write computer code). Code literacy may play a significant role in a digital divide reconstituted around literacy issues, with those competent in this area most easily able to escape the template-style strictures of commercial software; circumvent the censorware of meddlesome governments (Newton, 2009); and tailor digital channels to their own expressive and communicative needs (Prensky, 2008). This raises teacher training issues, but perhaps none is so pressing as the need for a shift of mind-set: Teachers must be ready to work in partnership with their students, combining their own pedagogical expertise with whatever levels of technological expertise their students bring to the classroom, especially those students who are already code literate.

Focus on information

It is not only language that is changing online. So, too, are the ways we access and assess information. Most people's online experiences begin with a search engine or portal. However, few possess the *search literacy* to make the most of search engines, for example by using finely differentiated search terms, opting for visual displays, or seeking multimodal results. Few are aware of the limitations of search engines, like their frequent commercial bias or their reliance on ruthless popularity contests that may disenfranchise minority perspectives. The hit or miss nature of many young net users' information searches (Livingstone, 2009, pp. 50–52; Weigel, James, & Gardner, 2009, p. 10) is compounded by an overreliance on the triumvirate of the Web (typically their first and only source of information), Google (typically the only search engine used, in its basic rather than its advanced formats) and Wikipedia (typically the first result in a Google search) (Carr, 2009). That does not mean that the Web, Google, and Wikipedia are not useful tools; but like all tools, they are better tailored to some contexts than others. We need to help students move outside their comfort zones to explore and critique a wide set of search engines: visual search engines like Quintura or Tag Galaxy; metasearch engines like Gnosh or WebCrawler; or a searchroll creator like Rollyo. Even if students opt to return to Google for their own searches, they will have a better sense of what Google (and all search engines) can and cannot offer them, and what they themselves must bring to the search process.

Of course, it is only possible to search for information that has been indexed, and the way we index information is shifting rapidly as we move away from the top-down, hierarchical taxonomies typical of Web 1.0 toward the bottom-up, organic folksonomies associated with Web 2.0. The latter depend on the principle of tagging. Students need a degree of *tagging literacy* to help them grasp the nature of "feral data" (Education.au, 2009)—that is, uncontrolled tags—and to appreciate the pros and cons of tag clouds, which may be flexible and extensible but simultaneously vague and inconsistent. Ultimately, students must learn to read taxonomies and folksonomies with and against each other (Pegrum, 2009, p. 37), juxtaposing the orderliness of the former with the openness of the latter. It is important, too, that students have the visual literacy not only to read tag clouds, as noted earlier, but to parse the many new applications, from Wordle to WordSift, which work with a tag cloud metaphor. In addition, students must become effective taggers themselves, recording metadata that will enable them to manage their own online journeys as well as contributing to managing the connections among disparate parts of the digital global storehouse. Students can begin making these contributions from within classroom walls, by publishing class folksonomies, adding to public folksonomies, or simply learning to carefully tag their own materials online.

Assessing information is just as important as accessing it. This is where the metaphor of the Web as a book or a library breaks down: All of us need to stop treating online documents as if they were pages in a book or books in a library. "[D]uring the Age of Paper," says Weinberger (2009b, n.p.), "we got used to the idea that authority comes in the form of a stop sign: You've reached a source whose reliability requires no further inquiry." But online texts are different, even if they are based on offline models. Take Web encyclopedias: Wikipedia tells us, for instance, that a kangaroo is "a marsupial from the family Macropodidae"; Conservapedia tells us that "[a]fter the Flood . . . kangaroos bred from the Ark passengers migrated to Australia"; and Uncyclopedia tells us that a kangaroo is "a FRIGGIN' HUGE MOUSE" (Pesce, 2007a, 2007b). There is not a lot of common ground here. In short: On the Web there is a pressing need for *information literacy* or, as Rheingold (2009c) calls it in a twist on an Ernest Hemingway quote, "Crap Detection 101."

The Web calls for a commonsense approach, with students assessing online information in light of what they already know. This means they require a baseline of knowledge to help them contextualize and evaluate new information. It turns out, then, that being able to look up everything is no good reason for not memorizing anything. Beyond this, students must learn to notice and see through slick graphic design; they must learn to evaluate the origins, authorship, history, accuracy, objectivity, completeness, currency, and relevance of every digital document they encounter; and they must learn to compare any given online source with other sources, online or offline. There is little doubt that "triangulation" is the future of information seeking. Unsurprisingly, given that the three encyclopedias cited above are online documents, the last two kangaroo entries have changed slightly from the 2007 versions quoted, and any of them might be (further) changed at any moment by just about any net user in the world. Reading the multivoiced, provisional, evolving documents of Web 2.0 as if they were edited, finished, stable print documents is another common failure of information literacy (Pegrum, 2009, p. 37). One way of developing students' skills is to start with spoof websites like those about *Dihydrogen monoxide* (www.dhmo. org) or the *Pacific Northwest Tree Octopus* (zapatopi.net/treeoctopus/), both of which have trapped many students in the past (e.g., Krane, 2006), before moving on to the analysis and evaluation of more challenging materials. Students must learn that people bend and stretch the truth to suit their contexts and purposes; and they must learn how, in the absence of gatekeepers like librarians or teachers, they can still find information that is suitable for their own contexts and purposes. In a sense, this is what information literacy is all about.

To be fair, we should give students the good news along with the bad. Approached the right way, digital documents can help liberate us from the tyrannical sanctity of print. Tracing the development of news stories through blogs and mainstream media is instructive in uncovering the shaping of journalistic "Truth." Wiki history and discussion pages reveal all the drafts written, all the points revised, and all the arguments buried in the process of constructing the current version of the "Truth" as presented on the main wiki pages themselves (Doctorow, 2008, pp. 169–170, on Wikipedia). We can encourage students to approach "Truth" backwards—deconstructively, if you like—by following its data trail into the past, an approach which will certainly give them, and indeed all of us, a healthier attitude toward the many "Truths" we encounter every day.

Yet there is simply too much information available for us to be able to access it all, let alone assess it. We are drowning in a morass of facts, figures, and opinions, many of them of questionable validity. Consider the number of terms coined in the last decade or so to highlight various aspects of what, back in 1970, Alvin Toffler (Toffler, 1970) called "information overload": information fatigue syndrome (Lewis, 1996, cited in Naish, 2008, p. 17); data smog (Shenk, 1997); infomania (Wilson, 2005, cited in "Infomania," 2005); Facebook fatigue (e.g., Malik, 2007); news fatigue (The Associated Press & the Context-Based Research Group, 2008); infobesity (Naish, 2008, p. 25); information obesity (Whitworth, 2009); and stream fatigue (Iliffe-Moon, 2009). What we have is information, lots of it. What we do not have is enough attention: "Value now lies not in information, but in its relevance: filtering, sorting, contextualizing that which 'speaks to us' " (Sasaki, 2009, n.p.). Or, as Shirky (2008b) put it in the title of his paper at Web 2.0 Expo NY: "It's Not Information Overload. It's Filter Failure." What is missing here is *filtering literacy.*

"If the news is that important, it will find me," one US college student observed recently (cited in Stelter, 2008, n.p.). Increasingly, we need to set up filters that ensure that the right information does make its way to us and we are not left drowning in a morass of data that exceeds our capacity to deal with it. First, we need to filter relatively static Web sources, which might include identifying and relying on appropriate mediation by librarians, editors, critics, journalists, or teachers. Second, we need to filter the real-time Web, keeping up with breaking news, which might involve setting up RSS feeds from trusted media sources, perhaps organizing those feeds through applications like RSS Voyage; keeping up with social news sites such as Digg or Reddit, perhaps focusing our attention through applications like OurSignal or Stack; or setting up Google Alerts for key terms trending in the news, on blogs, or on the Web at large. Third, we need to filter our own social networks, or, more exactly, to begin to understand our social networks *as* filters that can feed us commentary from our Facebook friends, our LinkedIn contacts, or those we follow on Twitter. Students would benefit from educational guidance on all these aspects of filtering.

Unsurprisingly, we are starting to hear discussions of *attention literacy* (Rheingold, 2009a). When confronted with too much undifferentiated information, we can become distracted by details and miss larger patterns (Wasik, 2009). There is growing evidence of the inefficiency and inaccuracy of multitasking, its advantages for lateral thinking notwithstanding (Small & Vorgan, 2008; Watkins, 2009). We are seeing rising stress levels (Stone, 2008) and a rise in attention-deficit disorders and their symptoms (Hallowell, 2007; Small & Vorgan, 2008). All of this suggests that from time to time we need to turn down or even switch off the flow of information and communication in order to create space to reflect. Any moderately sophisticated understanding of digital technologies must include an understanding of when, for personal, social, educational, or health reasons, to turn them off. This, too, is something we must communicate to students.

Focus on connections

If not having your own story is tantamount to being unfulfilled in late modern society (cf. Giddens, 1991), not having your own digital story is tantamount to not existing at all in digital culture—or being, at best, an object of stories others tell about you, or an extra in stories others tell about themselves. *Personal literacy* (Burniske, 2008) is therefore a crucial metaliteracy that empowers individuals to develop and shape their online presence. Only by gaining facility with digital literacies are we able to craft a Web presence that represents who we are or want to be, while reducing the risk of being misread or misunderstood. Students can be encouraged to experiment with self-presentation on blogs or in digital stories, in the process developing the digital public voices that will be essential to their professional and social futures. In this context, an understanding of media literacy, as mentioned earlier, will help students appreciate the extent to which commercially prepackaged roles and identities are being marketed to them online (Mayo & Nairn, 2009; Montgomery, 2007). Young people need to be warned, too, of threats to their digital identities from commercial and political surveillance and data mining (Martin, 2008, p. 174). Digital safety, as we will see, must be a core consideration.

The available evidence suggests that, far from being isolating, Internet use, especially for the younger generation, is largely about maintaining and strengthening social connections (Ito et al., 2010; Watkins, 2009). It is likely the future of the Web will be less about Google's algorithms than Facebook's vision of "a more personalized, humanized Web, where our network of friends, colleagues, peers, and family is our primary source of information, just as it is offline" (Vogelstein, 2009, p. 1). Indeed, social media are all about this kind of connectivity. Already, more and more of us are obtaining more and more of our information not through third party news websites but through our social networks: 33 percent of net users obtain news through Facebook and 19.5 percent through Twitter, according to one 2009 survey (MacManus, 2009; cf. Evangelista, 2010), while a 2010 report indicates that 75 percent of online news consumers receive news forwarded through email or social networking sites (Purcell et al., 2010). Consequently, social search—that is, search that ranks information based on its relevance to members of your social networks—has become a holy grail for Google and the other search giants of today.

Social media consultant Jerry Michalski advises: "Trust your community to filter and flow the right things to you when you need them" (cited in Hemp, 2009, p. 86). As Hemp notes, this works because Michalski "has at his disposal a set of powerful and personalized filters: social networks that gather, select, and value information for him." Michalski is a frontrunner of an emerging trend. To deal with information overload, our networks can—and must—become our filters. As the swing toward the social web continues, the result will be that if you belong to large and diverse social networks, you will be well informed; but if you do not, you will not. To put it another way: If, as indicated in the CIBER study mentioned earlier, many young people are already crowdsourcing their knowledge, then the number and range of their sources matter. "The connections we participate in form our identities," says Siemens (2010, n.p.). "We—you, I—know what our networks know." *Network literacy* is about knowing how to leverage your digital networks to stay informed and to obtain particular information (and even active support) as the need arises. But it is also about how far your own voice will carry as you "feed the network of people who follow you," as Rheingold (2009b, n.p.) writes of Twitter. In other words, network literacy is not just passive but is an active and empowering mode of literacy that allows individuals to shape their networks at the same time as they are shaped by them, and to leave their imprint on others' informational and communicative environments. The old offline saying is more relevant than ever online: The more people you know, the more things you can do. On the Web, it will come down, more and more, to networking.

That is the first reason we must not shut off access to Facebook and Twitter, MySpace and YouTube in schools and libraries: While kids from socioeconomically advantaged backgrounds will go home and begin to build their digital social and informational networks there, those from less privileged backgrounds will fall further and further behind (Ito et al., 2010, pp. 345–350; Pegrum, 2009, p. 61, p. 78). As the 2009 *Horizon Report* puts it: "Increasingly, those who use technology in ways that expand their global connections are more likely to advance, while those who do not will find themselves on the sidelines" (Johnson, Levine, & Smith, 2009, p. 5). If one of the purposes of education is to level the social playing field, it is crucial that we do not unwittingly help the digital divide to reconfigure itself around network literacy (which would compound any trend toward its reconfiguration around code literacy, as discussed earlier). While there are many promising ways of exploiting online networks in education, as emphasized in Siemens' (2005) work on connectivism, perhaps the most pressing educational intervention needed is just to give students time, space, and encouragement to begin building their own online networks.

Nevertheless, there are dangers here: If you open yourself to the network, you also expose yourself to the network. That, indeed, is the second reason we must not shut off access to Facebook and Twitter, MySpace and YouTube in schools and libraries. Most kids will find their way into these online spaces at some point, and we can either leave them to go it alone without any adult guidance, or we can be there when they take their first steps, offering advice on the advantages of such spaces as well as warnings about their inherent dangers. Opportunity and risk are correlated for youth online (Livingstone, 2009); we must find ways to maximize the former while minimizing the latter. At its best, the Internet provides space for experimenting with personal identity and exploring connections to others; at worst, it is a spatial and temporal panopticon (Mayer-Schönberger, 2009), which may tie users to past experiments and indiscretions forever. But it is not just about the information we intentionally put online. If, as suggested by a recent MIT study, a look at Facebook friend lists can accurately predict sexuality (Johnson, 2009), students need to carefully consider how any and all of their personal data may be used with or without their knowledge or consent, now and in the future. As Pesce (2009, n.p.) has asked:

> Do teenagers really understand how to use the network to their advantage, how to reinforce their own privacy and protect themselves? Do they know how easy it is to ruin their own lives—or someone else's—if they abuse the power of the network, that amplifier and accelerator of sharing?

The short answer is "no." Network literacy, then, must include a component of digital safety. Teachers have a duty, first, to educate themselves in this area and, second, to open up conversations about privacy, surveillance, safety, and responsibility with their students. Fortunately, both public and private organizations are now producing materials to support just these kinds of conversations (Pegrum, 2010).

Tim Berners-Lee, creator of the World Wide Web, originally conceived of it as a "read/write" web, but it took more than a decade for the shift to occur from Web 1.0, the informational Web, to Web 2.0, the social Web. As barriers to participation were lowered, ordinary net users could finally become creators and communicators in their own right, thereby unleashing the need for the swathe of literacies canvassed in this chapter. We now find ourselves part of a participatory culture enabled, largely, by Web 2.0 and the social media that build on it:

> Participatory culture shifts the focus of literacy from one of individual expression to community involvement. The new literacies almost all involve social skills developed through collaboration and networking. (Jenkins et al., 2006, p. 4)

Readers are expected to be writers. Listeners are expected to be speakers. And the more people who write as well as read, and speak as well as listen, the greater the potential. In the words of *Wired* editor Kevin Kelly: "Nobody is as smart as everybody" (cited by Wesch in Bayne, 2009, n.p.). Or in the words of Page (2007): "Diversity trumps ability." Developing *participatory literacy* means coming to appreciate how you can contribute to collective intelligence through your use of tools like blogs, wikis, folksonomies, or virtual worlds. It means recognizing how each of us shapes the Web environment through our digital networks, whether they exist on social networking, social sharing, or microblogging sites. It means learning how to leverage both social media and digital networks as we move back and forth across the porous virtual/real divide, engaging with the wider world offline as well as online.

There has been considerable discussion of the potential for youth activism online (Bennett, 2008; Palfrey & Gasser, 2008). There is some cause for optimism: A 2009 Pew Internet study, for example, reported that 37 percent of net users aged 18–29 use blogs or social networking sites as venues for political or civic involvement (Smith, Lehman Schlozman, Verba, & Brady, 2009). Discussing the US presidential race of 2008, Watkins (2009) has detailed signs of rising youth political engagement both online and offline, with the former feeding into the latter. Indeed, it has been suggested that Barack Obama was elected on a technologically enabled collaborative (and not just representative) democracy platform, inviting direct engagement by all sections of the US population (e.g., Noveck, 2009). The development of a truly participatory society or culture certainly impacts on, and is impacted by, the teaching and learning of literacy. After all, as Baron (2009, p. 23) observes, "the technologies of literacy control not just who can read and write, but also what can and can't be said."

But it is not just about contributing ideas in political forums at the request of Barack Obama or anyone else. Armed with digital technologies on the one hand and a certain level of participatory literacy on the other, activists everywhere, with youth at their forefront, are rewriting the rules of political participation. In varied contexts around the world, ordinary citizens are turning their tools and their literacies to keeping those in power under surveillance—or more accurately *sous*veillance (i.e., observation from below)—and even taking part in self-organizing smart mobs (Rheingold, 2002) or flash mobs (Shirky, 2008a), which have, in the most dramatic cases, brought down governments. Small wonder that *Forbes* reported recently on "China's Web 2.0 nightmare" (Epstein, 2009). In 2009, Western media focused obsessively on the—still somewhat unclear—role played in the coordination of the Iranian post-election protests by Twitter (which postponed planned maintenance downtime at the request of the US Government), Facebook (which launched a Persian beta version) and Google (which added Persian to Google Translate). "This is the moment," said Clay Shirky, "where the world participates in world politics" (cited in Vargas, 2009, n.p.). Yet Web 2.0 did not carry the day for the Iranian protesters. All over the world, in fact, governments are cracking down on the free communication enabled by the Internet and turning the tools of surveillance against dissidents and dissenters. When protesters are faced with police and soldiers, guns and jails, is it enough for them—or their supporters abroad—to rally on Facebook or Twitter? Likely not. Yet, although Twitter protests are obviously most effective in countries that already have democratic structures in place (Morozov, 2009), it is hard to say, for now, what role digital tools and digital literacies might eventually play in opening up or undermining more restrictive regimes. When reflecting on the ultimately uncertain impact of international Web protests on Iran, blogger Chas Danner put it this way: "Imagine if Anne Frank had been able to get online" (cited in Vargas, 2009, n.p.).

Participatory literacy is best taught through participation, and the ideal participatory tool is undoubtedly a wiki. After learning to collaborate on a wiki in a relatively safe classroom environment overseen by a teacher, students could venture onto the wider Web with assignments that encourage them to contribute information and insights derived from class research to Wikipedia, Simple English Wikipedia, or any number of other public wikis. Going further, and exploring the link between participatory literacy and participatory democracy, students could learn about civic engagement as they experience it first hand. For instance, they could hone their public voices by participating in social Web initiatives ranging from *TakingITGlobal* (www.tigweb.org) and *Blog Action Day* (www.blogactionday.org) to the US-based *Rock the Vote* (www.rockthevote.com) and the UK-based *Battlefront* (battlefront. co.uk). Of course, teachers must also prepare students for the darkly agonistic arguments and conflicts to which participatory culture sometimes gives rise (Lih, 2009, pp. 130–131; Pegrum, 2009, p. 39). Even more importantly, teachers need to warn students that in some contexts online activism carries risks of offline retribution. A responsible educational introduction to such a politicized and politicizing form of literacy must present its very considerable risks alongside its very considerable potential.

In a multilingual, multicultural world, participatory literacy overlaps with the multiliteracies touched on earlier. Ironically, the ebb and flow of languages and cultures online is leading to two real concerns. The first involves the increasingly polyglot nature of the Internet which—notwithstanding the continuing structural dominance of English and despite the apparent benefits of linguistic democratization—is beginning to throw up considerable barriers to international conversation, as Ethan Zuckerman observes (Funnell, 2009, n.p.). Joseph Lo Bianco has argued that "[t]here are two big disadvantages in this era of globalization: not knowing English if you're not a native English speaker, and being monolingual if you are an English speaker" (cited in Burgess, 2004, n.p.). This comment, made in a different context, applies absolutely to the linguistic diversification of the web. Urgent educational intervention is needed: Put simply, students must be given the opportunity to acquire and use foreign languages.

The second concern is that very different cultures will find more and more occasions to (mis-)communicate with each other online, and that we will see a continued rise in cultural clashes of the kind that have already started to occur (see Pegrum, 2009, pp. 82–83 for examples). Once again, urgent educational intervention is needed: Students must be given the opportunity to develop *cultural literacy,* which can help them "read" artifacts produced in a variety of cultural contexts, and *intercultural literacy,* which can help them communicate and negotiate more effectively with interlocutors from those contexts. For students of language(s) and culture(s), social media offer ideal tools for collaborative projects involving classes in different parts of the world. Examples abound of successful partnerships built on a variety of platforms, including discussion boards, blogs, wikis, podcasting, and vodcasting.

At the same time, more research is needed in this area. On the one hand, cultural and especially intercultural literacy have to be underpinned by an attitude of epistemological humility (Ess, 2007)—effectively, an acknowledgment that one's own perspective on the world is not the only, or even necessarily the best, one. On the other hand, such an attitude is itself reflective of a particular (often, but certainly not exclusively, Western) cultural positioning, which may sit uncomfortably with more absolute cultural or faith-based attitudes. Work is therefore essential on how to deal with the incompatibilities which may exist in cross-cultural partnerships, and how to turn clashes of perspectives into teachable moments. This is all the more vital because on a small planet with large problems we need to find ways of working collaboratively toward global solutions. Education must be our starting point.

Focus on remix

> If in analog times it was cool to *own* lots of books or music records or movies, in the digital age it is cool to *build on them*—to take the artifacts of our information culture and combine them into something new, something original. (Mayer-Schönberger, 2009, p. 61)

Remix involves taking preexisting images, sounds, and video from the culture around us and combining them in new ways to create new meaning (Lessig, 2007). As Lessig notes, TV and movie producers have long been able to do this; what has changed is that the tools of remix have been democratized, giving ordinary users of Web 2.0 a powerful voice. *Remix literacy* is, of course, a metaliteracy. Remix draws on a mind-boggling array of multiliteracies and on the media literacy necessary to decode cultural products. Its viral spread through networks, often in the form of memes (Lankshear & Knobel, 2006), takes network literacy to its logical conclusion, while its parodic politics push the expressive power of participatory literacy to an extreme. For those who possess the literacy skills to encode and decode its sophisticated and subversive messages, it is a powerful medium of social, cultural, and political communication.

Remix is, arguably, the hallmark of digital culture. It is often seen, too, as the hallmark of the digital generation. Yet, as discussed above, the construct of the "digital generation" is flawed on at least three counts: It ignores the diversity of youth access and use; it elides the distinction between the tech-comfy and the tech-savvy; and it overlooks adult expertise. To establish the nature of the link between youth and remix, we need to consider these points one by one.

On the first count: Two widely cited surveys by the Pew Internet & American Life Project show that the proportion of young online content creators rose from 57 percent of US 12- to 17-year-olds in 2004 to 64 percent in 2006 (Lenhart & Madden, 2005; Lenhart, Madden, Rankin Macgill, & Smith, 2007). The latter figure includes 26 percent who had remixed online content—far from a majority but, at over a quarter, a substantial proportion, and one likely to have increased further in the intervening years. Many of these young remixers would be among those identified in Ito et al.'s (2010) landmark study for the MacArthur Foundation as having moved along the continuum from "hanging out" online (the majority youth practice) via "messing around" with media (a potential bridging process) to "geeking out" (developing real expertise in new media and technologies). Yet even those who just hang out or mess around play essential roles in remix culture: as a receptive audience with the skills necessary to decode remixes, and as viral agents who can spread them through digital networks. Remixes are part of the currency of youth socialization: Circulating and responding to them is integral to building online identities and relationships.

On the second count: There is little doubt that those who "geek out" on remixes develop technological savvy, but they also develop a certain level of cultural and social savvy, since geeking out is not only about circumventing technological restrictions but about pushing social and legal boundaries, as well as spreading subversive "alternative readings of media" (Ito et al., 2010, p. 71) as part of an increasingly widespread, culturally knowing game (Wasik, 2009). Remix, then, is a subcultural practice that is gradually going mainstream—much like hip-hop, a once subcultural movement that has also gone mainstream and, perhaps not coincidentally, trades heavily in remixes or "mashups." While those who only circulate and respond to remixes certainly do not develop the same level of digital literacies as those who create them, and probably remain more tech-comfy than tech-savvy, they must develop at least some interpretive skills to join in this shrewd cultural game.

On the third count: While Ito et al.'s (2010) study, focused mainly on US 12- to 18-year-olds, reports a high rate of youth involvement in participatory media, echoing the Pew Internet studies, the authors note there is also considerable adult involvement (pp. 10–11). Again, this is not unlike hip-hop, with its famous adult creators and legions of young amateur adopters. If many of the slickest examples of remix come from adults, who may be seen as models or mentors, some of the edgiest examples come from youth, whom Ito et al. describe as "taking the lead in developing social norms and literacies that are likely to persist as structures of media participation and practice that transcend age boundaries" (p. 12). This is supported by Pew Internet figures that indicate that although, as noted above, 26 percent of youth had remixed content online in 2006, in 2007 only 17 percent of adults had done so (Lenhart, Madden, Rankin Macgill, & Smith, 2007). Thus, remix is an example of an area where the expertise of some youth exceeds that of many, though certainly not all, adults, leading to a "struggle over authority and control over learning and literacy" (Ito et al., 2010, p. 14).

In short, although it is important not to make easy assumptions about the "digital generation" in general or the "remix generation" in particular, remix culture is strongly associated with youth. It is a culture, though, in which many adults participate and that is rapidly becoming normalized. It is also a culture that draws much of its inspiration and source material from older generations of artists, designers, and musicians. I have argued elsewhere that Web 2.0 can be seen as a late flowering of the 1960s ideals which infused the inception of networked computing but had to wait three decades for the technology to mature (Pegrum, 2009). In the same way, remix, as perhaps the ultimate instantiation of Web 2.0, can be seen as a late flowering of postmodernism, another child of the sixties. Remix is Dadaism gone global. It is Warhol democratized. It is about practices formerly open only to elite artistic outsiders and/or elite cultural insiders being appropriated by ordinary people with day jobs—or school timetables.

If such an amorphous phenomenon as remix can be said to have a single message, it is this: that there is no single message. Words and images, stories and ideas are mixed together in ways that may be humorous, surprising, or challenging—or some combination of these—and often add up to incisive commentary. Sometimes remix takes on social themes, deflating overstated claims or overweening perspectives, as in the viral "I'mma let you finish" parodies of Kanye West's spotlight-grabbing speech at the 2009 MTV Video Music Awards. Sometimes remix takes on religion's claims to singular truthful narratives, as in the YouTube video *Jesus Will Survive—Jesus Christ! The Musical,* by self-described "digital-guerrilla-filmmaker" Javier Prato (www.javierprato.com), who conflates Jesus' story with Gloria Gaynor's liberational anthem *I Will Survive,* now a gay staple. Very often, remix takes on politicians and their particular claims to singular truthful narratives. In 2008, when news started to trickle out about the Australian Rudd Government's plans to censor the Internet, young and not-so-young Australians flooded the Web with parodic remixes, photoshopping the prime minister's image onto Chairman Mao's *Little Red Book* and into *Big Brother* posters, giving him a guest role in a *South Park* videoclip, and ironically reframing and reworking quotes from literature, film, art, and advertising to signal their discontent. But it is not just rich Web surfers in developed countries who are expressing themselves in this way. In 2009, when the Chinese government announced plans to install Green Dam Youth Escort filtering software on all new computers, Chinese netizens started circulating their own mashed up images and videos, drawing on elements as diverse as pictures of the "river crab" (an animal whose name, with a change of tones in Mandarin, becomes "harmonious" and, in reference to Beijing's push for a "harmonious society," is used as a slang expression for Internet censorship) and the mythical "grass mud horse" (whose name, with a change of tones, becomes an obscenity), as well as Japanese pornographic manga and Western references to Orwell's *1984* or the game show *Who Wants to Be a Millionaire?* Such remixes are not about speaking the truth. Rather, they are about undermining easy truths. They are a key form of expression on Web 2.0, occurring beneath the radar of those who cannot read them but informing the cultural politics of those who do.

There is growing appreciation of the place of remix in education. Jenkins et al. (2006) include "remix" under "Appropriation," one of nine key skills they associate with participatory culture. Churches (2008) lists remix under "Creating," the top level of his reworked "Bloom's Digital Taxonomy." In becoming active creators rather than passive consumers of media, students are able to develop a public voice—and no form of literacy requires a broader digital skills base or offers more expressive options than the metaliteracy that is remix. In addition, students can activate their growing digital networks to circulate, adapt, and respond to the remix products they create. Given that so much of young people's experience online, especially in educational contexts, is so limited—trapped within the walled gardens of virtual learning environments or the templates of proprietary software—remix holds great potential to enrich their learning.

Naturally, remix has its enemies. It can be undermined from within by those who plagiarize, rather than borrow from, the preexisting culture around them. It can be undermined from without by the twentieth-century cultural industries, which, through copyright law and technological blocks, seek to maintain the inviolability—and the profitability—of their content. And it can be undermined by those who, schooled in the modernist paradigm of the print era, recoil at its parodic postmodern playfulness. Educators must be aware of these and other concerns. Yes, we must guide students as they venture out onto the wild Web in search of source material; yes, we must caution them on copyright and plagiarism issues; yes, we need to steer their energies into educationally acceptable cultural production; and yes, we need to talk to them about when, and how, they might achieve social and political goals through combining remix with more traditional strategies, rather than through remix alone.

All these things we can and must do. While we should be wary of its potentially explosive power, remix, if handled carefully, could form the ideal lynchpin for any digital literacies program, bringing together students' energy, multiple digital literacies, and a focus on the real-world issues which, as adults, our students will inherit.

Obstacles and opportunities

The Australian Government is promoting a *Digital Education Revolution*. The EU has been focusing on *e-Inclusion*. The UK is working toward a *Digital Britain*. All around the Western world, there is growing governmental awareness of the need, in broad terms at least, for education in digital skills. But many educational institutions continue to resist the entry of social media into the classroom, fearing for their students' safety and their own loss of control over learning. Many teachers avoid social media because they are unprepared to use Web 2.0 technology, unconvinced of its benefits, or unwilling to vary tried-and-tested approaches. Others, having experimented with social media, have already retreated in the face of technical glitches, digital safety issues, cultural clashes, or simply the challenge of dealing with students who know more about technology than they do. Some learners, and indeed some teachers, balk at the collaborative, interactive learning fostered by social media and associated literacies. And many observers, from parents to politicians, query the shift toward more fluid forms of group, peer, and self-assessment, which fly in the face of international moves toward standardization and accountability.

None of these obstacles is insurmountable, though some of the objections should give us pause for thought. There is a real need for preservice teacher training and in-service professional development, coupled with effective dissemination strategies for relevant knowledge and skills. But embracing new literacies and new pedagogies is not an all-or-nothing proposition: Traditional literacies and pedagogies must continue to have their place, with contextually sensitive teachers seeking a balance between old and new. That, too, is partly a training issue. There is also a need for teachers to engage in learner training, talking transparently about the whys and hows of their teaching. Assessment strategies need careful (re-)development. Educating students about digital safety must be a priority. And finally, some of the most intractable issues, like cultural clashes, have no generic solutions and require careful investigation by researchers.

Those of us who see the value in new literacies have a responsibility to demonstrate what is possible in our own classrooms; to act as viral agents for the spread of good practice; to make a convincing case to educational leaders for institutional support; to participate in action research aimed at understanding and overcoming the challenges inherent in new technologies; and to find ways of compensating for the dangers and risks, as outlined throughout this chapter, which some of the new literacies entail. In the end, of course, the technologies themselves matter less than the literacies they enable (Rheingold, 2008). All of us, our students included, need these literacies to navigate digital culture and express ourselves there. If we do not work with social media and the associated literacies, not only do we deprive students of considerable educational benefits, but we will find that, for students, literacies acquired outside the classroom will come to seem more relevant than those acquired within it—at least for those on the right side of the digital divide that will, inexorably, reconstitute itself around literacy.

Acknowledgments

I would like to thank two of my past students, Miles Gaby and Peta Ranieri, for examples cited in this chapter, and my current student, Tosca Chen, for her help with the translation of Mandarin terms into English. I have also benefited from discussions of connectivism and connectivity with my colleague, Rose Senior.

References

Accenture (2010). *Jumping the boundaries of corporate IT: Accenture global research on millennials' use of technology.* Retrieved February 12, 2010, from http://nstore.accenture.com/technology/millennials/global_millennial_generation_research.pdf

The Associated Press & the Context-Based Research Group (2008, June). *A new model for news: Studying the deep structure of young-adult news consumption.* Associated Press. Retrieved February 12, 2010, from http://www.ap.org/newmodel.pdf

Australian Communications and Media Authority (2008, September). *Telecommunications today. Report 6: Internet activity and content.* Canberra: ACMA. Retrieved February 12, 2010, from http://www.acma.gov.au/webwr/_assets/main/lib310210/report_6_telecommunications_today.pdf

Baron, D. (2009). *A better pencil: Readers, writers, and the digital revolution*. New York: Oxford University Press.

Bayne, G. (2009). A sense of purpose. [Interview with Michael Wesch.] *EDUCAUSE Review, 44*(5). Retrieved February 12, 2010, from http://www.educause.edu/er/WeschInterview

Bennett, W.L. (Ed.). (2008). *Civic life online: Learning how digital media can engage youth*. Cambridge, MA: MIT Press. Retrieved February 12, 2010, from http://www.mitpressjournals.org/toc/dmal/-/1

boyd, d. (2008). Why youth ♥ social network sites: The role of networked publics in teenage social life. In D. Buckingham (Ed.), *Youth, identity, and digital media* (pp. 119–142). Cambridge, MA: MIT Press. Retrieved February 12, 2010, from http://www.mitpressjournals.org/doi/pdf/10.1162/dmal.9780262524834.119

Burgess, R. (2004, April 15). Australia must attune to Asia's voice. [Interview with Joseph LoBianco.] *The Guardian Weekly*. Retrieved February 12, 2010, from http://www.guardian.co.uk/education/2004/apr/15/tefl

Burniske, R.W. (2008). *Literacy in the digital age* (2nd edition). Thousand Oaks, CA: Corwin.

Carr, N. (2009, January 22). All hail the information triumvirate! *Rough Type*. Retrieved February 12, 2010, from http://www.roughtype.com/archives/2009/01/all_hail_the_in.php

Churches, A. (2008, April 1). Bloom's taxonomy blooms digitally. *Tech & Learning*. Retrieved February 12, 2010, from http://www.techlearning.com/article/8670

The Committee of Inquiry into the Changing Learner Experience (2009, March). *Higher education in a Web 2.0 world*. The Committee of Inquiry into the Changing Learner Experience. Retrieved February 12, 2010, from http://www.jisc.ac.uk/media/documents/publications/heweb20rptv1.pdf

Doctorow, C. (2008). *Content: Selected essays on technology, creativity, copyright, and the future of the future*. San Francisco: Tachyon.

Dudeney, G. (2009, May 26). The Luddite codex. *That'SLife*. Retrieved February 12, 2010, from http://slife.dudeney.com/?p=238

Education.au (2009). Linking data worldwide. *3C: Creative, capable, connected, 4*(3), p. 3. Retrieved February 12, 2010, from http://enewsletter.educationau.edu.au/link/id/67825644b2065fb71389P60c305526e6b5983e5ed/page.html

Epstein, G. (2009, October 8). China's web 2.0 nightmare. [Interview with Zhao Jing.] *Forbes.com*. Retrieved February 12, 2010, from http://www.forbes.com/2009/10/08/china-internet-facebook-twitter-youtube-technology-beijing-dispatch.html

Ess, C. (2007). Liberal arts and distance education: Can Socratic virtue (ἀρετυ) and Confucius' exemplary person (*junzi*) be taught online? In J. Lockard & M. Pegrum (Eds.), *Brave new classrooms: Democratic education and the Internet* (pp. 189–212). New York: Peter Lang.

Evangelista, B. (2010, February 15). Facebook directs more online users than Google. *SFGate*. Retrieved February 15, 2010, from http://www.sfgate.com/cgi-bin/article.cgi?f=/c/a/2010/02/14/BUU51C0AMN.DTL

Funnell, A. (2009, December 10). One beast, many tongues. [Interview with Ethan Zuckerman.] *Future Tense.* ABC Radio National. Retrieved February 12, 2010, from http://www.abc.net.au/rn/futuretense/stories/2009/2761911.htm

Giddens, A. (1991). *Modernity and self-identity: Self and society in the late modern age.* Cambridge: Polity.

Gilster, P. (1997). *Digital literacy.* New York: John Wiley & Sons.

Hague, C., & Williamson, B. (2009, August). *Digital participation, digital literacy, and school subjects: A review of the policies, literature and evidence.* Bristol: Futurelab. Retrieved February 12, 2010, from http://www.futurelab.org.uk/resources/documents/lit_reviews/DigitalParticipation.pdf

Hallowell, E.M. (2007). *Crazybusy: Overstretched, overbooked, and about to snap! Strategies for handling your fast-paced life.* New York: Ballantine Books.

Hampel, R., & Hauck, M. (2006). Computer-mediated language learning: Making meaning in multimodal virtual learning spaces. *JALT CALL Journal, 2*(2), 3–18.

Hargittai, E. (2010). Digital na(t)ives? Variation in Internet skills and uses among members of the "net generation." *Sociological Inquiry, 80*(1), 92–113.

Hemp, P. (2009). Death by information overload. *Harvard Business Review, 87*(9), 82–89.

Iliffe-Moon, S. (2009, June 9, 12:29pm). @timoreilly @sarahm The consequence of many consecutive tweets [...] *Twitter.* Retrieved February 12, 2010, from http://twitter.com/SonaMoon/statuses/2093368519

"Infomania" worse than marijuana (2005, April 22). *BBC News.* Retrieved February 12, 2010, from http://news.bbc.co.uk/2/hi/uk_news/4471607.stm

Ito, M., Baumer, S., Bittanti, M., boyd, d., Cody, R., et al. (2010). *Hanging out, messing around, and geeking out: Kids living and learning with new media.* Cambridge, MA: MIT Press. Retrieved February 12, 2010, from http://mitpress.mit.edu/books/full_pdfs/Hanging_Out.pdf

Jenkins, H. (2008). *Convergence culture: Where old and new media collide* (new ed.). New York: New York University Press.

———, Clinton, K., Purushotma, R., Robison, A.J., & Weigel, M. (2006). *Confronting the challenges of participatory culture: Media education for the 21st century.* Chicago: The MacArthur Foundation. Retrieved February 12, 2010, from http://www.digitallearning.macfound.org/atf/cf/%7B7E45C7E0-A3E0-4B89-AC9C-E807E1B0AE4E%7D/JENKINS_WHITE_PAPER.PDF

Johnson, C.Y. (2009, September 20). Project "Gaydar." *The Boston Globe.* Retrieved February 12, 2010, from http://www.boston.com/bostonglobe/ideas/articles/2009/09/20/project_gaydar_an_mit_experiment_raises_new_questions_about_online_privacy

Johnson, L., Levine, A., & Smith, R. (2009). *The 2009 Horizon report.* Austin, TX: The New Media Consortium. Retrieved February 12, 2010, from http://www.nmc.org/pdf/2009-Horizon-Report.pdf

Kaplan, A.M., & Haenlein, M. (2010). Users of the world, unite! The challenges and opportunities of social media. *Business Horizons, 53,* 59–68.

Krane, B. (2006, November 13). Researchers find kids need better online academic skills. *UConn Advance*. Retrieved February 12, 2010, from http://advance.uconn.edu/2006/061113/06111308.htm

Krotoski, A. (2010, January 24). Democratic, but dangerous too: How the web changed our world. *The Observer*. Retrieved February 12, 2010, from http://www.guardian.co.uk/technology/2010/jan/24/internet-revolution-changing-world

Lacasa, P. (2010). Learning in a participatory culture: A conversation about new media and education (Part one). [Interview with Henry Jenkins.] *Confessions of an Aca-Fan*. Retrieved February 12, 2010, from http://henryjenkins.org/2010/02/_children_and_young_people.html

Lankshear, C., & Knobel, M. (2006). *New literacies: Everyday practices and classroom learning* (2nd ed.). Maidenhead, Berkshire: Open University Press.

Lenhart, A., & Madden, M. (2005, November 2). *Teen content creators and consumers*. Washington: Pew Internet & American Life Project. Retrieved February 12, 2010, from http://www.pewinternet.org/PPF/r/166/report_display.aspx

Lenhart, A., Madden, M., Rankin Macgill, A., & Smith, A. (2007, December 19). *Teens and social media*. Washington: Pew Internet & American Life Project. Retrieved February 12, 2010, from http://www.pewinternet.org/Reports/2007/Teens-and-Social-Media.aspx

Lessig, L. (2007, March). *Larry Lessig on laws that choke creativity*. TED Talks. [Posted November.] Retrieved February 12, 2010, from http://www.ted.com/index.php/talks/larry_lessig_says_the_law_is_strangling_creativity.html

Lih, A. (2009). *The Wikipedia revolution: How a bunch of nobodies created the world's greatest encyclopedia*. London: Aurum.

Livingstone, S. (2009). *Children and the Internet: Great expectations, challenging realities*. Cambridge: Polity.

MacManus, R. (2009, November 10). 40% of people "friend" brands on Facebook. *ReadWriteWeb*. Retrieved February 12, 2010, from http://www.readwriteweb.com/archives/survey_brands_making_big_impact_on_facebook_twitter.php

Malik, O. (2007, July 29). Why do we have Facebook fatigue? *GigaOm*. Retrieved February 12, 2010, from http://gigaom.com/2007/07/29/facebook-fatigue/

Martin, A. (2008). Digital literacy and the "digital society." In C. Lankshear & M. Knobel (Eds.), *Digital literacies: Concepts, policies and practices* (pp. 151–176). New York: Peter Lang.

Mayer-Schönberger, V. (2009). *Delete: The virtue of forgetting in the digital age*. Princeton: Princeton University Press.

Mayo, E., & Nairn, A. (2009). *Consumer kids: How big business is grooming our children for profit*. London: Constable.

Montgomery, K.C. (2007). *Generation digital: Politics, commerce, and childhood in the age of the Internet*. Cambridge, MA: MIT Press.

Morozov, E. (2009, November 4). Engaged society vs Twittering society. *Foreign Policy*. Retrieved February 12, 2010, from http://neteffect.foreignpolicy.com/posts/2009/11/04/engaged_society_vs_twittering_society

Naish, J. (2008). *Enough: Breaking free from the world of more*. London: Hodder & Stoughton.

New London Group (2000). A pedagogy of multiliteracies: Designing social futures. In B. Cope & M. Kalantzis (Eds.), *Multiliteracies: Literacy learning and the design of social futures* (pp. 9–37). London: Routledge.

Newton, M. (2009, September 20, 12:25am). People clever enough to bypass censorware [...]. *Twitter*. Retrieved February 12, 2010, from https://twitter.com/NewtonMark/status/4120005536

Noveck, B.S. (2009). *Wiki government: How technology can make government better, democracy stronger, and citizens more powerful*. Washington: Brookings Institution Press.

O'Reilly, T., & Battelle, J. (2009). *Web squared: Web 2.0 five years on*. O'Reilly Media. Retrieved February 12, 2010, from http://assets.en.oreilly.com/1/event/28/web2009_websquared-whitepaper.pdf

Page, S.E. (2007). *The difference: How the power of diversity creates better groups, firms, schools, and societies*. Princeton: Princeton University Press.

Palfrey, J., & Gasser, U. (2008). *Born digital: Understanding the first generation of digital natives*. New York: Basic Books.

Pegrum, M. (2009). *From blogs to bombs: The future of digital technologies in education*. Crawley, WA: UWA Publishing.

——— (2010). Digital safety. *E-language*. Retrieved February 12, 2010, from http://e-language.wikispaces.com/digital-safety

Pesce, M. (2007a, July 13). *The inconvenience of truth (Part one)*. Paper presented to Education.au. Retrieved February 12, 2010, from http://www.youtube.com/watch?v=yosf621RbT8

——— (2007b, July 13). *The inconvenience of truth (Part two)*. Paper presented to Education.au. Retrieved February 12, 2010, from http://www.youtube.com/watch?v=zhDoBPURkW8

——— (2009, October 1). Nexus. *the human network*. Retrieved February 12, 2010, from http://blog.futurestreetconsulting.com/?p=211

Prensky, M. (2008, February). Programming is the new literacy. *Edutopia*. Retrieved February 12, 2010, from http://www.edutopia.org/programming-the-new-literacy

Purcell, K., Rainie, L., Mitchell, A., Rosenstiel, T., & Olmstead, K. (2010, March 1). *Understanding the participatory news consumer: How Internet and cell phone users have turned news into a social experience*. Washington: Pew Internet & American Life Project. Retrieved March 10, 2010, from http://www.pewinternet.org/Reports/2010/Online-News.aspx

Rheingold, H. (2002). *Smart mobs: The next social revolution*. Cambridge, MA: Basic Books.

——— (2008, August 20). *Social media classroom*. Retrieved February 12, 2010, from http://vlog.rheingold.com/index.php/site/video/social-media-classroom-co-laboratory-screencast1/

——— (2009a, April 20). Attention literacy. *SFGate*. Retrieved February 12, 2010, from http://www.sfgate.com/cgi-bin/blogs/rheingold/detail?entry_id=38828

Rheingold, H. (2009b, May 11). Twitter literacy. *SFGate*. Retrieved February 12, 2010, from http://www.sfgate.com/cgi-bin/blogs/rheingold/detail?blogid=108&entry_id=39948

——— (2009c, June 30). Crap detection 101. *SFGate*. Retrieved February 12, 2010, from http://www.sfgate.com/cgi-bin/blogs/rheingold/detail?entry_id=42805

Sandford, R. (2009, October). *Robots, drugs, reality and education: How the future will change how we think*. Coventry: Becta. Retrieved February 12, 2010, from http://emergingtechnologies.becta.org.uk/upload-dir/downloads/page_documents/research/emerging_technologies/sandford_robots_report.pdf

Sasaki, D. (2009, July 2). The expansion of ignorance is inevitable. *el-oso.net*. Retrieved February 12, 2010, from http://el-oso.net/blog/archives/2009/07/02/the-expansion-of-ignorance-is-inevitable/

Shenk, D. (1997). *Data smog: Surviving the information glut*. San Francisco: Harper Edge.

Shirky, C. (2008a). *Here comes everybody: The power of organizing without organizations*. New York: Allen Lane.

——— (2008b, September 18). *It's not information overload. It's filter failure*. Web 2.0 Expo, New York. Retrieved February 12, 2010, from http://www.web2expo.com/webexny2008/public/schedule/detail/4817

Siemens, G. (2005). Connectivism: A learning theory for the digital age. *International Journal of Instructional Technology and Distance Learning, 2*(1), 3–10. Retrieved February 12, 2010, from http://www.itdl.org/journal/jan_05/Jan_05.pdf#page=7

——— (2010, March 9). Collapsing to connections. *Connectivism: Networked and Social Learning*. Retrieved March 10, 2010, from http://www.connectivism.ca/?p=234

Small, G., & Vorgan, G. (2008). *iBrain: Surviving the technological alteration of the modern mind*. New York: Collins.

Smith, A., Lehman Schlozman, K., Verba, S., & Brady, H. (2009, September 1). *The Internet and civic engagement*. Washington: Pew Internet & American Life Project. Retrieved February 12, 2010, from http://www.pewinternet.org/Reports/2009/15 – The-Internet-and-Civic-Engagement.aspx

Stelter, B. (2008, March 27). Finding political news online, the young pass it on. *The New York Times*. Retrieved February 12, 2010, from http://www.nytimes.com/2008/03/27/us/politics/27voters.html

Stone, L. (2008, January 9). Fine dining with mobile devices. *The Huffington Post*. Retrieved February 12, 2010, from http://www.huffingtonpost.com/linda-stone/fine-dining-with-mobile-d_b_80819.html

Toffler, A. (1970). *Future shock*. London: Bodley Head.

Vargas, J.A. (2009, June 23). Does "Tiananmen + web = Tehran"? *The Washington Post*. Retrieved February 12, 2010, from http://www.washingtonpost.com/wp-dyn/content/article/2009/06/23/AR2009062301355_pf.html

Vogelstein, F. (2009). Great Wall of Facebook: The social network's plan to dominate the Internet – and keep Google out. [Interview with Mark Zuckerberg.]

Wired, 17(7). Retrieved February 12, 2010, from http://www.wired.com/techbiz/it/magazine/17–07/ff_facebookwall

Wasik, B. (2009). *And then there's this: How stories live and die in viral culture.* New York: Viking.

Watkins, S.C. (2009). *The young and the digital: What the migration to social-network sites, games, and anytime, anywhere media means for our future.* Boston: Beacon Press.

Weigel, M., James, C., & Gardner, H. (2009). Learning: Peering backward and looking forward in the digital era. *International Journal of Learning and Media, 1*(1). Retrieved February 12, 2010, from http://www.mitpressjournals.org/doi/pdf/10.1162/ijlm.2009.0005

Weinberger, D. (2009a, June 29). *Truth and transparency.* New York: Personal Democracy Forum. Retrieved February 12, 2010, from http://www.youtube.com/watch?v=o3qSDLF6lU4

————— (2009b, July 19). Transparency is the new objectivity. *JOHO the Blog!* Retrieved February 12, 2010, from http://www.hyperorg.com/blogger/2009/07/19/transparency-is-the-new-objectivity/

Whitworth, A. (2009). *Information obesity.* Oxford: Chandos.

CHAPTER 3

Research on Web 2.0 Digital Technologies in Education

Chaka Chaka

Introduction

Even though Web 2.0 technologies such as blogs, podcasts, wikis, and social networking sites (SNSs) are globally leveraged for teaching and learning purposes (Chapman & Russell, 2009; Hunter, 2009; Melville et al., 2009; Redecker et al., 2009), there is yet to be a widespread adoption of these technologies in the higher education sector worldwide. A myriad of complex factors are implicated in this regard: the digital divide; uneven digital literacies; variable learner and staff backgrounds and capabilities; staff attitudes toward Web 2.0 technologies and their readiness to embrace them; and institutional infrastructure and support (Luckin et al. 2008; Melville et al., 2009). Despite this lack of universal adoption of Web 2.0 technologies by most higher education institutions (HEIs), and notwithstanding the complex factors implicated in this process, there are an increasing number of case studies emerging, indicating that they have wide-ranging applications for teaching and learning. As such, they are regarded as having value-added educational offerings or affordances for students and staff (Banister, 2008; Heer, 2009; Minicha, 2009). Among such affordances are, for example, personalized and problem-based earning, collaborative learning, collaborative writing, reflective and expressivist writing, supplemental learning, collective intelligence, and learner-created content.

However, some of these affordances are not exclusive to Web 2.0 technologies alone. Instead, they also characterize conventional and other forms of traditional learning. Moreover, the last two affordances are not solely educational in nature; they apply to other Web 2.0 contexts as well. For instance, they are ascribed to diverse users of Web 2.0 technologies for whom learner-created content becomes user-generated content. In spite of all this, these affordances tend to assume a pride of place when harnessed by Web 2.0 technologies within educational contexts as they help emphasize the same educational value these technologies have in relation to other traditional forms of learning. Most importantly, they also help highlight the added efficiencies of these technologies in teaching and learning, and to education in general (Crook et al., 2008; Heer, 2009). These last two points are exemplified by the educational affordances offered by the six Web 2.0 technologies employed in the twelve case studies discussed in this chapter and the teaching and learning purposes these technologies served in the context of their application. The six Web 2.0 technologies are blogs, podcasts, a microblog (e.g., Twitter), a collaborative writing tool (e.g., Google Docs and Spreadsheets, Google D & S), and two SNSs (e.g., Facebook and YouTube). These technologies were selected for their foregrounding of the following affordances: reflection, engagement, higher-order learning, and expressivist writing; problem-based learning (PBL) and pod creativity; language learning and use case; collaborative learning and concurrent collaborative spreadsheeting; supplemental learning and collaborative knowledge creation; and fostering multiple intelligences.

Web 2.0 digital technologies in education: A concise overview

A myriad of Web 2.0 technologies are currently used at numerous learning institutions for educational purposes around the world. Examples of such institutions are universities in the UK (Chapman & Russell, 2009; Crook et al., 2008), the European Union (Redecker et al., 2009), Australia (Hunter, 2009), the United States and South Africa (Melville et al., 2009).There are three generic senses with which Web 2.0 technologies are associated in this chapter. First, Web 2.0 technologies are, collectively, composite tools and applications harnessed by the participatory and Social Web that enable users to engage in a number of value-added user-driven services. Some of the main areas of focus for these technologies are participation, content creation/repurposing, sharing, and collaboration. Second, they are, mostly, convergent platforms hosting tools, applications, and features, and offer diverse customized uses, services, and data to potential users (Crook et al., 2008; Redecker et al., 2009; Simões & Gouveia, 2008). Third, Web 2.0 technologies are perennially in a beta state. They are never fully developed, thereby allowing users to add to their development (Chaka, 2009a, 2010a, 2010b; see Crook et al., 2008).

Overall, Web 2.0 technologies are a set of technologies complementing each other in their respective offerings. Typical examples, on the one hand, are blogs (weblogs), microblogs, instant messaging, podcasts, wikis, SNSs, tagging and social bookmarking, virtual worlds, massively multiplayer online games (MMOGs)/massively multiplayer online role-playing games (MMORPGs), mashups; RSS (really simple syndication), and VoIP (voice over Internet protocol). In contrast are instances such as SlideShare, Scribd, and Google D & S. This last set of examples represents presentation applications.

In relation to education especially, there are Web 2.0 technologies specific to and designed for educational use. Typical instances of such technologies are edublogs (educational blogs), educational wikis, and educational social networking platforms. These technologies are exemplified by Elgg, which is a multipurpose open-source blogging and social networking application (Franklin & Van Harmelen, 2007; Minocha, 2009); MediaWiki and PBWiki (Barsky & Giustini, 2007); the Mechanica blogging platform and wikiMechanica (Li & Suo, 2007); Connect, which is a social networking platform (Oradini & Saunders, 2008); Ning, which is a social networking platform used as an alternative to virtual learning environments (VLEs) (Minocha, 2009), and Eduspaces.

While Web 2.0 technologies are almost pervasive and ubiquitous in most developed countries, such technologies are not yet well entrenched in a developing region such as Africa. Mostly, efforts related to the use and application of Web 2.0 technologies in this region are, if anything, sporadic and individualistic initiatives offered at unit or course levels as opposed to a universal uptake of such technologies by universities and faculties. Added to this are the lack of infrastructure and the deepening digital divide characterizing most universities in Africa. In fact, it is now no longer access to the Internet per se that is a critical challenge for most African universities but it is the use (Harle, 2009) of Web 2.0 technologies and to what extent they have been embraced by academic staff. However, despite all this, there are instances of documented initiatives involving the use of certain Web 2.0 technologies for teaching and learning purposes at course or unit levels in certain African universities, especially in South Africa. Two such instances are Butgereit's

(2007, 2009) MXit and Bosch's (2009) Facebook initiatives. The first initiative—which is a joint venture between the Meraka Institute and the University of Pretoria's engineering students—entails the tutoring of mathematics through MXit. The latter is a mobile instant messaging service run on mobile phones. This project is targeted at previously disadvantaged high school learners who interact with Dr Math (a tutoring service) in attempting to learn mathematics outside of school hours. The second initiative relates to the use of Facebook by Film and Media Studies students and their engagement with their lecturer at the University of Cape Town.

In a different but related educational context, there are arguments for Education 2.0, Learning 2.0, and E-Learning 2.0 modeled on Web 2.0 technologies (Chaka, 2009b; Gokhale & Chandra, 2009). Similarly, there are views for both Education 3.0 (Keats & Schmidt, 2007) and the Educational Semantic Web, which tend to borrow from and emulate Web 2.0 and the Semantic Web respectively. These are all attempts to apply Web 2.0 digital technologies in educational contexts. Above all, the timeless beta state of Web 2.0 technologies tends to dovetail well with the notion of lifelong learning, which is an endless form of learning. Moreover, Education 2.0 is often contrasted with Education 1.0, both of which correspond, respectively, to Web 1.0 and Web 2.0.

Selected Web 2.0 technologies as applied in higher education institutions

First, this part presents a literature review of case studies that focus on the use of six selected Web 2.0 technologies. These six selected Web 2.0 technologies are blogs; podcasts, a microblog (e.g., Twitter), a collaborative writing tool (e.g., Google D & S), and two SNSs (e.g., Facebook and YouTube). The main objective of this section is to delineate both the educational benefits and shortcomings associated with such technologies as documented in the case studies reported here.

Blogs and podcasts

Blogs and podcasts (a blend of *iPod* and *broadcast*) as examples of Web 2.0 technologies have been trialed and used in many universities for teaching and learning purposes (Belanger, 2005; Carney, 2009; Edirisingha, Salmon & Fothergill, 2007; Quinn, Duff, Johnston & Gursansky, 2007; Vallance, Vallance & Matsui, 2009). While blogs may be deployed as stand-alone teaching and learning tools, podcasts are often used as supplementary learning resources. The latter also lend themselves well as device-neutral, platform-independent, online and offline resources. Additionally, they are both location and space independent. This section of the chapter, then, reports on seven case studies focusing on the use of blogs and podcasts in four universities highlighting the successes and failures.

Reflection and engagement through blogging

The first three case studies were conducted at the University of South Australia (UniSA) (Quinn et al., 2007). The first took place in 2006 with 32 students and was related to an online blog (the UniSA online journal blog) used in an elective course, *Aged Care and Social Work*. Its main objective was to develop students' reflective writing skills using blogs: It required students to reflect, after each lesson, on their learning through reflective writing skills. Throughout the duration of the course, students had to engage in regular journaling in their blogs, and this helped them develop their reflective writing. Thus, students were able to change their perceptions toward the aged through blogs, thereby exhibiting a transformative learning trajectory (Carney, 2009; Quinn et al., 2007).

The second case study (the CIS-Quest blog) was conducted in 2007 and initiated by UniSA's School of Computer and Information Sciences (CIS). It required commencing undergraduate students to search for a *treasure hunt* so as to orientate themselves to campus, school, learning, their careers, and each other. Students had to complete the quest and blog their experiences working in groups of six to ten, over two days. The groups were encouraged to develop content and use a discussion board to share their blogs. They also had to engage in a group reflection about the future of mobile telephony. All this was characterized by self-disclosure, creativity, and reflection. In this case study, blogs played a vital role in establishing both identity and social presence for students, and in building a community for students, academics, and university support staff (Carney, 2009; Murray & Hourigan, 2008; Quinn et al., 2007).

The third case study—the Scientists Write! blog—was initiated by learning advisers at UniSA. It was intended for a community of scientific writers (computers scientists and engineers), and its purpose was to foster academic learning and promote controversy and critique. Using Google Blogger, Scientists Write! brought together science academics, students, librarians, and learning advisers. Besides points of contention and controversy, Scientists Write! modeled the struggles experienced by scientific writers for new postgraduate students (Li & Suo, 2007; Quinn et al., 2007).

These case studies indicate that blogs have both benefits and short-comings as Web 2.0 teaching and learning tools. In respect of the former, Quinn et al. (2007) contend that blogs have the potential to serve various educational and communicative purposes (Carney, 2009). For example, blogs promote self-direction, active inquiry, independence, and individuality. In addition, they foster self/group reflection; they facilitate transformative learning; and they help students and teachers establish online communities of interest. Moreover, blogs, Quinn et al. (2007) maintain, encourage student engagement and enjoyment. However, there are drawbacks associated the deployment of blogs. First, as demonstrated by the three case studies, the effectiveness of blogs as teaching and learning tools is inchoate and compromised by limited and, sometimes, one-off anecdotal data sourced from a small sample of participants. If anything, such data are highly contextual and thus only applicable to the specific contexts from which they have been drawn. Second, while issues such as self-direction, reflection, independence, individuality, engagement, and enjoyment are essential for teaching and learning, they are nonetheless more meta-cognitive, meta-learning, and meta-methodological in nature.

Blogging and higher-order learning and blogs as expressivist and socio-cognitivist approach?

The fourth case study is Farmer, Yue, and Brooks' (2008) project, which explored the use of blogging in a large cohort, first-year arts subject at the University of Melbourne. Deploying a blogging system—*CultureBlogging*—as an integral part of learning in the Cultural Studies Program on a trial basis and involving more than 225 students, the case study set out to evaluate the effectiveness of blogs as a tool for facilitating higher-order learning skills in the first semester of 2007. *CultureBlogging* was preferred to other Web 2.0 applications as it was believed that it would offer the opportunity to promote meta-cognitive reflection on the part of students. Moreover, it was regarded as an appropriate tool that would enable students to engage in associative thinking necessary for contemporary culture and media. Thus, it was integrated into *Cultural Studies* as a formative assessment instrument (Banister, 2008; Farmer et al., 2007).

In this regard, the blog exercise constituted 30 percent of the final assessment grade, and students were required to maintain their blogs for the entire duration of their twelve-week-long semester. Students were also informed about the objective of the blog activity: to reflect upon and discuss course content and/or issues emanating from their learning experiences or to use their blogs for their own personal purposes as long as they avoided inflammatory or offensive content. The blog project had a 93 percent usage rate from participating students. Some of the preliminary results of the evaluation of the project sourced from such evaluation methods as online observation, content analysis and questionnaires, as reported by Farmer et al. (2007), included the following. First, judging by the quality of their blog entries, some students proved to be accomplished writers. Similarly, other students—albeit a few—produced creatively and critically reflective posts accompanied by multimedia and characterized by traditional prose. Second, the project supported the view that blogging is a valuable tool for large cohort university teaching. For instance, the project managed to facilitate student–student interaction in which students had to comment on each other's posts as a requirement for assessment.

On the downside, the following key observations were made. There was tension for teaching staff between wanting to support and offer sufficient pedagogic scaffolding and encouraging independent learner thought, commentary, and creativity. Students could not reach the expected level of self-reflexivity due to a lack of explicit guidelines about what constituted self-reflexivity. In addition, they could not engage the notion of identity as well as they were expected to. As such, they failed to critically and actively apply their contemporary culture and media knowledge and to integrate it into their intellectual growth (Farmer et al., 2007).

The fifth case study in this regard is Murray and Hourigan's (2008) blog project. Involving students enrolled for a second-year Language and Technology course at the University of Limerick in Ireland, the case study—which was initially a pilot study on the potential of blogs in second language acquisition—set out to identify specific pedagogical roles for blogs in language learning. The Language and Technology course draws students from diverse modern foreign languages courses: These range from Language and Cultural Studies, Applied Languages, Applied Languages and Computing, to Erasmus. The students span both lower-intermediate and advanced levels of proficiency, with the main languages studied being English as a foreign language (EFL), Irish, French, Spanish, and German.

The main task for the learners participating in this case study was to create and maintain a reflective blog that focused strictly on their experiences as language learners over a twelve-week semester. It constituted

50 percent of the final mark for the module. Students had to fulfill two criteria: (a) to create and maintain a blog so as to reflect upon the process of language learning; and (b) to write a three thousand word essay in English concerning integrating the blog by using the different entries as examples in their analysis. It was hoped that this reflective blog—which was popular among Erasmus students doing the course—would provide a space for students to explore their strategies and approaches toward language learning. Most significantly, the blog exercise employed three approaches: an expressivist approach (which was implemented earlier); a socio-cognitivist approach (which was introduced later); and a process/post-process approach to writing. However, even though the blog activity was intended for a twelve-week span, it was presented to the students as a potential task that could be continued even after they had completed the course (Carney, 2009; Murray & Hourigan, 2008).

Student blogs were to be evaluated according to content analysis and structure, linguistic performance, and the depth and development of ideas. There are varied results that emerged from this blog project. This relates especially to lower-intermediate and advanced learners. On the one hand, the lower-intermediate learners displayed inconsistent structures in terms of their second language (L2) written production. For instance, they exhibited poor performance with respect to punctuation, capitalization, vocabulary, sentence construction, and syntax. Additionally, this group of learners tended to produce descriptive and reflective blog entries that were too general in nature. In contrast, the advanced learners' blog postings displayed a critically focused reflective style of writing. Their blog postings engaged, in particular, issues such as proofreading, writing style, reading material, vocabulary acquisition, and culture (Murray & Hourigan, 2008). Finally, of the three approaches on which the authors contend their blog project focused, it is the individualist-expressivist approach that occupies pride of place.

Podcasting: PBL and pod creativity

There are two case studies under the spotlight here. The first one concerns Petrovic, Kennedy, Chang and Waycott's (2008) case study focusing on the use of podcasting in PBL. This was a fourteen-week pilot study intended to support informal peer learning in a medical curriculum. Involving eighty-five students out of a cohort of 319 second-year medical curriculum students at the University of Melbourne, the pilot study investigated the use of student-generated podcasts as learning resources. The context for the investigation was a PBL curriculum at the same university. This PBL curriculum employed ill-defined problems while it progressively disclosed information to encourage students to identify learning issues through critical thinking and reasoning about the information provided. Once learning issues had been identified, students investigated them by means of self-directed learning. In this regard, the main interest of the pilot study was to see whether a parallel informal peer-based learning environment using audio-based podcasting rather than text would be embraced by so-called Net Generation students.

Participating students had access to a podcasting activity throughout the fourteen-week semester and each week they had to undertake a new PBL case. Before the start of a semester, students were informed about the forthcoming podcasting activity. Once the semester had begun, e-mails were sent to the cohort reminding them of the podcasting activity and offering them advice in creating and publishing podcasts. Accordingly, a podcasting system called *Problm* was developed. It comprised a Web database application custom-built to provide an interface to a podcasting activity with the functionalities for users to subscribe, listen, publish, upload, rate, and comment on podcasts related to each of the fourteen-weekly PBL cases encountered during the semester. Using this system, students could create short podcasts that communicated their understanding, difficulties, or opinions to their peers about the weekly clinical problem under investigation. The *Problm* home page displayed a table of contents with the title of each PBL case as a link to another page containing the titles of podcasts created for that PBL case. All these were displayed in a reverse sequential format, with the most recently posted podcasts at the top of the page. Students could upload a podcast from this page as well. This self-same page included an embedded Flash-based MP3 player for playback. In addition, students could download the podcast, rate it, or post a comment about it. There were three categories of podcasts that students could create: *Aha!*, *Huh?* and *IMHO* (Edirisingha et al., 2007; Petrovic et al., 2008).

Of the eighty-five students who participated in this podcasting activity, six students made a podcast. The majority of students (65) were "listeners," who either downloaded podcasts or played them online. There were twenty-eight "visitors" (students that came to the podcast Web site but did not listen to or upload podcasts). In addition, there were "commenters" (8) (students who wrote an observation about the podcast) and scorers (students who rated a podcast on a scale featuring 1 to 5 points). Of the three categories of podcast, twenty-eight were *Aha!*, six were *Huh!* and fourteen were *IMHO*. Overall, the pilot study indicated that podcasting activities needed to be integrated into and aligned with both formal curricula and assessment practices (Edirisingha et al., 2007; Petrovic et al., 2008).

The second case study relates to Wallace's (2007) creativity-driven podcast project. Exploring the potential podcasting had as a creative tool in an art classroom, this case study had one primary objective: to determine what art teachers needed to know for them to effectively adapt the podcasting technology in their own classrooms. It involved a group of ten preservice Art Education student teachers at the University of Florida and sought to answer two questions: (a) How can art teachers use podcasting to enhance and transform art education?; and (b) What do art teachers perceive as significant barriers to practicing podcasting? The case study was informed by two objectives: promoting creativity through a choice-based approach and minimizing potential anxieties associated with learning new technologies by allowing the preservice teachers to offer instruction in areas of familiarity.

In addition, it comprised two phases: working with a group of pre-service Art Education teachers on a podcasting project course *ARE 2456 Digital Media in Art Education*; and developing a Web-based resource guide for art teachers to engage their students in learning about art through podcasts. All students were offered eighty-gigabyte (GB) video iPods in which they were to download and view a podcast they preferred most. They were allowed to work in pairs so as to produce a two-minute art tutorial podcast based on their own subject matter. One pair chose to produce two such podcasts.

In the first phase, which had elements of action research, students were required to produce visual podcasts. However, they were permitted to choose between enhanced podcasts or vodcasts. In this regard, four groups decided to produce enhanced podcasts while one group worked on a vodcast. Enhanced podcast topics chosen included: *How to draw a manga character*; *How to collograph*; *How to create a cyanotype*; *How to stencil*; and *How to tone a canvas*. The vodcast topic selected was *How not to be a starving artist*. The second phase entailed developing both a resource guide for art teachers and a Web site. The guide comprised designated resources from the podcasting project. The Web site (designed by the researcher) was used to host students' two-minute tutorial podcasts (Wallace, 2007; see Edirisingha et al., 2007; Vallance et al., 2009).

Microblogging

Microblogging is one of the relatively recent additions to the Web 2.0 family of technologies. Thus, due to its late entry into the consumer market, it does not yet enjoy a widespread adoption and usage in most learning institutions. This digital technology, which is an upshot and a customized version of blogging, lends itself well as a form of supplemental learning and instruction even though its educational affordances have not yet been extensively investigated and trialed. Considering its maximum character quota of 140, especially as exemplified by Twitter, some of the few educational affordances it might offer are notifications or alerts about study material and module/course content; posting assignment topics; monitoring students' learning progress; assessing or evaluating student performance; spontaneity and immediacy of response, feedback or communication; and serving as a delivery platform for nano-learning or chunk learning.

Twittering for language learning

Among case studies or experiments investigating the use of microblogging for learning purposes, two are a focus of this part of the chapter. The first is Borau, Ullrich, Feng, and Shen's (2009) project leveraging the microblogging tool Twitter. Focusing on the usefulness of the latter tool in an EFL classroom environment, the project was carried out for seven weeks and two days in the 2007 summer term at Sanghai Jiao Tong Distance College (Online-SJTU). It comprised ninety-eight students who had enrolled for an English course meant for Chinese native speakers. A personal Twitter account was created by an instructor and students were prompted to create their own accounts and link them to their instructor's so they could receive messages (tweets) from both their instructor and their fellow students. All the participating students were required to post at least seven microblogging messages (tweet updates) per week and to read incoming tweets from their fellow students.

One of the reasons for implementing the Twitter project was that the class sizes at the Online-SJTU were such that all students could not have the opportunity to communicate with the instructor during class periods to practice English skills. But most importantly, the Twitter project was intended to enable students to practice both communicative and cultural competence. Twitter participation contributed to the students' final grades. In this regard, grading was determined solely by the number of tweets posted and not by the linguistic correctness of the updates. Overall, a total of 5,574 updates were posted, which translates into 796 average updates a week or 113 per day. At the end of the project, the students were given a questionnaire to complete. First, Twitter proved to be a tool for learning communicative and cultural competence anytime, anywhere. In addition, it lent itself well as a medium for social and collaborative learning if used appropriately. Third, the questionnaire responses tended to substantiate the claim that Twitter serves as a quick and easy medium for informal communication and reading (Borau et al., 2009).

The second case study is Al-Khalifa's (2008) pilot study that leveraged Twitter as a microblogging technology and platform. The study was conducted at King Saud University in the second semester of the 2007–2008 academic year. It was intended for 190 students enrolled for the Introduction to Operating Systems (IOS) course. However, only sixty students signed up for the Twitter project. There was a dual objective for this pilot study: to test the effectiveness of Twitter as a tool for keeping the IOS students connected to the blog meant for their course and to enable students to receive classroom announcements and news posted on the course blog. Toward the end of the semester, a survey was posted to poll students' experiences with Twitter. Based on the students' adoption and usage of this microblogging tool, there are pros and cons that were observed. The pros included the following: There were timely announcements without the need for a reliable Internet service; students were better connected as they all had mobile phones; and students saved time as they did not have to visit the IOS blog daily. Among the disadvantages the following were noted: the service was both unstable and unreliable throughout the trial period and there was a shortened message space occasioned by the use of Arabic language. For their part the survey results indicated that 93 percent of the students preferred receiving text announcements via Twitter to visiting the course blog for updates. Nonetheless, only 37 percent of the students expressed the desire to continue using Twitter beyond the project for nonacademic purposes (Al-Khalifa, 2008).

A collaborative writing tool—Google D & S

Google Docs and Spreadsheets is one of the recent additions—after the wiki—to the Web 2.0 family of collaborative writing tools. Like the wiki, it has a number of potential educational offerings for a broad spectrum of teaching and learning. These encompass the following: enabling multiple users to write, edit, and share the same documents simultaneously; collaborative authorship, editorship, and publishing; fostering beta-reading and beta-writing, that is, endless reading, drafting, revising, and editing; experimenting with different writing genres (e.g., social, fictional, academic, technical, scientific, medical writing, summaries, etc.); cocreating, co-owning, comanaging, co-disseminating, and sharing knowledge and information; serving as a medium for knowledge/learning repository; and allowing users to export documents to and import them from other applications (Chaka, 2010a). Although at the time of writing there are not many documented trials and uses of Google D & S, there are some case studies that are beginning to explore its use in relation to teaching and learning. Two such case studies are the focal point of the next section.

Collaborative learning and concurrent collaborative spreadsheeting?
The first case study is Blau and Caspi's (2009) experiment involving the use of Google Docs. Targeting 118 undergraduate students in the Department of Education and Psychology at the Open University of Israel, this study was designed to test the differences between sharing and collaboration on a written assignment. In particular, it focused on the influence of sharing and collaborating with documents using Google Docs on psychological ownership, perceived learning, and perceived outcome quality. Participants were randomly assigned to one of five experimental conditions that differed in types of collaboration. These conditions were control, publishing, reading, suggesting, and editing. The same conditions also served as five randomly constituted groups, four of which were experimental groups while the fifth one was a control group. Two experimental groups shared their draft with either an unknown audience or known peers whereas the other two groups collaborated by either suggesting improvements to or editing each other's draft. The control group members had to keep their draft to themselves (Blau & Caspi, 2009).

There are findings emanating from the study that have a significant bearing on this chapter. First, in terms of the psychological ownership the suggesting and publishing groups had a significantly higher sense of ownership compared to the editing group, with the publishing group rating their ownership highest overall. Second, in respect of the perceived quality of the document, the average perceived quality after revision was higher than prior to revising, implying that students generally thought that revising the document had improved it. Third, participants in all groups believed that collaboration had resulted in better documents. Thus, this study tends to support the usefulness of Google Docs as a collaborative social writing platform. Most importantly, the findings supported the perceived importance of collaboration as the quality of a revised document was viewed as higher only after collaborative learning (Blau & Caspi, 2009).

The second case study concerns Silverstein's (2008) project, which employed Google Spreadsheets. This project set out to investigate the viability of a concurrently collaborative online spreadsheet to improve the effectiveness of student teams in solving chemical engineering problems. It involved students in two chemical engineering courses at the University of Kentucky Extended Campus in Paducah (United States). It examined four questions of which, the following are relevant to this chapter:

- Are online spreadsheets adequate for solving problems not requiring advanced spreadsheet capabilities?
- Does the collaborative nature of the online spreadsheet contribute to training students to function effectively as a team?

Prior to the project, students were given basic instruction in group problem solving, concentrating especially on planning a solution and task distribution. Then, eight students were each assigned group problems to solve as a team using Google Spreadsheets. Of these, five were sophomores (second-year students) in a material and energy balances course while the other three were in a senior-level engineering economy course. Students in the sophomore course were given a problem that required completing a spreadsheet to calculate the compressibility of a mixture using the Peng–Robinson equation of state. They were to complete selected portions of the spreadsheet based on equations provided on the assignment. The spreadsheet was color coded to indicate cells the students had to edit and those representing inputs to the problem.

The senior students in the engineering economy course were expected to develop a spreadsheet to enable users to compare the total costs of living for buying and renting a home. They were not provided with any template for this assignment. Lastly, all the students were required to use computers spread across multiple locations within the university and to communicate with each other through the instant messaging system built into Google D & S (Silverstein, 2008).

Feedback indicated students were satisfied with the capabilities of the online spreadsheet. However, they were uncomfortable with the nonavailability of familiar features that would have been useful for the assigned problems. Sophomores expressed a greater appreciation for the value of planning and organization in team projects leveraged through Google Spreadsheets than the seniors. Finally, both groups felt that the collaborative nature of the spreadsheet was appealing and that the problems were solved rapidly with everybody contributing simultaneously (Silverstein, 2008). Based on the preceding pointers, this project, together with its results, highlights the value of Google Spreadsheets as a collaborative social writing platform facilitating not only collaborative problem solving but collaborative learning as well.

Social networking—Facebook and YouTube

Both Facebook and YouTube are instances of SNSs. However, the latter is more of a media-sharing site. Each of these SNSs—notwithstanding the privacy and security threat they both pose—has potential educational affordances. For example, Facebook can be deployed for the following educational purposes: establishing individual or group profiles for students; establishing and fostering educational or learning networks; a communication and discussion medium; posting course or module discussion/assignment topics; and sharing information with other students or with faculty staff. For its part, YouTube can be put to the following educational uses: creating or producing educational video clips that can serve as learning objects; sharing educational video clips; embedding educational video clips into relevant institutional Web sites and into learning content; and a knowledge base or a database for educational video clips. Even though both Facebook and YouTube still trail the other Web 2.0 technologies in terms of educational trials and experiments, there are some case studies that have explored the educational uses of these SNSs. Three such case studies are briefly discussed in this section.

Supplemental learning and collaborative knowledge creation

The first of these case studies is Schroeder and Greenbowe's (2009) Facebook pilot study. It was undertaken at Iowa State University during the 2007 fall semester and compared students' use of Facebook and WebCT. It involved 128 undergraduate students enrolled in an introductory organic chemistry laboratory for non-chemistry majors. One of the reasons for implementing this pilot study was a low level of student participation inside and outside introductory chemistry laboratory courses. So, Facebook seemed a viable alternative platform to WebCT—which students did not utilize as well as they were expected to—for promoting student communication about course work. As such, the major focus here was the effectiveness of Facebook as a communication and discussion tool. And the primary question the study set out to answer was *Would students discuss chemical concepts outside of regular class time in a Facebook group more frequently than they did in WebCT?*

Students were invited, during the first meeting of each laboratory section, to join the Facebook group *Chemistry 231L*. As registered members of the Facebook group, all students could view the group home page, post to, or view the discussion board, photos, videos, and posted items. However, they first had to get their instructor's approval to do all of this. The Facebook group, like the WebCT forum, served as an informal venue for students to ask, among other things, questions about their laboratory experiences. One of the Facebook features that the students used most is the one that enabled them to upload photos to supplement related text. This same function allowed any group member to respond to a comment, explanation, or observation using relevant figures, diagrams, or graphics. Additionally, the instructor utilized this function to draw step-by-step chemical reactions or chemical structures, and to post spectral data that had to be referenced accordingly. Overall, there were differences in students' use of the two platforms. For instance, judging by the frequency of posts, Facebook posts were 400 percent more than WebCT posts, and these postings had raised more complex topics and generated more detailed replies than WebCT postings. However, students avoided providing direct answers on Facebook in their replies to their classmates (Schroeder & Greenbowe, 2009).

The second case study is Molnár, Kárpáti, and Aoki's (2009) pilot study. This study employed hybrid Web 2.0 technologies—Facebook, Google Docs, Voicethread, and Tokbox—and involved twenty-nine international students. The latter comprised twelve third-grade Hungarian undergraduate students from Károly Gáspár University majoring in *Japanese Studies* and seventeen Japanese undergraduate students from the Kanda University of International Studies doing *Media Communication*. A joint course was set up for Japanese and Hungarian students so as to create an authentic avenue for them to contact each other, communicate with each other and learn about each other's culture. Students chose topics for visual and verbal interpretation in groups. They then had to collect information about their own culture (e.g., facts, pictures, videos, music, etc.) and about their partner's, prepare documents and make collaborative presentations. All these tasks were managed online through social software tools.

Some of the observations from this study, especially those related to Facebook, which are of significance to this chapter, are briefly highlighted here. Hungarian students selected seven topics about Japanese culture (e.g., audience reception of foreign television dramas in Japan; life and works of Haruki Murakami, a world-famous Japanese writer; transportation mechanisms in Japan; "geek culture" in Japan; anime and manga culture; Japanese idols and the concept of beauty in Japan; and music in Japan). In contrast, Japanese students selected five topics about Hungarian culture (e.g., sports in Hungary; tourism in Hungary; Hungarian gastronomy; coming of age—youth entering adult life; and classical music in Hungary). Both groups' final presentations were shared on Facebook (Molnár et al., 2009).

Fostering multiple intelligences

The third and last case study is the one by Lance and Kitchin (2007). It took place during the November 2008 autumn semester at London Metropolitan University and was targeted at a student cohort enrolled for two Marketing Management oriented modules, Masters levels *Sports Management* and *Events Marketing Management*. As such, it assumed a case study within a case study format: It was a case study that comprised two case studies. The focus of the double case study was on the significance of the inclusion of YouTube Web-based video clips in teaching and learning the two related modules and on promoting individual learning styles by leveraging students' nine multiple intelligences (MIs) through the use of YouTube video clips. The MIs in question are verbal/linguistic, logical/mathematical, musical/rhythmic, bodily/kinaesthetic, interpersonal, intrapersonal, visual/spatial, naturalistic, and international intelligences.

The first of these two related case studies involved twelve students in the *Events Marketing Management* module, the content of which introduced students to the theory of the events industry with a view to enabling them to apply marketing practices in response to this theory. YouTube video clips were periodically shown throughout the semester to support or illustrate theoretical concepts. Some of the video clips used were, a television (TV) advertisement for the Innocent Drinks Company, a McDonalds TV advertisement promoting McDonalds Happy Meals, a video clip of the Innocent Drinks Company Fruitstock Festival, and a promotional video clip of the Daily Mail Ski & Snowboard Show. The second of the two linked case studies consisted of twenty-three students enrolled for the *Sports Management* whose content introduced students to the theoretical underpinnings of the sports marketing. The module required students to use the traditional approach to marketing and to apply it to a sport situation in the UK and internationally. Here, too, a series of YouTube video clips was periodically displayed throughout the semester for illustrating or supporting historical and social contexts and marketing communications campaigns. Two such video clips were the 2006 Grand National and the London Nike 10K (Lance & Kitchin, 2007).

A research instrument employed in the double-case study was a self-delivered paper-based questionnaire, which was distributed to the students during their seminar sessions. It consisted of two sections. The first section required students to identify their preferred learning styles, based on eleven questions that described the eight MIs. The second section asked students to identify the general benefits to them of watching YouTube video clips, and to identify, using the same list of the intelligences from section one, whether any of these intelligences had been initiated, improved or enhanced by watching YouTube video clips. For example, in *Events Marketing Management*, interpersonal intelligence remained unaffected while the percentage increase for the other intelligences was 8 percent.

In contrast, in *Sports Management*, the impact for verbal/linguistic, logical/mathematical, and bodily/kinesthetic intelligences remained constant whereas the other intelligences improved, with the most improved being musical/rhythmic intelligence. Moreover, among the *Events Marketing Management* group, the overall group change in MIs after the exposure to YouTube video clips within a teaching environment was an 11 percent increase in incidence. Most importantly, the value of YouTube video clip inclusion lay in the varieties of intelligences that were impacted upon or enhanced (Lance & Kitchin, 2007).

Future directions

Web 2.0 technologies herald a new era of teaching and learning leveraging new digital technologies. In this regard, based on the case studies presented in this chapter, three key factors are likely to dominate the future use of Web 2.0 technologies in education, and especially, in the higher education domain. These are the move from pilot or one-off projects to sustainable longitudinal studies, universal adoption, and easy accessibility. Pilot or one-off studies on Web 2.0 technologies as explored and discussed in this chapter are a good starting point. However, there is a need to move away from piloting these projects to more sustainable longitudinal studies so as to further evaluate the usefulness and effectiveness of Web 2.0 technologies in relation to their teaching and learning affordances. Universal adoption refers to a wholesale and ubiquitous adoption of Web 2.0 technologies by numerous higher educational institutions, faculties, academics, and students for teaching, learning, and research across the globe. Alongside this factor is the effectiveness and utility of Web 2.0 technologies: They need to demonstrate their added value and effectiveness as media of choice for teaching and learning. Only then will their profile and image improve significantly. Tied to universal adoption is easy accessibility: Web 2.0 technologies must be easily accessible to all the stakeholders intent on leveraging them if they are to make a substantial inroad into the teaching and learning market. One way of doing so is by imploring governments and education authorities worldwide to roll out and market these technologies in their respective countries.

Conclusion

This chapter has explored and presented fourteen case studies documenting the implementation of some of the educational affordances leveraged by six Web 2.0 technologies at 12 HEIs from eight different countries. While the chapter has foregrounded the usability of these technologies within given HEIs—together with some of the likely benefits derived from them—it concludes by contending that the success of these technologies in and their adoption by most HEIs hinges on other critical factors not mentioned in the discussion. Some of these factors are blurring the divide between informal and formal learning, mainstreaming Web 2.0 technologies, narrowing the digital divide, and content copyright, and privacy and security issues. Blurring the divide between informal and formal learning refers to *informalizing* and *casualizing* teaching and learning to reflect the informal and casual nature of Web 2.0 technologies. This means that Web 2.0 technologies should be mainstreamed and harnessed to blur the classical divide between informal and formal learning. Allied to mainstreaming Web 2.0 technologies is the need to incorporate them into official teaching and learning assessment and evaluation practices such as semester assignments, tests, and examinations as in the case of Farmer et al.'s (2007), Murray and Hourigan's (2008), and Borau et al.'s case studies reported in this chapter (2009). Alongside mainstreaming these technologies is the imperative to narrow the digital divide between students and academics. Most crucially are content copyright and privacy and security issues. Even though a lot of content offered by most Web 2.0 technologies (e.g., Flickr and YouTube) is freely available, top-quality content needed for teaching and learning purposes is mostly copyrighted. Moreover, some Web 2.0 technologies (e.g., Facebook and MySpace) often pose both privacy and security problems for users.

References

Al-Khalifa, H. S. (2008). Twitter in academia: A case study from Saudi Arabia. Retrieved August 30, 2009, from http://elearnmag.org/subpage.cfm?section=case_studies&article=42-1

Banister, S. (2008). Web 2.0 tools in the reading classroom: Teachers exploring literacy in the 21st century. Retrieved May 21, 2009, from http://ijttl.sicet.org/issue0802/4_2_3_Banister.pdf

Barsky, E., & Giustini, D. (2007). Introducing Web 2.0: Wikis for health librarians. Retrieved June 17, 2008, from http://pubs.nrc-cnrc.gc.ca/jchla/jchla28/c07-036.pdf

Belanger, Y. (2005). Duke University iPod first year experience final evaluation report. Retrieved August 10, 2007, from http://cit.duke.edu/pdf/ipod_initiative_04_05.pdf

Blau, I., & Caspi, A. (2009). What type of collaboration helps? Psychological ownership, perceived learning and outcome quality of collaboration using Google Docs. Retrieved March 4, 2009, from http://telem-pub.openu.ac.il/users/chais/2009/noon/1_1.pdf

Borau, K., Ullrich, C., Feng, J., & Shen, R. (2009). Microblogging for language learning: Using Twitter to train communicative and cultural competence. Retrieved June 19, 2009, from http://www.carsternullrich.net/pubs/ICWL78.pdf

Bosch, T. E. (2009). Using online social networking for teaching and learning: Facebook use at the University of Cape Town. *Communication*, *35*(2), 185–200.

Butgereit. L. (2007). Math on MXit: Using MXit as a medium for mathematics education. Retrieved February 28, 2010, from http://researchspace.csir.co.za/dspace/bitstream/10204/1614/1/Butgereit_2007.pdf

Butgereit, L. (2009). How Dr Math reaches pupils with competitions and computer games by using MXit. Retrieved March 1, 2010, from http://researchspace.csir.co.za/dspace/bitstream/10204/3391/1/Butgereit_2009.pdf

Carney, N. (2009). Blogging in foreign language education. In M. Thomas. (Ed.). *Handbook of research on Web 2.0 and second language learning* (pp. 292–312). Hershey, PA: IGI Global.

Chaka, C. (2009a). From classical mobile learning to mobile Web 2.0 learning. In R. Guy (Ed.), *The evolution of mobile teaching and learning* (pp. 79–102). Santa Rosa, CA: Informing Science Press.

Chaka, C. (2009b). *Education 2.0: Teacher and learner transformation and 21st century learning approaches and pedagogies.* Unpublished manuscript.

Chaka, C. (2010a). Enterprise 2.0: Leveraging Prosumerism 2.0 using Web 2.0 and Web 3.0. In S. Murugesan (Ed.), *Handbook of research on Web 2.0, 3.0, and X.0:Technologies, business, and social applications* (pp. 630–646). Hershey, PA: IGI Global.

Chaka, C. (2010b). E-learning 2.0: Web 2.0, the semantic web and the power of collective intelligence. In S. Yuen & H. Yang (Eds.), *Handbook of research on practices and outcomes in e-learning: Issues and trends* (pp. 38–60). Hershey, PA: IGI Global.

Chapman, A., & Russell, R. (2009). Shared infrastructure services landscape study: A survey of the use of Web 2.0 tools and services in the UK HE sector.

Retrieved February 24, 2010, from http://ie-repository.jisc.ac.uk/438/1/JISC-SIS-Landscape-report-v3.0.pdf

Crook, C., Cummings, J., Fisher, T., Graber, R., Harrison, C., Lewin, C., et al. (2008). Web 2.0 technologies for learning: The current landscape—opportunities, challenges and tensions. Retrieved 21 May, 2009, from http://partners.becta.org.uk/upload-dir/downloads/page_documents/research/web2_technologies_learning.pdf

Edirisingha, P., Salmon, G., & Fothergill, J. (2007). Profcasting—A pilot study and guidelines for integrating podcasts in a blended learning environment. Retrieved February 23, 2010, from https://lra.le.ac.uk/bitstream/2381/404/3/Edirisingha%20et%20al%20Profcasting%20book%20chapter.pdf

Farmer, B., Yue, A., & Brooks, C. (2008). Using blogging for higher order learning in large cohort university teaching: A case study. *Australasian Journal of Educational Technology, 24*(2), 123–136. Retrieved May 21, 2009, from http://www.ascilite.org.au/ajet/ajet24/farmer.html

Franklin, T., & Van Harmelen, M. (2007). Web 2.0 for content for learning and teaching in higher education. Retrieved October 12, 2007, from http://www.jisc.ac.uk/media/documents/programmes/digital_repositories/web2-content-learning-and-teaching.pdf

Gokhale, P. A., & Chandra, S. (2009). Web 2.0 and e-learning: The Indian perspective. Retrieved June 17, 2009, from http://publications.drdo.gov.in/ojs/index.php/djlit/article/viewFile/511/274

Keats, D. W., & Schmidt, J. P. (2007). The genesis of Education 3.0 in higher education: The potential for Africa. Retrieved June 01, 2009, from http://elearn.uwc.ac.za/usrfiles/content/fsoftelearn/documents/education-3.0-V3.pdf

Harle, J. (2009). Digital resources for research: A review of access and use in African universities. Retrieved April 25, 2010, from http://www.acu.ac.uk/publication/download?id=173

Heer, R. (2009). Social networking technologies: Implications for teaching and learning. Retrieved May 21, 2009, from http://www.celt.iastate.edu/pdfs-docs/SocialNetworkingApril09a.pdf

Hunter, J. (2009). A landscape study of shared infrastructure services in the Australian academic sector. Retrieved February 24, 2010, from http://ie-repository.jisc.ac.uk/439/1/Aust-SIS-Landscape-report-final.pdf

Lance, J., & Kitchin, P. (2007). Promoting the individual learning styles of master students studying marketing-related modules through the use of YouTube video-clips. Retrieved September 02, 2009, from http://www.londonmet.ac.uk/londonmet/library/x61001_3.pdf

Li, T., & Suo, Z. (2007). Engineering education in the age of Web 2.0. Retrieved October 28, 2007, from http://www.imechanica.org/files/Engineering%20Education%20in%20the%20age%20of%20Web%202.0%20%20Li%20and%20Suo%20(2007).pdf

Luckin, R., Logan, K., Clark, W., Graber, R., Oliver, M., & Mee, A. (2008). "KS3 and KS4 learners" use of Web 2.0 technologies in and out of school—Summary. Retrieved May 22, 2009, from http://partners.becta.org.uk/upload-dir/downloads/page_documents/research/web2_technologies_ks3_4_summary.pdf

Melville, S. D., Allan, C., Crampton, J., Fothergill, J., Godfrey, A., Harloe, M. et al. (2009). Higher education in a Web 2.0 world. Retrieved February 23, 2010, from http://clex.org.uk/CLEX_Report_v1-final.pdf

Molnár, P., Kárpáti, A., & Aoki, K. (2009). Social Web applications for intercultural projects: Results of a Japanese-Hungarian collaborative teaching experience. In A. Szucs (Ed.), *Proceedings of the LOGOS Open on Strengthening the Integration of ICT Research Effort* (pp. 155–166). Budapest: European Distance and E-Learning Network.

Minicha, S. (2009). A study of the effective use of social software by further and higher education in the UK to support student learning and engagement. Retrieved August 25, 2009, from http://www.jisc.ac.uk/media/documents/projects/effective-use-of-social-software-in-education-finalreport.pdf

Murray, L., & Hourigan, T. (2008). Blogs for specific purposes: Expressivist or socio-cognitivist approach? Retrieved March 1, 2009, from http://www.melbourne2008.com/article/call1.pdf

Oradini, F., & Saunders, G. (2008. The use of social networking by students and staff in higher education. Retrieved August 11, 2008, from http://www.eife-l.org/publications/proceedings/ilf08/contributions/improving-quality-of-learning-with-tech-Oradini_Saunders.pdf

Petrovic, T., Kennedy, G., Chang, R., & Waycott, J. (2008). Podcasting: Is it a technology for informal peer learning? Retrieved May 30, 2009, from http://www.ascilite.org.au/conferences/melbourne08/procs/petrovic.pdf

Redecker, R., Ala-Mutka., K., Bacigalupo, M., Ferrari, A., & Punie, Y. (2009). Learning 2.0: The impact of Web 2.0 innovations on education and training in Europe. Retrieved February 24, 2010, from http://ftp.jrc.es/EURdoc/JRC55629.pdf

Quinn, D., Duff, A., Johnston, H., & Gursansky, D. (2007, July). Blogging—infusing engagement, enjoyment (joy) and reflection into learning. *Proceedings of the 30th HERDSA Annual Conference [CD-ROM], Adelaide, Australia.* Retrieved June 18, 2009, from http://www.herdsa.org/au/wp-content/uploads/conference/2007/PDF/REF/p190.pdf

Schroeder, J., & Greenbowe, T. J. (2009). The chemistry of Facebook: Using social networking to create an online community for the organic chemistry laboratory. Retrieved June 18, 2009, from http://www.uh.cu/static/documents/AL/The%20Chemistry%20ofFacebook.pdf

Silverstein, D. (2008). AC 2008-228: Using a concurrently collaborative spreadsheet to improve teamwork and chemical engineering problem solving. Retrieved March 4, 2009, from http:www.engr.uky.edu/~aseeched/papers/2008/228_USING_A_CONCURRENTLY_COLLABORATIVE_SPREA.pdf

Simões, L., & Gouveia, L. B. (2008). Web 2.0 and higher education: Pedagogical implications. Retrieved May 22, 2009, from http://web.guni2005.upc.es/media/0000000500/0000000523.pdf

Vallance, M., Vallance, V., & Matsui, M. (2009). Criteria for the implementation of learning technologies. In M. Thomas. (Ed.). *Handbook of research on Web 2.0 and second language learning* (pp. 1–19). Hershey, PA: IGI Global.

Wallace, T. (2007). Podcasting as a creative learning tool in the art classroom. Retrieved June 17, 2009, from http://traceywallace.org/Podcast%20Paper.pdf

CHAPTER 4

The Role of Adult Educators in the Age of Social Media

Rita Kop and Paul Bouchard

Introduction

In a world where the authority of knowledge is challenged by self-generated networks of fluid meaning, learners and educators alike should familiarize themselves with the intricacies of epistemology and power distribution that are implied in the notion of learner control. The idea that limitless information and cost-free connectivity provides accessible opportunities for learning does not take into account the required agency of the learner. In particular, adult educators have questioned the commodification of knowledge and simultaneous relativization of meaning in many-to-many communication, while pointing to necessary shifts in epistemic beliefs and in the importance of self-direction in learning. In this context, adult educators must examine the social, political, and psychological dimensions of the new learning environments and re-define their role as facilitators of learning.

The rise of technology has, apart from its perceived influence on the economic competitiveness of nations, also pressurized society in a different way. It has led to the increasing bureaucratization of institutions. Foucault mentioned the stifling influence of technological systems on hospitals, prisons, and education, while Illich discussed the restriction on freedom, the "enclosure of the commons," the increased policing and surveillance of everyday life (Foucault, 1977; Illich, 1992, p. 51).

Illich saw, at the heart of the educational revolution in the 1970s, the need

> (1) to liberate access to things by abolishing the control which persons and institutions now exercise over their educational values; (2) to liberate the sharing of skills by guaranteeing freedom to teach or exercise them on request; (3) to liberate the critical and creative resources of people by returning to individual persons the ability to call and hold meetings—an ability now interestingly monopolized by institutions which claim to speak for the people; and (4) to liberate the individual from the obligation to shape his expectations to the services offered by any established profession—by providing him with the opportunity to draw on the experience of his peers and to entrust himself to the teacher, guide, adviser, or healer of his choice (Illich, 1971, p. 103).

Illich's vision was to see people take ownership of the learning process rather than institutions controlling their education. In order for agency and participation to return to the learning experience, Illich (1971) called for "the possible use of technology to create institutions which serve personal, creative and autonomous interaction and the emergence of values which cannot be substantially controlled by technocrats" (p. 2). He saw that the alternative to "scholastic funnels" would be true communication webs. However, his vision related to community webs between real people in face-to-face communities, rather than the current virtual nodes on networks. How then could this apply to educational institutions? Would it be advantageous to move from an institutionally controlled learning environment with hierarchical systems and course structures toward an Internet-based, open environment where nodes of networks would communicate with one another and tag information? This would create several problems and raise some important questions, starting with the effectiveness for learning of this type of technology. Would communication with global communities of (possibly the same) interest help in knowledge construction? What would happen to traditional adult education values in learning, such as awareness rising of inequalities in society and learner autonomy?

Web 2.0 technology and the role of the adult educator

The rapid development of technology and exponential growth in the use of the Internet, its Web 2.0 and mobile developments, make new and different structures, educational organizations, and settings a possibility. The personal online and face-to-face networks that people build up throughout their lives could provide expertise and knowledge in addition to the guidance that local tutors would provide. The learner would be at the center of the learning experience, rather than the tutor and the institution and would be instrumental in determining the content of the learning in addition to deciding the nature and levels of communication and who would participate.

Some researchers of e-learning (Downes, 2009a; Dron, 2002) propose that the increasing influence of the Internet and online connectedness of people might mean that the role of the tutor could not only change, but disappear altogether. People can move from a learning environment controlled by the tutor and the institution to an environment where they direct their own learning, find their own information, and create knowledge by engaging in networks away from the formal setting. They still communicate with others, but their personal interests and preferences, rather than institutional requirements and choices, are the main drivers for their engagement with more knowledgeable others in their learning.

The networks in which people communicate can be small or vast, but the main characteristics for networks to support knowledge development would be that they are diverse, open, autonomous, and connected (Downes, 2009a). There are parallels with how Illich saw his community webs. Online networks also come together as interest groups of autonomous participants, but Illich envisaged his webs in community settings and aimed at bringing local people together, learners and "people with knowledge." Networks might be open and facilitate connections, but local culture and values cannot be incorporated very easily as the online networks are global, with diverse participants, each bringing their own ideas and background to the fore. This might stimulate debate, but the local community and its development would be of less importance than the dominant culture on the network. There have also been concerns about the lack of critical engagement online (Norris, 2001; Walters & Kop, 2008), because of the temptation of connecting with like-minded people rather than in more challenging transactions, with experts such as the teacher in a classroom, whose role it is to make people aware of alternative points of view. Critical educators such as Freire (Freire & Macedo, 1999, p. 48) thought it to be essential that teachers have a directive role. In this capacity, teachers would enter into a dialogue "as a process of learning and knowing" with learners, rather than the dialogue being a "conversation" that would remain at the level of "the individual's lived experience." I engage in dialogue because I recognize the "social and not merely the individualistic character of knowing." Freire feels that this capacity for critical engagement is not present if educators are reduced to being facilitators. Moreover, in a connectivist online environment, with an emphasis on informal learning and the possible individual's choice of engaging with experts outside the classroom, this critical localized influence could be lost completely. The lack of critical engagement by a tutor, on top of the diminishing level of control by the institution would also imply a high level of learner autonomy.

Social media to support a "pedagogy of abundance" or "a pedagogy for human beings"?

It is clear that the proliferation of information and communications technology (ICT) has blurred the boundaries between home, work, leisure, learning, and play, and has reshaped our lifestyles and social interaction, while creating a new form of literacy (Partnership for 21st Century Skills, 2009). Being able to read books is not enough to function well in society; "effective" citizens also have to be able to "read" new media, understand and learn from interactive learning programs, and adjust to new ways of communication (Downes, 2009b; Selwyn, 2006).

Who could have foreseen ten years ago, the inception of online places to share photographs, video, and music, or social bookmark/information sharing sites, such as del.icio.us? Moreover, the explosion of mobile phone photography, blogs, and wikis and their fast distribution and linkage via RSS (Really Simple Syndication) feeds to networks of people in the blogosphere has already had its influence on the traditional media and even disrupted them and pushed their development into new directions (Huffington, 2006).

Adult educators have been rather reluctant to engage with these technological developments and have more likely than not seen such developments as undermining the traditions of adult education (Martin, 2006). Technology has been too widely used by politicians to push for an economic discourse with an agenda of upskilling of the workforce. Moreover, the naïve enthusiasm of learning technologists and the failure of initial high-profile and high-funding e-learning programs (Bacsich & Bristow, 2004) also contributed to a skepticism of what ICT could offer adult education.

Some adult educators have now seen that perhaps technology is not just a burden but can have a meaningful place in education. Theorists have started thinking about how the changes that technology and the complex world in which we now live affect pedagogy. Weller (2009), for instance, suggests that a move toward a "pedagogy of abundance" could be a positive step in a technology-rich learning environment. He argues that on the Web, among other issues, content is free and varied and can be shared easily as social interaction is at the heart of the new social media, and is not taxing as it is at the level of a conversation rather than of a dialogue; it is lightweight and easy to organize (Weller, 2009), although he foresees problems to match this unstructured learning with university requirements (Weller, 2010). Learning can take place on informal networks rather than in formal institutional structures. In the current complex times, however, others feel that adult educators also have a duty to be critical of the technologies and teach adults what the implications of the technologies are for their lives. The views as expressed by Wheelahan (2007, p. 145) seem more fitting than Weller's. She promotes a "pedagogy for human beings," where "pedagogy itself must be characterized by uncertainty, with knowledge loosely framed, provisional, and open-ended." She would see different forms of knowledge as being required to be able to live and learn successfully in uncertain times. It is not just the Internet that has brought changes to learning and living; in post-modern society education and work are being organized in quite new ways from before, which means that lifelong and lifewide learning have become part of everyday existence. The commodification of knowledge and its relationship to work, play, and life has put an emphasis on a different type of knowledge (Delanty, 2001; Lyotard, 1984). The move toward lifelong learning means that propositional knowledge as part of institutional education might no longer be sufficient; it might have to be related to real life situations and the workplace, as an educational tool in practice (Wheelahan, 2007).

However promising the new social networking environments appear to be, we must be cautious of not overgeneralizing this potential across the population of adult learners. There is individual variability in the self-efficacy and self-regulatory abilities of learners, just as there is variability in the contexts in which they evolve. The question is, how do these variables intersect with the new potential of Web 2.0 and how can adult educators be of assistance in resolving some of the tensions that will inevitably appear?

What knowledge?

The emergence of virtual learning environments and social media has given rise to the belief in a future that abounds with new opportunities for learners and the notion that learning and knowledge are being redefined as epistemological concepts in themselves. This enthusiasm has been sparked in great part by the possibility for persons to quickly and efficiently gather in networks that are not limited by contingencies of time or space, thus offering limitless possibilities of interconnectedness. In the context of the recent rise in popularity of social constructivist learning theories, it comes as little surprise that networked connectivity is heralded as the new age of learning. However, there are some natural limitations to the actual promise of networked learning that seem to be lost in the shuffle to extol the exciting and unheard-of possibilities of Web 2.0. Several of these theoretically predictable limitations are being encountered every day by persons wishing to use networked learning for specific purposes, but somehow their voices hardly resonate outside their immediate surroundings. In the age of cost-free publishing and infinite networking potential, this seems somewhat odd. Or is it?

One observation that is repeatedly made by network enthusiasts is that because of the democratic space created by networks, the nature of knowledge is changing from that of a top-down, authority-based world of certainty to one of fluctuating boundaries and "people-based" content, and that "the world of expert, clearly-defined, and well-organized knowledge formed by ancient philosophers and deciphered by subsequent thinkers, has today given way to continual flux" (Siemens, 2008, p. 5).

This apparent shift in what constitutes "valid" knowledge is attributed to the velocity at which information and meaning are transported across Web networks, so that it becomes quite impractical to congeal knowledge in accepted formulas while ignoring the information revolution unfolding before our eyes. While this seems self-evident at first glance, psychologists have described in some detail the journey of all persons from their initial beliefs in the absoluteness of truth and knowledge to the more uncomfortable spheres of approximation and uncertainty that characterize a *mature* system of epistemic beliefs (Baxter-Magolda, 1992; Perry, 1970). To posit that this maturation occurs in persons because they are offered the possibility of connectivity is an attempt to explain a known phenomenon with a heretofore unknown cause. Certainly, navigating countless nodes of divergent opinions on any given topic makes one ponder the validity of each one and the criteria we should apply to establish such degrees of validity. Could it be that the "new knowledge" network theorists are experiencing an epistemic shift themselves and are merely (1) attributing it falsely to their newfound connectivity; and (2) projecting it unconsciously on to others? Whatever the case, we cannot assume that the "new" knowledge will be constructed in the same manner by all individuals. In many foreseeable instances, there will be a need for learners to have access to a trusted "knowledgeable other" in order to negotiate the complex tasks of epistemic growth.

If the new connectivity encourages such reflections in some people, it certainly carries the potential for doing precisely the opposite for others. The likeliness that persons will congregate to networks that share their own values and beliefs is much higher than for them to participate in groups that are hostile to their views (Barabási, 2003; Norris, 2001). This can only foster a form of close-knit tribalism that encourages adherence to self-proclaimed truths. Many of these can be readily found on the Web, and they range from the mildly delusional to the downright frightening. This is also a shift in epistemic belief, but this time from the rational to the irrational, which can just as likely be associated with social media as with any other cause. Again, caring adult educators can be instrumental in helping develop a critical awareness of the nature of human congregations.

Interestingly, the notion that knowledge is constructed by people, and therefore is equally valid and "true" for those people, has been described in the developmental literature as the "relativist" phase of epistemic growth, which precedes the quest for validity that is based on considerations other than social appurtenance. This evolving quest for truth is not only considered normal by psychologists of adult development, it is considered essential by some philosophers. As Boghossian (2007) puts it, "If science weren't privileged, we might well have to accord as much credibility to archeology as to Zuni creationism, as much credibility to evolution as to Christian creationism" (p. 6).

Putting information and inference to the test of inherent validity requires specific skills without which the navigation of blogs and wikis might be a journey toward futility, or worse, toward falsehood and superstition. In this context, careful guidance from ethically motivated adult educators may prove to be an invaluable resource for Web 2.0 cyberlearners.

The new environment

One striking feature of the new media is that it relies on artifacts that are quite separate from the literacies that were normally associated with the culture of "high knowledge." The practice of aggregating and distributing unedited Web links attached to a blog acts much like the scholarly practice of paraphrasing and synthesizing historical works before adding one's contribution to the existing body of literature, with the difference that the sender evacuates all need to provide a synthesis, since the original works are all appended easily and cheaply. The sender needs only add a few words to make a complex point, and indeed there is a discernible movement on the Web to value network communications that are as short as possible.

The rise of a kind of monosyllabic "geek" literacy (Boyd, 2008), regardless of its true power to communicate ideas, has prompted cries of warning against the impeding "literacy crisis" brought about by the information age (Goodfellow & Lea, 2007). These new Web literacies are seen as challenges to the traditional literate culture that has been the central value of our education system, and we are indeed witnessing a kind of "literacy guerrilla" between so-called digital natives and conventional academia whose complaints about the new "literacy crisis" are heard throughout the world (Greenfield, 2006). This plea for prudence relies on two arguments: (1) that new media replaces the need for complex written language; and (2) that a rising generation of "digital natives" are quite comfortable with that fact (see Bennett, Maton, & Kervin, 2008).

There is nothing new about this "literacy crisis." The fear of the return to the dark ages of illiteracy surfaced when the first radio receivers hit the market at the turn of the twentieth century then again at mid-century with the advent of the television (Goodfellow & Lea, 2007). Some of us remember the prediction that with the invention of instant-playback VCRs (a magnetic tape video recorder), we would see the end of books and of all formalized cinematography. These fears turned out to be unfounded simply because new media provided opportunities for *more* communicative possibilities, not less.

The second argument, that our culture is being transformed by the Net Generation, has not been supported by research. Persons who were born after the popularization of the PC do not seem to be any more adept or interested, on average, in the more complex functions of their machines (Bennett et al., 2008; Selwyn, 2006). Teenagers use their computers just as they would any other communication gadget—to chat, twit, and gossip. Their older counterparts do much the same, but are more preoccupied with functions compatible developmentally with their own age group. For this reason, they are in fact more likely to develop deeper computer sophistication than the teenage twitters. Overall, the main difference between persons who spend time learning and mastering arcane computer functions lies in their interest in doing so, regardless of their age group (British Library & JISC, 2008).

The real clash of cultures is apparent when we consider *who* is actually threatened by the rise of computer networking. Anyone who has recently set foot in a contemporary, technologically advanced university will be startled to find that these institutions are at the most retrograde end of the spectrum when it comes to acknowledging the new media. It appears they are still recovering from the expectation that they offer Web-based courses (in the form of managed learning systems [MLS] designs). Apart from a few notable exceptions such as MIT and the UK Open University (both of which provide open-access course materials), higher-learning institutions generally guard their wares quite jealously and regularly threaten noncompliers with breach-of-copyright suits. They also routinely set higher fees for online courses than for the classroom equivalent. One university in the United States boasts that it does not rely on Web-based tools for their education, but proudly delivers everything face to face. A recent memo circulated in a Canadian institution warned that social networking software such as Facebook and Twitter were considered contrary to scholarly values and are to be discouraged in designing course materials. More and more, ethically motivated university instructors are moving away from their alma mater's mainframe and turning to networks that are less vulnerable to administrative scrutiny and control.

There is evidence in the history of technology of institutions and their resident professions not only being challenged to change by new technology but also literally disappearing altogether for lack of relevance. Shirky (2008) mentions the example of medieval clerical scribes becoming irrelevant after the advent of the printing press and also predicts the soon-to-be redundancy of newsrooms and the extinction of the profession of journalist due to the fact that their existence relied on their privileged access to a scarce resource, publishing. Today of course, publishing is cost free for anyone who owns a computer. From medieval publication to modern era journalism, there is but a small step toward challenging the traditional guardian of knowledge and culture, the contemporary university. Without resorting to futurist rhetoric, it is safe to say that the mastodon seems aware of its predicament.

Authority of knowledge, stability of knowledge

Over the past decades the authority of knowledge has shifted. In the enlightenment era, the university clearly held the position of authority of knowledge. This all changed in post-modern time. Lyotard (1984) and Readings (1996) claimed that the university has changed into a largely bureaucratic type of institution without a "moral purpose." The university is no longer the dominant producer of knowledge. Other institutions, such as think tanks, research institutes, multinational corporations, have become major producers as knowledge is related to the performance of society (Lyotard, 1984; Readings, 1996). In addition, what counts as knowledge has changed. It is more dynamic and related to the social, political, and cultural climates of the time (Delanty, 2001). Lyotard laments these changes:

> [T]he process of delegitimation and the predominance of the performance criterion are sounding the knell of the age of the Professor: a Professor is no more competent than memory bank networks in transmitting established knowledge, no more competent than interdisciplinary teams in imagining new moves or new games. (Lyotard, 1984, p. 53)

However, Delanty saw a new role emerging for the university:

> This restructuring in the mode of knowledge implies not the end of the university but its reconstitution. The great significance of the institution of the university today is that it can be the most important site of interconnectivity in what is now a knowledge society. There is a proliferation of so many different kinds of knowledge that no particular one can unify all the others. The university cannot reestablish the broken unity of knowledge, but it can open up avenues of communication between these different kinds of knowledge, in particular between knowledge in science and knowledge as culture (Delanty, 2001, p. 6).

Delanty proposed that communication is the new tie at the heart of contemporary society and could be the unifying factor in our complex society. He refers to Habermas' ideas on communication in the public sphere. Of course, mass media and commerce are already heavily engaged in the arena of public communication and have shaped it to a certain extent. However, this was before Web 2.0 developments and they were in a "broadcasting" mode. The new digital media allow for a two-way exchange. They are increasingly changing the mass media themselves: There is interactive television, and newspapers have blogs and podcasts and ask their audience to engage and produce content. Matheson speaks of an online news blog as a model of "knowledge-as-process, rather than knowledge-as-product" (Matheson, 2004, p. 447).

The new "bottom up" developments in communication through social software on the Internet could ensure a new platform of public communication and dialogue. A substantial number of academics are already involved in communication of this nature (Glaser, 2004; Jenkins, 2007; Mortenson & Walker, 2002; North, 2006). As is shown in the development of the Wikipedia, anybody interested can get involved in the debate and development of knowledge, but the meaning of knowledge is changing.

It appears inevitable that educational programs, and particularly those populated by adult learners, will need to adapt to the new reality of open-source learning. The new semantics of Web conversations require a sophisticated view of meaning-making, which needs to be supported by dedicated adult educators. Perhaps this is where the future of our teaching institutions lies.

The problem of self-directed learning

One related consequence of "liberating" knowledge from its traditional institutional guardians and setting it free on the network is the impact on academic credentials. One convenient way of not having to demonstrate one's competencies and skills each time they are required, has been to obtain a credible, documented opinion about them in the form of a degree, diploma, or other form of educational credential. Although it is quite practical, there are important drawbacks to this system, such as the exaggerated power it gives to the educational institutions, and the underuse of countless expertise due to lack of documentation (Livingstone, 2009).

Much has been said about the desirability of Prior Learning Assessment, but the main problem with such a system is that it would necessarily be controlled by the same educational institutions that it wishes to bypass in the first place. One solution would be to shift the role of the university faculty from that of evaluator of learning *outcomes* to that of witness of learning *processes* (Thomas, 1998). This of course, would be a radical departure from current views on the role of higher education and its renewed emphasis on performance and end results, while some authors point out that this shift is pretty much inevitable in the context of the new media (Walton, Weller, & Conole, 2008).

The problem of learning outside the institution has existed as an object of theoretical discussion for nearly half a century (Candy, 1991; Knowles, 1972; Long, 1993). The problems associated with self-direction in learning have been scrutinized by experts for decades, and many advances have been made toward elucidating its most prominent features. The fact that the new networked environments are confronted with the issue of learner control only makes the continued study of self-directed learning more relevant today.

The first obvious property of networked learning is that it allows learners to freely choose what it is that they want to learn. The control over the object—or content—of one's learning is a central element that distinguishes informal learning from the formal and the other-directed from the self-directed. However, it is not the only one. Learners can exercise control not only over what they learn, but also why they learn, and where, how, at what cost, and with whom. In order to put some order in these disparate questions, Bouchard (2009) proposed a four-dimensional model of learner control, or learner autonomy (see Figure 4.1).

The conative dimension

Before deciding what to learn, we must decide whether to learn at all, and why. This area of learner control includes the motivational and the affective domains that influence learners in their journey. In the workplace or the classroom, persons may be simply told to learn something without being told why, or how, thereby being allowed a low degree of conative control. In the real world, which includes networks of all kinds, influences such as socioeconomic status, cultural origin, values, and attitudes will largely determine whether a person engages in a personal quest for knowledge, and the nature of that quest. In the conative domain, learner control is determined by external as well as internal factors.

The algorithmic dimension

In recent literature on networked learning, the notion of learner control has been largely taken to be synonymous with the possibility for learners of selecting their own learning resources. This is one of the reasons that networks are valued, in that they are powerful learning tools and they are devoid of external control. One direct consequence of the networked autonomy is that learners are empowered to choose *what* they learn. This is not to say, however, that learners spontaneously set pedagogical goals for themselves. Several studies in the 1980s and early '90s have found that self-directed learners do not typically follow the "algorithms" that are prescribed by professional instructors, such as setting learning goals, but tend rather to follow more fluid and opportunistic paths to achieving their learning. Other algorithms of learning include scheduling, pacing, searching, filtering, monitoring, following up, and evaluating. Together, they form the algorithmic dimension of learner-control.

The semiotic dimension

With the outburst of new technologies, the traditional formats of conveying information—namely print and film—are being supplanted by virtual environments that utilize a range of communication and archiving tools that share few of the features of conventional media. At first, Web 1.0 technologies were considered quite revolutionary from a semiotic point of view. The notion of navigating between "pages" of information linked together by "hyperlinks" brought with it many metaphors for renewed meaning making. Now, Web 2.0 is providing a means of communication that allow cost-free self-publication and so-called many-to-many networking, thereby challenging us to interpret information obtained in new ways such as aggregating, filtering, and blogging.

The economic dimension

Formal degree-granting institutions are facing competition on several fronts. Learners can complete similar courses at any faraway institution that offers equivalent programs online, and similar knowledge can often be obtained from non-credit outfits anywhere in the world. But now, Web 2.0 does away entirely with the notion of organizations or institutions as sources of knowledge (e.g., MLS) and replaces them with the notion of the network. This brings about a shift in the value of knowledge, both as a commodity that one purchases and as the knowledge-as-capital that one possesses.

Variable degrees of learner control

Learners rarely have absolute control in any learning environment, not even Web 2.0, but rather follow a personal progression somewhere along each of these four independent continuums, depending on two factors: (1) the degree of control allowed by the particular learning environment; and (2) the degree of control of which the learner is capable within that environment. Adult educators have been among the strongest advocates of "matching" their interventions to the degree of autonomy manifested by the learner, meanwhile helping learners to access higher degrees of autonomy. Hence, a highly dependent learner requires more direction from a tutor than a more autonomous one. Knowing this—and applying it along the four dimensions detailed above—is an important task of adult educators.

Similarly, learning environments, from formal education settings to MLS to network aggregates, allow for different levels of learner autonomy with social media obviously at the top offering the most possibilities for individual expression. This is not to say however, from an educator's perspective, that all learners are prepared to face the conative, algorithmic, semiotic, and economic complexities of the Web 2.0 networked learning.

The mediation of learner control requires metacognitive skills that are not universally distributed among the population. Networked learning theories such as connectivism (Siemens, 2006) equate learning with networking itself, but remain seemingly oblivious to the important corollary that successful learning requires successful networking. In an environment that purposefully avoids attaching specific value to any of its multifarious components, except perhaps the overarching value of "net-neutrality," the task of sense-making becomes overwhelming for anyone who is not adequately familiarized with the intricacies of epistemology and power distribution that are implied in the notion of learner control.

The question of successful Web 2.0 navigation mandates the mediation of external agents, such as flexible MLS environments populated with trained adult educators acting as guides or facilitators during some parts of the learners' journey. What would such a hybrid environment look like? What parameters should guide its inception and limit its potential for interference? These are the questions that are faced by educational institutions in general and adult educators in particular.

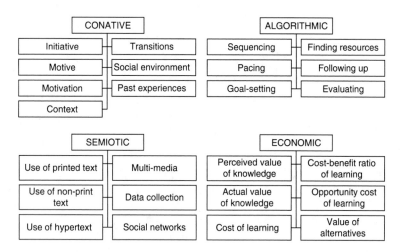

Figure 4.1   The four dimensions of learner autonomy.

Toward hybrid learning environments

Clearly, an understanding of how people learn is imperative in order to create a good educational experience and is implicit in a sound teaching strategy. In addition, an awareness of the factors of importance to foster learner autonomy while designing an online adult learning experience is crucial as learning at a distance implies a certain level of self-direction by the learner. This knowledge will allow tutors to relinquish control if and when appropriate and provide learners with additional choices, without them feeling overwhelmed by uncertainty about the new unknown that there is to be learned. It is of course in the nature of new learning to make people feel insecure and uncomfortable; to cause them to struggle in understanding new concepts and in processing vast amounts of information and in the making of choices.

Dron and Anderson (2007) and Carroll, Kop, and Woodward (2008) argue that the closer people are involved with other participants in the learning activity, the more the experience will attract them and influence how much time and energy they will be willing to invest in the undertaking. Carroll et al. (2008) suggest that the creation of a place where people feel comfortable and trusted will aid in this development; the level of "presence" of learners and tutors in a learning environment, it was suggested, would be important in their level of engagement. Dron and Anderson (2007) make distinctions between learning in groups (typically in a classroom or online learning situation), learning on networks (where the nature of the network would mean that the distance between participants in the learning activity would be larger), and collectives (which they see as environments where the connections are made through "tags" that would make sure that people are further removed again from the people who made the connection), which suggests that people will be more involved and engaged in groups than on networks.

Research has shown that communication and interaction with other learners and with educators are at the heart of a quality online learning experience, and that communication does not necessarily have to happen through a text-based medium (Kop, 2010). The mixed use of multisensory social media in a flexible manner, "if and when required," can be very powerful. The emergence of social media and digital technologies and their combined use can help in the facilitation of an authenticity of interaction and communication in the learning process that will help learners to become more self-directed. Figure 4.2 shows how multisensory, interactive materials foster a higher level of engagement from learners.

Text-based recourses	Multi-sensory, interactive resources	
Low level of engagement	Medium level of engagement	**Low level of presence**
Medium level of engagement	High level of engagement	**High level of presence**

Figure 4.2   Relation between tutor and student "presence," resources, and level of student engagement.

Research carried out on an online adult education program that used Web 2.0 tools with the aim to foster self-direction among learners and a high level of communication, highlighted that "presence" was not only achieved through the social "chat" tool and through "video and sound podcasts," although these tools were important in creating an immediacy of interaction between participants in the learning experience, but also through a high level of metacognition. Reflection by the learner on his own learning and also a high level of reflection by the educator on her teaching were achieved by using blogs as reflective diaries. These were also used by students and educators as a space for one-to-one communication, achieving a high level of personalization of the learning (Kop, 2010). Sandbothe argues that the "comprehensive and systematic development of reflective judgment at all levels of the population and on a global scale is the central task for a democratic educational system in the twenty-first century" (Sandbothe, 2000, p. 67).

If knowledge is developing in a more communal way than in the past, the validation of knowledge will be different from that in the era of accountability and individual knowledge development. If the learner finds information on the World Wide Web and communicates in the "blogosphere" to make sense of that information according to his own interests and experiences while learning away from the institution in collaboration with others, the institution will still have to devise structures to fit the learning into its quality systems. It is a paradox that technology has facilitated a closer control on assessment and validation of knowledge, while what will be required to use the new technologies effectively are flexibility, creativity, and a willingness to adapt to a new assessment practice. There will be an important negotiating and facilitating role for the local educator in linking the online learning to a local community of practice and accreditation structure.

The new P2P learning environments offer much potential for distancing oneself from standardized knowledge but at the same time require caution when attributing value to content and interaction on the Web 2.0. The new many-to-many network and its apparent quality of absolute democracy hide a structural reality that does nothing to upset the constants of power distribution and social stratification in the world today (and may, in fact, serve to reinforce them).

There are three layers to the new interactive network. The first is the network itself, a quasi-infinite number of "nodes" (people, really) that are linked together in a horizontal pattern where each node is theoretically linked to all the others, but where in fact there is fierce competition for recognition and notice in a kind of "economy of attention" (Lanham, 2007).

The second layer is built up of the software platforms that are necessary to navigate the network, link up, search, filter, share, aggregate, or otherwise mash up and organize information. These platforms are often repositories of user-generated content, or what Mejias (2008) calls "monopsonies," a reverse form of monopoly where there is but one buyer for a multitude of "sellers" (e.g., YouTube).

The third layer is the globalized economy without which networks could not exist. The startling levels of technological innovation that are changing our lives would not be possible without the support of the global capitalist logistic, which exploits all network "peers" while excluding the multitude of the "peerless" (Mejias, 2008).

The process of negotiating the complex social and political ramifications of Web 2.0 requires a high level of sophistication in the way learners interpret the interactive world. To help strengthen this capacity, adult educators must engage in the ongoing critical discussion on connectivity and the way it can enhance, assist, and help learning, but also in the ways that it can threaten the diversity of world views, epistemologies, and judgment.

References

Bacsich, P., & Bristow, S. (2004). *The e-university compendium: Volume one*. York: Higher Education Academy.

Barabási, A. L. (2003). *Linked: How everything is connected to everything else and what it means*. New York, London, and Toronto: Penguin Books.

Baxter-Magolda, M. B. (1992). *Knowing and reasoning in college: Gender-related patterns in students" intellectual development*. San Francisco: Jossey Bass.

Bennett, S., Maton, K., & Kervin, L. (2008). The "digital natives" debate: A critical review of the evidence. *British Journal of Educational Technology, 39*(5), 775–786.

Boghossian, P. (2007). *Fear of knowledge: Against relativism and constructivism.* Oxford: Clarendon Press.

Bouchard, P. (2009). *Some factors to consider when designing semi-autonomous learning environments. Electronic Journal of e-learning, 7*(2), 93–100. Retrieved November 24, 2009, from http://www.ejel.org/Volume-7/v7-i2/v7-i2-art-2.htm

Boyd, D. (2008). None of this is real. In J. Karaganis (Ed.), *Structures of participation in digital cultures* (pp. 132–157). New York: Social Science Research Council.

British Library & JISC (2008). *Information behaviour of the researcher of the future.* Retrieved January 11, 2008, from www.ucl.ac.uk/slais/research/ciber/downloads/

Candy, P. (1991). *Self-direction in learning: A comprehensive guide to theory and practice.* San Francisco: Jossey Bass.

Carroll, F., Kop, R., & Woodward, C. (2008). *Sowing the seeds of learner autonomy: Transforming the VLE into a third place through the use of web 2.0 tools.* In ECEL-European Conference on e-Learning, University of Cyprus, Cyprus, November 6–7, 2008, 152–160.

Delanty, G. (2001). *Challenging knowledge: The university in the knowledge society.* Buckingham, UK: Open University Press.

Downes, S. (2009a). *New tools for personal learning.* Presentation delivered at the MEFANET 2009 Conference, Brno, Czech Republic. Retrieved November 26, 2009, from http://www.downes.ca/presentation/234

Downes, S. (2009b). *Speaking in lolcats: What literacy means in the digital era.* Seminar for Educational Computing Organization of Ontario, Richmond Hill, Ontario, Canada.

Dron, J. (2002). *Achieving self-organisation in network-based learning environment.* Unpublished PhD thesis. Brighton, UK: University of Brighton.

Dron, J., & Anderson, T. (2007). Collectives, networks and groups in social software for e-learning. Paper presented at the World Conference on E-Learning in Corporate, Government, Healthcare and Higher Education (ELEARN), Quebec City, Quebec, Canada.

Foucault, M. (1977). *Discipline and punish: The birth of the prison.* Peregrine Press: London.

Freire, P., & Macedo, D. (1999). *Pedagogy, culture, language and race: A dialogue.* In J. Leach & B. Moon (Eds.), *Learners and pedagogy* (pp. 46–58). London: PCP in association with the Open University.

Glaser, M. (2004). Scholars discover weblogs pass test as mode of communication. *Online Journalism Review,* USC Annanberg, May 11, 2004. Retrieved February 23, 2009, from http://ojr.org/ojr/glaser/1084325287.php

Goodfellow, R., & Lea, M. (2007). *Challenging e-learning in the university: A literacies perspective.* Maidenhead: Society for Research into Higher Education and Open University Press.

Greenfield, S. (2006). Education: Science and Technology, Speech in The UK House of Lords, Vol. 2006. Retrieved May 21, 2007, from http://www.

publications.parliament.uk/pa/ld199900/ldhansrd/pdvn/lds06/text/60420-18.
htm#60420-18_spopq0

Huffington, A. (2006). Now the little guy is the true pit bull of journalism. *The Guardian*. Retrieved January 20, 2009, from http://www.guardian.co.uk/comment/story/0,,1730326,00.html

Illich, I. (1971). *Deschooling society*. London: Marion Boyars.

Illich, I. (1992). *In the mirror of the past*. New York, London: Marion Boyars Publishers.

Jenkins, H. (2007). *From YouTube to YouNiversity*, The Official Weblog of Henry Jenkins. Retrieved November 30, 2008, from http://www.henryjenkins.org/2007/02/from_youtube_to_youniversity.html

Knowles, M. (1972). *Self-directed learning: A guide for learners and teachers*. New York: Association Press.

Kop, R. (2010). *Networked connectivity and adult learning: Social media, the knowledgeable other and distance education*. Unpublished PhD thesis. Swansea, UK: Swansea University.

Lanham, R. A. (2007). *The economics of attention: Style and substance in the age of information*. Chicago: University of Chicago Press.

Livingstone, D. (2009). *Education & jobs: Exploring the gaps*. Toronto: University of Toronto Press.

Long, H. B. (1993). *Emerging perspectives of self-directed learning*. Research Center for Professional and Continuing Education: University of Oklahoma.

Lyotard, J. (1984). *The postmodern condition: A Report on Knowledge*. Manchester: University of Manchester Press.

Martin, I. (2006). In whose interests? Interrogating the metamorphosis of adult education. In A. Antikainen et al. (Eds.), *From the margins: Adult education, work and civil society* (pp. 11–26). Rotterdam, The Netherlands: Sense Publishers.

Matheson, D. (2004). Weblogs and the epistemology of the news: Some trends in online journalism. *New Media and Society, 6*(4), 443–468.

Mejias, U. (2008, April 17). *Networks and the politics of the paranodal*. Paper presented at Politics: Web 2.0: An International Conference, New Political Communication Unit, Department of Politics and International Relations, Royal Holloway, University of London. London, UK.

Mortenson, T., & Walker, J. (2002). *Blogging thoughts: Personal publication as an online research tool*. *Intermedia, 11*, 249–279.

Norris, P. (2001). *Digital divide: Civic engagement, information poverty, and the internet worldwide*. Cambridge: Cambridge University Press.

North, M. (2006). Political debate is thriving as academics blog on. *Times Higher Education Supplement,* September 22, 2006.

Partnership for 21st Century skills (2009). The MILE Guide: Milestones for improving Learning & Education, Tucson, USA. Retrieved November 11, 2009, from http://www.21stcenturyskills.org/documents/MILE_Guide_091101.pdf

Perry, W. G. (1970). *Forms of intellectual and ethical development in the college years*. New York: Holt, Reinhart, & Winston.

Readings, W. (1996). *The university in ruins.* Cambridge, MA & London: Harvard University Press.

Sandbothe, M. (2000). Media philosophy and media education in the age of the internet. *Journal of Philosophy of Education, 34*(1), 53–69.

Selwyn, N. (2006). *Dealing with digital inequality: Rethinking young people, technology and social inclusion.* Keynote presentation at Cyberworld Unlimited Conference: Digital Inequality and New Spaces of Informal Education for Young People, February 19, Bielefeld, Germany.

Shirky, C. (2008). *Here comes everybody: The power of organizing without organizations.* New York: Penguin Press.

Siemens, G. (2006). *Connectivism: Learning theory or pastime of the self-amused?* Elearnspace blog. Retrieved January 19, 2009, from http://www.elearnspace. org/Articles/connectivism_self-amused.htm

Siemens, G. (2008). *New structures and spaces of learning: The systemic impact of connective knowledge, connectivism, and networked learning.* Paper presented at Encontro Sobre Web 2.0. Braga, Portugal, October 10, 2008.

Thomas, A. M. (1998). The tolerable contradictions of prior learning assessment. In S. Scott, B. Spencer, & A. M. Thomas (Eds.), *Learning for life: Canadian readings in adult education.* Thompson Educational Publishing: Toronto.

Walters, P., & Kop, R. (2009). Heidegger, digital technology and post-modern education: From Being-in-cyberspace to meeting on MySpace. *Bulletin of Science, Technology & Society. 29*(4), 278–286.

Walton, A., Weller, M., & Conole, G. (2008). Social:Learn—Widening Participation and Sustainability of Higher Education. Proc. EDEN 2008: Annual Conference of the European Distance and E-Learning Network. June 11–14, 2008, Lisbon, Portugal.

Weller, M. (2009). *The pedagogy of abundance.* Invited speaker Connectivism and Connective Knowledge 09 course, University of Manitoba and National Research council Cananda. Retrieved November 16, 2009, from http://www. slideshare.net/mweller/a-pedagogy-of-abundance

Weller, M. (2010). The centralisation dilemma in educational IT. *International Journal of Virtual and Personal Learning Environments, 1*(1), 1–9.

Wheelahan, L. (2007). "What are the implications of an uncertain future for pedagogy, curriculum and qualifications?" In M. Osborne et al. (Eds.), *The pedagogy of lifelong learning: Understanding effective teaching and learning in diverse contexts* (pp. 143–154). London & New York: Routledge.

CHAPTER 5

Educational Networking in the Digital Age

Cristina Costa

Introduction

The emergence of the Web as a dynamic, user-centered platform for interaction and congregation of social capital has been said to impact different levels in our society (Ferlander, 2003; Rheingold, 2000; Wellman, 2001). It is changing some of the fundamental aspects of how people connect, interact, share, and work (Attwell, 2007; Cross, 2007), and a new networking culture seems to be evolving as a result. Academia is not an exception in this respect. These days it is said to be imperative to foster new forms of engagement with one's field and even beyond. For knowledge workers especially, keeping up with the continuous advancements in their subject areas is not only important, but necessary to survive in a competitive world. Engaging with the possibilities the digital age offers beyond what institutions formally provide in terms of collaboration and personal and professional development is thus more crucial than ever. Understanding the implications of one's online presence as part of practice, learning, and life in general, is a new skill to be acquired. This chapter will focus on learning and networking online, with special emphasis on academic researchers' professional networking activity. Hence, we will explore the obstacles, as well as the advantages and implications of adopting a Web 2.0 approach in the context of academic research and practice. In this chapter we will attempt to provide a holistic reference to what it means to be a *networked researcher* in light of the network society (Castells, 2000)—while approaching related themes such as networked learning, digital literacy, and digital identity, as well as the opportunities and challenges the Web presents when it comes to the publication and dissemination of research activity.

Knowledge in the digital age

The use of the Web to communicate scientific knowledge is probably one of the major transformations academic practice has gone through in the last decade. It is a rising movement that is transforming academic communication culture. Nevertheless, scholarly communication practices are as diverse as the disciplines they represent. Different areas of knowledge feature different communication conventions, which are largely determined by the very nature of the field as well as the rituals and practices associated with it (Fry, 2004, 2006). In a broad view, disciplines requiring greater levels of interdependency are more open to establishing collaborative links, and using the Internet as a vehicle for both communication and cocreation of knowledge, than those whose research practice presents lower levels of mutual dependency (Whitley, 1984). Yet, none of this is new. The broad research community has long engaged in a networking culture. Voltaire, for instance, was probably one of the most networked scholars of his time, with more than a thousand European correspondents (Pehn, 1999). Networks of correspondence were quite important throughout several centuries. They represented a way of establishing and maintaining influential links with the outside world. The communication flow, although rather informal, became a meaningful way of disseminating knowledge and connecting (to) like-minded people who were separated by geographical boundaries. Other scholars also made use of the epistolary genre to establish their networks beyond their local whereabouts. Erasmus and Samuel Formey, among others, were also prominent thinkers who sustained their learning relationships through correspondence circles (Berkvens-Stevelinck, Bots, & Häseler et al., 2005). With the emergence of Web 2.0 with its read and write features, networking has taken on a new dimension. Its importance has only just started to be acknowledged. In fact, digital technologies have brought a renewed awareness to the single individual's networking activity as a meaningful informal learning activity as well as a useful strategy for effective dissemination, both of which can raise a professional profile and enhance learning and practice. Consequently, it can also have an impact on the institution the individual represents.

Hence, it is no surprise that research councils, academia, and governmental agencies have been trying to introduce information and communications technology (ICT) in education for the last two decades in particular (Research Information Network, 2009; Times Higher Educational Supplement, 2009), with the purpose of giving learning, teaching, and research a more twenty-first-century look and thus prepare the current and new generations of learners for the future ahead. Yet, it is important not to forget that academic practice has a long tradition. The "way things are done around here" became accepted norms that are passed on from generation to generation in a rather standard way. Making the transition from an analog culture into a digital one can be a complex task that requires a close look at how research, in given areas, operates. In order to develop new approaches, improve practice, and, above all, transform the working culture and mind-sets of knowledge workers, it is crucial not to neglect their context. Such transformations present medium- to long-term challenges, as each discipline has its own pace and rhythm of adaptation. But such transformations will offer sustained results on how technology can be deployed to maximize the learning experience and research process and thus capitalize on its outcomes via interactive dissemination and communicative means.

Heterogeneity in scholarly communication

Different disciplines have different approaches as to how they make sense of their field of work and develop knowledge in their area. As Fry (2004) states, "knowledge is not a homogeneous whole, but a patchwork of heterogeneous fields" (p. 1). Fields of knowledge are more easily distinguished when considered within the framework of academic disciplines they belong to. They feature contrasting characteristics regarding their cultural conventions anchored in disciplinary habits and practices, which consequently give them an identity as a discipline or a subdomain of a given area.

The emergence of the participatory Web has offered academia a suitable kit of tools and platforms for the exchange of knowledge and human congregation. Indeed, academic communication is no longer restricted to face-to-face events or conservative communication methods. The Internet has not only mediated new forms of informal interaction, it has equally enhanced formal and scholarly communication. As Fry (2004) points out, "channels for the formal communication of scholarly work [have] expanded far beyond the local collections of academic libraries" (p. 304). The open-access movement and related initiatives, such as institutional repositories imply changes concerning how knowledge is being shared. Nevertheless, such institutional mandates for the openness of formally published work does not inform us how academic researchers are networking in the digital age and which influence and impact the use of ICT has on their learning and practice as researchers. Making their research available through pre-print services is not necessarily the same as engaging with technology in an interactive way. The greatest advantage of Web 2.0 in enhancing scholarly communication resides in the "human tone" (Forrester, 2009) it is able to convey.

As Pehn (1999) reminds us, "networking is an organic development which stems from the need of individuals to establish contacts, exchange ideas and work together" (p. 48). Networking does not necessarily have to be solely online, as it was not only face-to-face in past ages, for instance. Multiple forms of intercommunication can coexist. But networking does require active engagement from and with individuals. These days, online environments have become part of the networking equation, especially with the availability of numerous social networking sites (SNS) and interaction possibilities. Still, the limited research in this area asserts that the adoption of such approaches does not happen across the board, and it is linked with the nature and traditions of the disciplines and knowledge fields researchers belong to (Fry, 2004; Kling & McKim, 2000) rather than the availability of the technology itself.

Each area of knowledge has its own conventions and traits that influence the way people conduct their practice. As Kling and McKim (2000) have concluded, academic research activity online is a mere reflection of one's face-to-face practice. For example, disciplines that have a greater tendency to collaborate and share ideas in physical settings are more likely to establish an online presence for the same purpose, whereas disciplines whose ongoing shared practices are more infrequent are less likely to adopt an online communication strategy. In other words, the authors argue that the online practices of academic researchers are emblematic of the collaborative nature of the disciplines they represent.

Bearing in mind that we are moving toward a heavily inter- and multidisciplinary world, the need to collaborate and engage with different areas will become even more important than it is today. Digital technologies will be a core aspect of interaction and cooperation between different fields of expertise, sectors, and institutions. Therefore, it is imperative to understand the differences between disciplinary approaches (their habits, traits, and cultural identity) as to develop theories and frameworks, which will help us understand how we can best introduce and mentor academic researchers from different epistemological backgrounds as to the benefits and implications of the Web in contextual ways. The Web may have become accessible to the intellectual community, but it has not been appropriated across all disciplines and fields of expertise in a consistent way.

In this sense, there is still a path to be identified. When it comes to engaging different disciplines in contextual lifelong learning and providing guidance and mentoring on how to use the Web effectively and efficiently there is still work to be done. More importantly, personalized and contextual training and mentoring need to be developed as indicated by the PLA ICT Cluster report (2008).

Lifelong learning within communities

During the last two decades the concept of Communities of Practice (CoP), as part of professional and personal development, has grown popular. Lave and Wenger (1991) conducted research on how people learn in organizations and workspaces and discovered that one's learning and professional development is contextually and socially bound. Hence, the authors proposed a definition of CoP as follows:

> a set of relations among persons, activity, and world, overtime and in relation with other tangential and overlapping communities of practice. A community of practice is an intrinsic condition for the existence of knowledge.... It does imply participation in an activity system about which participants share understandings concerning what they are doing and what that means in their lives and for their communities. (p. 98)

Academics join groups of interest and congregate in social circles in which they feel they can benefit from the experiences shared and the stories and artifacts (Wenger, 1998) that are built as part of that same social practice and communal engagement. Such learning circles are often formed informally and maintained at the cost of peer participation. They are based on individuals' learning needs and the willingness of like-minded people to codevelop deeper understanding and practice about relevant areas. When Lave and Wenger started looking at this phenomenon they based much of their fieldwork on face-to-face communities (i.e., circles of people with close bonds, who shared the same geographical space, belonged to the same company, or were connected for a specific reason). Usually "this reason" was closely related to the involvement in similar practices, the sharing of interests, or learning goals. Since then, the concept and approach to communities of practice has gained a new dimension.

With the widespread use of the Internet and the transformation of the Web from the mere consumption of static information to interactive content and collective participation, which O'Reilly (2005) coined as Web 2.0, Wenger, McDermott & Snyder (2002) have also been looking at the Web as a new space for the congregation of social capital and the development of shared practices. The transformation of a static Web to a dynamic, participant-led environment has largely influenced the way communities of practice are formed and sustained in the first decade of the twenty-first century. Furthermore, the participatory Web, with its communication bridging facilities (the easy and ready to use online tools), has equally facilitated the development of networks, which predominantly operate informally, and are centered on the individual and their personal interests rather than on the purposes of a given community. In the present moment both networks and communities coexist in cyberspace, providing different opportunities for participation and the emancipation of the learner within their social and professional interests.

Networked learning

White (2009) states that the difference between communities and networks relies on the bonds that the individual establishes with the others. It is equally also linked to the way individuals act in the collective environments. White (2009) asserts that in a community "we give up a little bit of 'Me' on the service of the 'We.'" Thus, the concept of identity shifts from the individual's interests to the communal goals. In contrast, networks can be seen as an agglomeration of people with intersecting interests, whose interrelationships are relatively casual and more likely to be ephemeral when compared with those often established in communities. But as White goes on to say, the connections that start in one's networks can, at any given moment, evolve into a communal practice, provided the bond grows to sustain the learning relationship.

Networks are more dispersed in their nature than communities, but both are useful as part of the individual's learning process at different stages of their learning path and career. In other words, one does not necessarily exclude the other. Yet, with the growing popularity of the Web as an easy vehicle for self-presentation and representation of work and learning, networking, as part of personal learning and professional activity, has acquired a new meaning when it comes to online activity. Networks are based on individuals' contributions and help raise the profile of those who actively engage with their own learning in such open and connected spaces. As Siemens (2006) puts it, "a network...imbues individual nodes with personal voices...and finds its value in aggregating, not overwriting (marginalizing) nodes not in line with the thinking of the majority" (n.p.). It may be correct to say that whereas the network celebrates the individual, the community focuses on the collective effort. In a plain approach, we can say that the first is more self-centered and the latter more altruistic.

The main value of the Internet, as it stands today, is in the way it allows single individuals to independently interact with others, how knowledge emerges as a result of those connections, and how individuals can thus develop their practice and raise their professional profiles by effectively disseminating their work and working processes. The truth is that individuals no longer have to rely on institutional provision to learn, interact, or even present their work. The realization of the Web as an open channel for communication with the wider community is no longer news. Nevertheless, the fact that these days the individual has access to better and more modern tools than what most institutions and organizations are able to provide might constitute an element of surprise (Forrester, 2009) to the more conservative scholars. Although technology is leading to major changes at different levels of our society, the transformation of practices is a progressive process, which happens at different speeds in different contexts. Academia is no exception (Kling & McKim, 2000), and even there we can see differing approaches and Web-based practices in different disciplines and knowledge areas (Fry, 2004; Matzat, 2009).

Personal and professional learning networks: Emancipation of the individual

As cyberspace becomes more open to user-generated activity, we see an increase in the number of communities and networks running in complement of the local circles of interest and learning provision. Seminars, conferences, or local reading groups, for instance, are no longer the only way knowledge workers have access to learning opportunities, networks, or make their ideas and practices known. The Web, as the twenty-first-century user is experiencing it, has helped develop new contexts for the constitution of personal and professional learning networks (PLNs), which grant the single learner personalized forms of cultivating connections and participating in events relevant to his/her own practice and based on his/her own needs and choices.

In an attempt to describe this phenomenon, Warlick (2009) refers to a PLN as

> an individual's topic-oriented goal, a set of practices and techniques aimed at attracting and organising a variety of relevant content sources, selected for their value to help the owner accomplish a professional goal or interest. (slide 3)

Each individual has his or her own PLN, which he or she engages with in the attempt to create connections with other like-minded people. These links are cultivated by this dialectic of providing and acquiring relevant information and personal perspectives about topics that matter to the individual in particular, but to which others also have something to add. The PLN is meant to suit the individual in learning, and thus enhance his or her practice, in a networked environment. It is thus as peculiar as its owner chooses it to be. Hence, we can say that PLNs are crucial in connecting the individual to living resources, that is, other individuals, through Web 2.0 tools. The practice of cultivating a PLN online contributes to the emancipation of the self.

Individuals increasingly gain prominence in such channels, hence, raising their personal and professional profiles across contexts, spaces, and time. Academics as well as individuals in other areas can benefit hugely from the opportunities the Web currently offers. Indeed, online, the learning landscape has become highly distributed, yet it has also become more connected than ever before. Furthermore, it has become highly customizable and personalized.

With the continuous emergence of Web 2.0 tools the individual is also empowered to create their own personal learning environment (PLE), which individuals themselves will manage and direct. As Lubensky (2006) states a PLE is "a facility for an individual to access, aggregate, configure and manipulate digital artefacts of their ongoing learning experiences" (n.p.). This represents a major shift in practice and attitude. For academics, in particular, this allows them to "break free" from institutional walls and present and represent their learning and research activities in forms that best suit them. Web 2.0 has come to augment academic practice through non-standard ways, augmenting the scope for non-standard, creative, and personalized initiatives. Furthermore, Web 2.0 stimulates academics to reinvent themselves and their practice within their disciplinary contexts.

All of this innovation in communicating and learning with others does not come without a price, as we will explore in the sections below.

The transition from a private, reserved sphere into open, publicly accessible spaces is the predicament of a society, which, having gone through a very fast transformation, is still striving to make sense of the advantages and implications of being digitally and globally exposed. This is particularly true for knowledge workers, to whom the Web represents a new source of information, collaboration, maturing of joint knowledge, and also knowledge diffusion. However, the new forms of interaction presented to us by the participatory Web leads to several dilemmas, especially those related to the communication of information and the construction of knowledge in given disciplines. The way learning communities and networks operate online are not always compatible with the practices and working cultures of the disciplines single individuals represent. Hence, such activities are not always seen as a natural approach to certain academic disciplines. Changing academic practice is therefore a complex process, which requires a deep understanding of one's own context as well as professional and cultural identity. Additionally, the personal and social traits of the individual will also have an impact on how they regard the use of ICT in their practice.

With the advent of the Web new practices are progressively developing. As a direct result of this, a new literacy has also been created (Gilster, 1997; Lankshear & Knobel, 2006). Hence, new skills need to be acquired (Jenkins et al., 2006). Being digitally savvy is not necessarily a synonym of knowing how to use a computer or learning how to register for an account in a given Web application. Working and interacting online requires a new set of soft skills that will enable individuals to create a reputable image of themselves and their professional practice, but the opposite can also happen. Given that the participatory Web is a fairly recent phenomenon, many of us are still struggling to make sense of what it means to "be online," and what the implications our Web presence may have in the future. Hence, it becomes crucial to create awareness regarding this new literacy. Providing digital literacy training might be the way forward. Nevertheless, it is important to develop contextual approaches that will match the needs, traits, and knowledge fields of our students and faculty staff.

Digital literacy: A third basic skill

For many decades literacy and numeracy were regarded as the two fundamental skills. Preparing individuals to read, write, and do their maths was the initial goal of mandatory education. With the introduction of computers in the workplace, information technology (IT) courses have been offered to provide individuals with basic, technical computer skills. It aimed to make them more competitive in the job market. Hence, computers introduced a new dimension to the performance of knowledge workers, in particular, as it became an essential tool for their work. In fact, computer skills, alongside personal and social skills, have become a common item in job specifications, which are highly ranked. These days, being able to work with a computer is seen as an essential requirement. As Solomon and Schrum (2007) put it, "companies use technology to become lean and efficient" (p. 8). Nevertheless, knowing how to use a keyboard or print a document is just a minor element of the whole range of subskills today's knowledge workers needs to acquire in order to cope with the digital world as well as digital education. It is in this line that we feel the need to adopt the approach presented by the British Department for Education and Skills (DfES, 2003) and to introduce the concept of digital literacy as a third basic skill for the Information Age. Initiatives as those developed by UNESCO, the European Commission, the 21st Century Skills or the Realising our Potential (UK) project to name a few, are already exploring ways through which we can educate our citizens to be more digitally literate. Nevertheless, it is still early days regarding the outcomes and impact of such programs. Furthermore, much of the training that is offered in this current age is still mainly focusing on the technical use of the tools, rather than exploring the possibilities and implications of appropriating them for personal and professional use. The latter, in our opinion however, are key to the mentoring of digitally literate individuals. This is even true for our young users, who have grown accustomed to participating in online environments from an early age. It becomes also important for individuals with established careers (in our particular case, established academic researchers), not only because the Web may represent a novelty for their practice, but also because they are the mentors, and role models, of new generations of scholars.

Studying how individuals in different areas are using the Web to actively interact with their own learning and research is crucial to understand the challenges people face, beyond the common technical problems. Such studies become even more pertinent as such understanding will support the development of tailored strategies that will help shift the practice of scholarly communities, within their knowledge domains, to the digital age. This takes us to another issue—that of developing a digital identity, a topic that has generated quite a few discussions in recent times.

Digital identity: Growing professionally in public

Within the educational context, "digital identity" has acquired a growing importance. Broadly speaking, it can be understood as the way academics, educators, and learners, in general, present themselves toward their (learning) communities and networks and the impact it has on his/her personal learning and/or professional practice toward a wider community.

With the advent of Web 2.0, learning and networking online also means to cultivate a digital presence as it evolves over time and across social spaces, communities, and networks. Whereas in the past, academics were mostly known by the work they published in renowned journals or formal events they participated in, in this day and age, more interactive strategies for the dissemination of academic work have started to emerge in parallel to the more traditional ones. Web 2.0 is enabling additional forms of communication and interaction with academic work and among academics themselves. Web 2.0 environments can stimulate the creation of critical dialogues and active engagement with and between academics. The social aspect of the Web is not only related to the realization of new forms of collaboration; it is also about allowing new levels of connectivity. In the particular case of academics this means having direct access to a wider and diverse critical cohort of like-minded people. It also implies that scholars can develop a more approachable facet of themselves and their work since contact is no longer limited to their students or peers at their home institutions or to any sporadic events. Web 2.0 enables information sharing, debating, and the creation of knowledge in a borderless world. It can bring more visibility into academic work. Nevertheless, we can also argue that people's work and performance are more vulnerable to wider scrutiny as a result. It should not be forgotten that online users create a traceable historical thread recounting their path online (Keegan, 2009). This, of course, presents advantages, but it may also introduce disadvantages, especially when our online activity is not developed in consistency with our professional practice. The key is to be aware of the implications and act accordingly. By consistency we mean the development of an online presence that reflects the academic practice of researchers. It is crucial to consciously cultivate our online presence in such a way that it works for our own advantage.

In short, the read and write Web has become a powerful space for the retrieval, creation, and dissemination of knowledge, as well as the presentation of work and ideas in progress. Web 2.0 environments do present a fresh opportunity for academics to learn, enhance their work, and extend their networks. But Web 2.0 also poses a challenge: that of maintaining and maturing our online presence into a respectable professional identity in public.

Digital identity: Managing reputation

In 2005, in his keynote on Identity 2.0, Hardt argued that modern identity has been based mainly on photo ID (passport, driving license, and even student card). Its current digital, Web 2.0 form, however, provides a bigger picture of the individual's activity. The searchability of the Web makes it easier to identify what, where, and when we create and publish information online. The judgment others make of us, based on our participation, and the information they have access to, will also have an impact on our profile (Williams, Fleming & Parslow, 2010).

Hence, digital identity is not just about creating an online profile; it is especially about individual reputation in a connected environment. In educational settings, in particular, digital identity is based on our academic and social performance. Online, academics also have a status to preserve, as the information they display and the activities they take part in constitute tangible artifacts regarding their character and social and intellectual behavior. The picture others create of them can work for as well as against them. Therefore, it is important to develop examples of awareness regarding the online identity management of academics as they will, implicitly, influence the digital identity of those they mentor and influence, namely their students and also their peers. Learning how to develop and manage a professional online presence is of prime importance in today's world. With the Web allowing academics to showcase their roll of activities while making themselves more available to the wider community, it is crucial they learn how to manage their digital footprint. Initiatives such as the "This is Me" project led by the University of Reading in the UK have been looking at these issues and are trying to create awareness and resources to help academics and learners to manage the complexity of having and maintaining a coherent identity in a digital world.

In a nutshell, a digital identity resembles an enhanced business card to which an extensive list of examples of the person's practice and professional activities are attached. In the case of knowledge workers it can comprise their publications and academic memberships, but it will also include the networks and communities they belong to (PLN), as well as their PLEs. In this sense, one's professional digital identity is a dynamic representation of one's learning process and professional development.

Digital identity: Belonging to an open world

Establishing an online presence implies a greater deal of (ongoing) exposure within a wider community than any other form of traditional scholarly communication format has ever required. Online, individual researchers end up unveiling more about who they are, what they research, and how they conduct their research. Hence, their professional and social identity is taken to a new dimension and scale.

This has its added value for academics, but it can equally conflict with their research culture. Some scientific areas are more sensitive than others, and there is a presumption that certain disciplines do not lend themselves well to online environments. As Cronin (2003) confirms "the world of research and scholarship comprises many disciplines and a mélange of epistemic cultures. This heterogeneity of behaviors and practices mean that ICTs are deployed differently" (p. 13) and at different paces.

In *Academic Tribes And Territories*, Becher (1989) claims that in areas where the creation of new knowledge is seen more as an isolated activity, the use of the Web for both dissemination and interaction with peer researchers is less common, whereas in knowledge fields that require teamwork and/or cross-discipline collaboration, the use of ICT is more widely accepted and used. This often tends to lead to a separation between the so-called hard and soft sciences. Nevertheless, as the Web becomes more prominent among scholarly practice, faculty are progressively reconsidering "some of their engrained practices" (Cronin, 2003, p.14).

Knowledge is no longer restricted to the institution, nor is it only accessible through local libraries. In fact, those are precisely the places where knowledge is being less accessed and definitely less produced. The shift from an analog to a digital culture is changing the way individuals search for and access knowledge. The open access movement is unquestionably influencing the way people publish their work and access the work of their peers. The phenomenon of self-publishing, peer review, and regulations regarding validation and assessment of content are other important issues that we will not be able to explore here, but which can also create feelings of mistrust in the most conservative scholars. They can thus hinder the process of transition into the digital sphere. Still, there are some innovative practices being implemented in this area, as is, for instance, the case of the new peer-reviewed journal in education

(http://ineducation.ca), which seeks to bring a participatory component to academic publications, or the Virtual Research Environments
Programme run by JISC, which aims to support research activity in a
collaborative environment. We are convinced that such initiatives will
bear fruits in the medium to long term, as technology becomes not only
more integrated, but also more invisible, in daily practice. Such projects
will help academics perceive the value of open participation. Ultimately,
such experiences will hopefully generate meaningful debates about
opening up the academic "knowledge safes" to the wider public and the
impact it will have on academics' digital identity.

Indeed, the participatory Web is progressively making a difference
about how knowledge workers can collaborate across space and time,
with people in their areas, but also from other disciplines. Such is the
case of Scivee.TV project, which aims to promote researchers' work in
a collaborative, DIY, Web 2.0 environment. The informal networking
activities have been amplified to a more global level and the impact on
one's practice thus becomes wider than before. Yet, if making the transition to the digital world is that straightforward, why are we still trying
to convince the "laggards" to enter this post-modern age?

The networked researcher

Being a networked scholar is not as simple as it might seem, as cultural
change is implied (Becher, 1989; Cronin, 2003; Fry, 2004; Kemp &
Jones, 2007). Research in the past suggests that disciplinary differences
can determine academic activity (in our particular case: research practice). The take-up of technology presents a direct correlation with the
context of scholarly tradition and is shaped by disciplinary rituals and
practices (Fry, 2004, p. 301). Ideally, however, the networked academic
researcher would not differ much from the notion of the networked
teacher as presented by Couros (2006). When looking at approaches of
knowledge workers, of both educators and researchers, the epistemological background seems to be quite similar. Based on the definition of
networks formulated by Jarvis (2006), who says:

> Networks are about sharing now; they used to be about control.
> Networks are two-way; they used to be one-way. Networks are about
> aggregation more than distribution; they are about finding and being
> found. Networks are now open while, by their very definition, they used
> to be closed. You join networks and leave them at will; you can join any
> number of networks at once and content can be found via any number

of networks, there is no practical limit. Networks used to be static. Now networks are fluid (n.p.).

Couros (2006) supports the idea that the networked teacher is one who "embraces and participates in an open and distributed culture" (p. 174).

That is not much different from what we envisage a networked researcher to be. Knowledge workers need to be where knowledge is developed. Today the Web constitutes a productive platform for knowledge cocreation and collaboration in a rather dynamic way. With it emerges one's digital professional ID. Learning does not happen in isolation, and the participatory Web is allowing its social nature to become more visible than ever. The recognition and valorization of inter- and multidisciplinary knowledge by research councils, academic institutions, and other funding bodies is setting the agenda for new forms of research practice and dissemination. All of this, allied to the fact that online networking is starting to get the attention of researchers because of its "affordances and reach" (boyd & Ellison, 2007), lead us to believe that the networked researcher is one who explores connections beyond traditional boundaries and becomes engaged in activities that will benefit his or her practice as well as the practices of others.

Nevertheless, it is important to remember that taking people away from their comfort zone is a difficult task. Changing culture is a gradual and long process, which needs to be based on a logic that corresponds to the epistemological background of the culture we aim to transform. Research suggests that hard sciences tend to be more proactive in the creation of a Web presence. Even so, it has also been noticed that humanities and arts are also following the steps of the hard sciences in adopting the digital world (Thelwall & Price, 2003). Nonetheless, most of the studies that have been conducted regarding the online presence of researchers focus primarily on new forms of formal publications and dissemination and not on the informal interaction and networking activity of this scholarly cohort (Palmer, 2005). In this sense, the networked researcher as an active participant in an open, highly interactive culture of shared practice and knowledge creation is still in its early days of development.

Conclusion

The Web has become a prosperous environment for the development of interconnections, in which individuals have the option to both contribute to and benefit from distributed networks. In their study about social network sites (SNSs), boyd and Ellison (2007) assert that SNSs are formed around individuals rather than interests. This, in the words of the authors, "introduc(es) a new organizational framework for online communities, and with it, a vibrant new research context" (boyd & Ellison, 2007).

So far, very little has been published on the use of such technologies and approaches to enhance one's academic research experience and practice. Documentation on networking practices of researchers, the usage of the Web for dissemination and valorization of one's research, or the building of one's profile as a researcher is still scarce. Moreover, how this particular group, academic researchers, develop and nurture their informal networks and identity beyond the boundaries of the institution is an area that needs further examination (Redeker, 2009). So far, the majority of studies are based on teaching staff (teacher training) and learners' experience (Ala-Mutka, Punie & Redecker, 2008).

This, in a way, reflects the changing environment that characterizes the first decade of the twenty-first century. As Mason and Rennie (2008) state:

> Web 1.0 was an improvement over print as a means of transmitting and consuming research. What is different with web 2.0 technologies is that real interaction, peer commenting and collaborative research are actually happening in a distributed, global, environment. Knowledge is created, shared, remixed, repurposed, and passed along. In Short, web 2.0 is a research network as well as a learning network. (p. 10)

Even those studies that focus on the research community centre their attention particularly on the publication of research results rather than on networking practices.

Yet, it is widely recognized that the engagement of academic researchers with the Web is strongly dependent on the epistemological background of the disciplines they represent. Academic disciplines present different patterns of communication and collaboration (Becher, 2001; Kling & McKim, 2000; Fry 2004), which can be subject to disciplinary publishing conventions, group habits, or even interpersonal features. Yet, such frames of reference according to Fry (2004) are limited in terms of understanding the pattern of academic communication, "because it tends to focus on communication products, such as journals, [and] articles, rather than on informal communication at the process level, such as collaborative practices" (p. 305).

Further research needs to conducted in order to study how academic researchers in different disciplines are networking in the digital age and in their digital education contexts and which similarities and differences such practices present and why. Only then can we develop adequate training and mentoring. Additionally, it becomes essential to devote more attention to the processes of participation in networked learning rather than merely focusing on one's own formal digital publishing activity.

References

Ala-Mutka, K., Punie, Y., & Redecker, C. (2008). ICT for Learning, Innovation and Creativity, EC, Joint Research Centre, IPTS. Retrieved May 8, 2010, from http://tinyurl.com/yj8mn8n

Attwell, G. (2007). Personal Learning Environments—the future of eLearning? *2*(1). Retrieved May 10, 2010, from http://www.elearningeuropa.info/files/media/media11561.pdf

Becher, T. (1989). *Academic tribes and territories: Intellectual enquiry and the cultures of disciplines* (1st edition). Buckingham: Study for Research into Higher Education (SRHE) and the Open University Press.

Berkvens-Stevelinck, C. Bots, H., & Häseler, J. (2005). *Les grands intermédiaires culturels de la république des lettres: études des réseaux de correspondances du XVIe au XVIIIe siècles.* Paris: Honoré Champion.

boyd, d. m., & Ellison, N. B. (2007). Social network sites: Definition, history, and scholarship. *Journal of Computer-Mediated Communication, 13*(1), article 11. Retrieved May 15, 2010, from http://jcmc.indiana.edu/vol13/issue1/boyd.ellison.html

Castells, M. (2000). *The rise of the network society, the information age: Economy, society and culture*, Vol. I. Cambridge, MA; Oxford, UK: Blackwell.

Couros, A. (2006). *Examining the open movement: Possibilities and implications for education.* Unpublished Doctoral thesis, University of Regina, Canada. Retrieved May 10, 2010, from http://www.scribd.com/doc/3363/Dissertation-Couros-FINAL-06-WebVersion

Cronin, B. (2003). Scholarly communication and epistemic cultures. *New Review of Academic Librarianship, 9*(1), 1–24.

Cross, J. (2007). *Informal learning, rediscovering the natural pathways that inspire innovation and performance.* San Francisco, CA: Pfeiffer, an imprint of WILEY.

DfES (2003). The skills strategy white paper, 21st century skills: Realising our potential: Individuals, employers, nation. Retrieved September 10, 2010, from http://webarchive.nationalarchives.gov.uk/tna/+/http://www.dcsf.gov.uk/skillsstrategy/uploads/documents/21st%20Century%20Skills.pdf

Ferlander S. (2003). *The Internet, social capital and local community.* Unpublished Doctoral thesis. University of Stirling, UK.

Forrester, I. (2009). From backstage to open innovation. Guest lecture at the University of Salford, UK. Retrieved May 15, 2010, from http://www.slideshare.net/cubicgarden/tv-20–1643191

Fry, J. (2004). The cultural shaping of ICTs within academic fields: Corpus-based linguistics as a case study. *Literary and Linguistic Computing 19*(3), pp. 303–319.

Fry, J. (2006). Studying the scholarly Web: How disciplinary culture shapes online representations. *Cybermetrics: International Journal of Scientometrics, Informetrics and Bibliometrics. 10*(1). Retrieved May 10, 2010, from http://www.cindoc.csic.es/cybermetrics/vol10iss1.html Last accessed 14/12/2009

Gilster, P. (1997). *Digital literacy.* New York: Wiley Computer Pub.

Hardt, D. (2005). Identity 2.0. Keynote presentation for Identity 2.0 Conference. Retrieved May 10, 2010, from http://identity20.com/media/OSCON2005/

Jarvis, J. (2006). Everybody's a network. Retrieved September 10, 2010, from http://www.buzzmachine.com/2006/05/21/everybodys-a-network/

Jenkins, H., Clinton, K., Purishoyma, R., Robison, A., & Weigel, M. (2006). *Confronting the challenges of participatory culture: Media education for the 21st century,* a white paper. Retrieved May 10, 2010, from http://digitallearning.macfound.org/atf/cf/%7B7E45C7E0-A3E0–4B89-AC9C-E807E1B0AE4E%7D/JENKINS_WHITE_PAPER.PDF

Keegan, H. (2009). *Public vs. private: Conflict and compromise in converging social networks.* 2nd digital cultures workshop: Social media publics. Salford, UK.

Kemp, B., & Jones, C. (2007). Academic use of digital resources: Disciplinary differences and the issue of progression revisited. *Educational Technology & Society, 10*(1), 52–60.

Kling, R., & McKim, G. (2000). Not just a matter of time: Field differences and the shaping of electronic in supporting scientific communication. *Journal of the American Society for Information Science and Technology, 51*(14), 1306–20. Retrieved September 10, 2010, from http://xxx.lanl.gov/ftp/cs/papers/9909/9909008.pdf

Lankshear, C., & Knobel, M. (2006). *New literacies: Everyday practices and classroom learning* (2nd edition). New York: Open University Press.

Lave, J., & Wenger, E. (1991). *Situated learning: Legitimate peripheral participation.* Cambridge: Cambridge University Press.

Lubensky, R. (December 18, 2006). The present and future of personal learning environments (PLE). Retrieved May 10, 2010, from http://www.deliberations.com.au/2006/12/present-and-future-of-personal-learning.html

Mason, R., & Rennie, F. (2008). *E-Learning and social networking handbook: Resources for higher education.* New York: Routledge.

Matzat, U. (2009). Disciplinary differences in the use of internet discussion groups: Differential communication needs or trust problems? *Journal of Information Science, 35*(5), 613–631.

O'Reilly, T. (2005). What is web 2.0: Design patterns and business models for the next generation of software. Retrieved May 10, 2010, from http://oreilly.com/web2/archive/what-is-web-20.html

Palmer, D. (2005). A motivational view of constructivist- informed teaching. *International Journal of Science Education, 27*(15), 1853–1881.

Pehn, G. (1999). *Networking culture: The role of European cultural networks.* Council of Europe: Council of Europe Publishing.

PLA ICT Cluster Report (2008). E-skills and digital literacy and partnerships for LLL strategies. 8 October 2008, Thessaloniki, Greece. Retrieved September 10, 2010, from http://www.kslll.net/PeerLearningActivities/PlaDetails.cfm?id=76

Redeker, C. (2009). *Review of learning 2.0 practices: Study on the impact of web* 2.0. Innovations on. Education and Training in Europe, EC, Joint Research Centre, IPTS. Retrieved May 10, 2010, from http://tinyurl.com/ygcnauc

Research Information Network (2009). *Patterns of information use and exchange: Case studies of researchers in the life sciences.* A report by the Research Information Network and the British Library. Retrieved May 10, 2010, from http://www.rin.ac.uk/our-work/using-and-accessing-information-resources/disciplinary-case-studies-life-sciences

Rheingold, H. (2000). *The virtual community* (revised ed.). Cambridge, MA: MIT Press.

Siemens, G. (2006). Groups vs networks, in elearnspace. Retrieved May 10, 2010, from http://www.elearnspace.org/blog/2006/09/22/groups-vs-networks/

Solomon, G., & Schrum, L. (2007). *Web 2.0: New tools, new schools.* Eugene, Oregon: International Society for Technology in Education.

Thelwall, M., & Price, E. (2003). Disciplinary differences in academic web presence. A statistical study of the UK. *Libri, 53*(4), 242–253.

Times Higher Educational Supplement (2009). *The research life cycle: A report produced by TSL Education Limited to a brief agreed with JISC.* Retrieved May 10, 2010, from http://www.timeshighereducation.co.uk/story.asp?sectioncode=26&storycode=409097

Warlick, D. (2009). The art of cultivating a personal learning network. Retrieved May 10, 2010, from http://www.slideshare.net/dwarlick/personal-learning-networks

Wellman, B. (2001). Physical place and cyberplace: The rise of network individualism. *International Journal of Urban and Regional Research,* 25(2), 227–252.

White, N. (2009). Group Facilitation vs. Network Facilitation—Video interview. Retrieved May 10, 2010, from http://www.youtube.com/watch?v=KpiKMhOdMYI

Whitley, R. (1984). *The intellectual and social organization of the sciences.* Oxford: Clarendon Press.

Wenger, E. (1998). *Communities of practice: Learning, meaning and identity.* Cambridge: Cambridge University Press

Wenger, E., McDermott, R., & Snyder, W. M. (2002). *Cultivating communities of practice.* HBS press.

Williams, S., Fleming, S., & Parslow, P. (2010). This is me—digital identity for careers. Odin Lab. Retrieved May 10, 2010, from http://tinyurl.com/y8kz7ep

21st Century Skills—Realising our Potential (2003). Department for Education and Skills, national skills strategy, white paper. Retrieved May 10, 2010, from http://www.dius.gov.uk/skills/skills_strategy/21st_century_skills

CHAPTER 6

Integrating Digital Technologies in Education: A Model for Negotiating Change and Resistance to Change

Thomas Berger and Michael Thomas

Introduction

The integration of learning technologies in educational institutions is a complex process and presents stakeholders with potential opportunities as well as significant points of resistance. Understanding this process is crucial in the age of digital education, as without the active involvement of educational managers, teacher trainers, curriculum coordinators, and administrators there is a high risk that new digital technologies will stay in the hands of a few core enthusiasts or "missioners" (Miller & Glover, 2010) and potentially marginalize nonparticipants rather than engage them in meaningful ways. There is also a danger that the technologies and the gains made from deploying these technologies may disappear again when those core enthusiasts change roles or organizations. The high turnover of trends, technologies, and ideas in information and communication technology (ICT) is one reason why they generate both excitement and skepticism in almost equal measure. Learning technologies is a constantly moving area with new applications appearing with high frequency and significant barriers to integration, both intrinsic and extrinsic, exist. The main factors in terms of instructors include "lack of confidence, lack of competence, and lack of access to resources" (Bingimlas, 2009, p. 243). Attempts to articulate the history of educational technology often reinforce the existence of these challenges (Cuban, 1986), and it is important to understand the forces and stakeholder interests influencing technology integration.

This chapter is targeted at both instructors and educational administrators and aims to provide support to teachers who would like to integrate Web 2.0 digital technologies in particular (Gonella & Pantó, 2008) as well as the new teaching methods associated with them and who have already experienced resistance to new learning practices or expect potential resistance in the future. Furthermore, it introduces an approach to change management in educational contexts that attempts to resignify resistance as a productive rather than destructive force. In what follows, the framework presented is primarily based on a "train the trainer" model developed by the European project consortium entitled VITAE or Implementation of Innovation in Vocational Training and Education (VITAE, 2008). The VITAE project, which concluded in 2009, articulates a model of "learning by mentoring" with the aid of Web-based applications. The change management perspective discussed in the chapter is one of the buildings blocks of the VITAE model, and thus the model and the experiences of pilot implementations of the project serve as an important reference point (http://www.vitae-project.eu).

The role of new media in changing the learning culture

The relationship between the new media and education has been a source of controversy in recent years. Some see a new generation of learners growing up together with digital technologies as well as new forms of literacy (Prensky 2001; Tapscott, 1998, 2009); others question the almost evangelical undercurrents that promote ICTs and lead to unrealistic expectations. Though widely disseminated, the idea of a distinct generation of digital learners has been subject to sustained critique over the last few years (Bennett, Maton & Kervin, 2009; Schulmeister, 2008) and a growing amount of empirical research argues that by eliding significant differences between learners (based on socioeconomic class, gender, and ethnicity to name but a few variables) the concept is in fact potentially dangerous. By no means all young people possess more than fairly rudimentary skills of searching and accessing digital information, and the widespread use of digital technologies owes perhaps far more to the skills of the so-called "digital immigrants" than to their children.

While largely discredited in terms of an identifiable "generation," then, the number of people who are blogging or contributing to a virtual community is nevertheless growing as the number of Internet users grows. But many Internet studies confirm that the majority of people who use blogs, discussion forums, or similar platforms remain passive "lurkers" rather than active contributors (Fisch & Gscheidle, 2008; Mediascope Europe, 2008; Nielsen, 2006; Rheingold, 2000). This means that for a majority of people, use of the Internet still conforms to traditional patterns of media consumption such as watching television rather than to computer-mediated forms of social interaction and the collaborative production of content—attributes that O'Reilly (2005) identifies with Web 2.0.

Independent of the exact role the new media is given, opportunities for enhancing social and collaborative strategies for learning cannot be neglected. Socioeconomic (globalization, demographic change) and political developments (European Integration, European reform processes such as the Lisbon, Bologna, or Copenhagen processes) have had an influence on expectations relating to the structure of learning environments and the role of digital literacies within them (Lankshear & Knobel, 2007). It is also a fact that the Internet offers new learning opportunities, although the extent to which learners and trainers take advantage of those opportunities (e.g., through intercultural exchange and virtual mobility, new ways of expression, ad hoc access to a huge amount of learning resources and contact with experts) is another issue.

The organizational development perspective

The concept of "learning culture" helps to provide a wider perspective on the relationship between education, digital technologies, and the new forms of social media enabling the integration of management and organization perspectives. The term "culture" reveals the underlying influence of values, traditions, and norms on learning activities and environments. Based on Sindler (2004), learning culture can be described as an interrelation of five main perspectives:

- *Learner perspectives*: Includes their motivations, emotions, and learning strategies
- *Trainer perspectives*: Includes the design of learning environments for the learner to facilitate learning (methods, tools)
- *Institutional framework perspective*: Includes the organizational framework, the learning infrastructure, structures and processes of the educational organization

- *Organization perspective*: Includes strategic development plans and management decisions of an educational organization
- *Social perspective*: Includes the sociocultural framework conditions, matters of social power, and social environments (milieus)

According to Kirchhöfer (2004), one of the main factors for the current change process concerning the learning culture consists of the dissolution of boundaries. In turn, this process consists of a number of interrelated factors:

- *Time*: learning takes place across all stages of life (the concept of life-long-learning)
- *Space*: digital technologies allow independence from special learning organizations (such as schools, colleges and universities), thus enabling learners to construct their learning spaces in different locations
- *Resources*: digital technologies allow almost unlimited access to learning resources
- *Content*: the relative importance of knowledge is decreasing against the importance of competences, especially those of meta-competences (e.g., the ability to learn, to further develop and maintain competences relevant to a professional field, and self-management abilities)
- *Social form*: in a self-directed learning process, the social functions of learning and teaching can no longer be separated
- *Institution*: traditional institutions have to deal with new forms of learning (e.g., learners seek recognition and accreditation of informal and nonformal learning)
- *Biography*: after school, the degree of freedom to decide about content, time, and duration of learning increases

The dissolution of these boundaries is a reaction to and catalyst for wider sociocultural developments. They are reflected in the ongoing reforms of national and international educational systems such as, for example, the promotion of life-long-learning through the UNESCO and EU bodies or the shift to learning outcomes and a competence orientation as part of the Bologna and Copenhagen processes (CEDEFOP, 2008). Kirchhöfer (2004), however, underlines that these changes to the nature of learning culture are not part of a linear or unidirectional process; instead traditional and new learning cultures will in all likelihood coexist beside one another and both types of learning culture will develop further.

New digital and social media can be important factors in the process of change vis-à-vis learning culture but their appearance does not automatically mean they can become a catalyst for change (Sindler, 2004). The conflict between enthusiasts and skeptics concerning the role of new media in education is often rooted in a misunderstanding. Learning culture changes because traditional boundaries begin to dissolve but new media can support this process as well as work against it (Parker, 2004).

The dynamic developments of the Internet, particularly Web 2.0 tools, such as blogs, audio-blogs (podcasts), microblogs (e.g., Twitter), and social networking platforms (e.g., Ning), often come with the expectation that these new tools will be used in educational organizations, and that by using them the quality of the learning experience will be enhanced. A concomitant feature is that this enhancement of learning will be immediate—a factor reinforced by the marketing campaigns that often accompany each new generation of educational technology. When new media tools become the focus of attention rather than the wider aspects of the learning culture, disappointment about the effects and the infrequent use of expensive learning platforms and software is often the result. Moreover, new media can also be used to support very traditional forms of pedagogy. Computer or Web-based training such as preparatory courses for the International or European Computer Driving Licence (ECDL Foundation, 2010) or other popular training programs using multiple choice tests to control the learning progress are examples of traditional learning cultures being facilitated by new digital media.

On the other hand, networking among educational institutions and learners independent of their location is practically impossible without the help of new media. Networking can also be seen as the basis of a new learning approach called connectivism (Gonella & Pantò, 2008; Siemens, 2005). The process of learning is a constant effort to connect information, ideas, and concepts but also learners with other learners and experts. A decision about the relevance of a certain connection is part of the effort involved in the learning process itself.

With reference to Kirchhöfer (2004) discussed above, Table 6.1 shows specific examples of a new learning culture in operation, indicating how it is possible to ground the learner-centered perspective in an approach based on the organization of a personal learning environment within the framework established by the UNESCO (2008) ICT standards. The most prominent example of this is the use of a mentoring process to underline a cooperative approach to technology integration.

Table 6.1 Promoting Change Between Traditional and New Learning Cultures Using the VITAE Model

Criteria	Examples from VITAE model
Position of individuals in the learning process	Emphasis on the organization of a personal learning environment (PLE).
Learning Content	Definition of learning outcomes and competences according to UNESCO (2008) ICT standards and national qualification frameworks.
Learning Sector	The different pilot runs taking place in different institutional settings and sectors have demonstrated the flexibility of the model. For instance, Module 1 of the VITAE template provides examples of how the social environment becomes part of the personal learning environment.
Learning Method	The Learning Portfolio (including the digital version called e-Portfolio) is a documentation method of a self-reflective learning process but it also symbolises learner independence.
Learning Biography	The VITAE model promotes learning which is fully integrated into the professional life of trainers.
Learning Goals	Although there are institutional and in some countries even governmental qualification standards the VITAE model had to take these into account (as reminiscence of the traditional learning culture). The whole model is based on building a personal learning environment. The diversity of learning experiences and learning outcomes of the pilot runs demonstrate its flexibility.
Organization of Learning Cooperation	The VITAE model promotes learning within a community of practice and promotes active networking beyond a traditional course or institution. The practical implementation however shows that language barriers and other constraints might still lead to (albeit new forms of) segregation rather than fluid networks.
Learning Certification	The VITAE model describes learning outcomes according to the UNESCO ICT-standards (UNESCO, 2008). The documentation of learning results using the portfolio in combination with the standardised references to certain levels of competence, allows recognition and certification in a wide range of contexts, whenever and wherever required. The current development of the ECVET (European Commission, 2010) system will facilitate this form of European-wide certification in the future.
Teaching Culture	The mentoring component is the most prominent example of how a cooperative and learner-centric culture is promoted by the VITAE model.

Gonella and Pantò (2008) interlink the change of learning culture with the change of organizations. The organizations that the trainers and their trainees are working in have an immediate influence on the learning culture. But it is also influenced by a new learning culture in a mutual relationship. As in the case of the development of a learning culture, organizational development should not be connected to a linear process. All organization models from Taylor's (2006) production model (inspired by behaviourism from the industrial age) to postindustrial developments toward a learning and knowledge-based organization can still be observed today. Terms such as Enterprise 1.0 and 2.0 as well as E-learning 1.0 and 2.0 intend to illustrate the change but might also give the impression that there is a linear development. Nevertheless, Gonella and Pantò (2008, p. 9) illustrate the relationship of organizational and pedagogic models as well as technical, structural, and theoretical developments.

According to Gonella and Pantò, the VITAE model can easily be linked to E-learning 2.0 as it uses the Web platform Ning as a learning community environment. It no longer depends on fixed learning objects as part of a learning management system (LMS such as WebCT) but rather makes use of the diversity of social networking applications such as a group on Flickr and a collection of bookmarks on Delicious.

However, from an organizational perspective, it is also apparent that the VITAE model is not compatible with traditional production models, organizational structures, and other models. This has consequences for the implementation of the VITAE model. It demonstrates that the implementation of new media in adult and vocational learning organizations is a question of change in the learning culture and consequently a question of organizational development. However, most teachers do not have a management background and rather underestimate the importance of this organizational perspective. The focus on the organizational development of the perspective, as one of the important factors of learning culture, will be addressed with reference to the following question:

> Might resistance to change of the learning culture and to implementation of new media be also rooted in resistance to a "(self-) evaluation culture" and to the implementation of a "control society"?

When we look back at the description of a new learning culture as described above, it is clear that an individual's responsibility for the learning process has increased. Terms such as "self-organized," "self-regulated," or "self-reflective" illustrate this development. This is also reflected in the description of new organizational cultures, where employees take more responsibility for their own career as well as for their organization (e.g., as a consequence of flat and fluid hierarchies) and are expected to develop an entrepreneurial spirit (in educational organizations this is often perceived as increased economical pressure).

The dissolving boundaries described by Kirchhoefer can also be studied as dissolving boundaries between employed and self-employed people. Haecker (2007) refers to Sennet and Foucault, when he describes how the interplay of the power and logic of markets and economic pressure to adapt competences to market conditions implies the danger of a control society. In such a society, individuals take over the role of controllers and by their self-control they unconsciously subjugate themselves completely to purely economic market rules. Finally, those individuals see their own subjectivity as a result of social norms and discipline. Such a perspective of self-reflective life-long learning and personal development turns into life-long self-marketing and self-promotion. While their learning outcomes and competences are dictated by market rules and market requirements, individuals are required to self-regulate and self-organize their learning process to achieve certain learning objectives and gain certain competences, often outside institutional boundaries (e.g., in informal or nonformal settings).

Promising Web 2.0 learning tools (e.g., online social networks and e-portfolios) might turn into tools of (self-)control. The growing number of tools and services that help to manage one's "online reputation"—the image someone presents in his or her social networking profiles and contributions to forums and blogs—seem to confirm the potential of such a development (Reputation Defender, 2010; Schawbel, 2009).

In order to address the unease which many educators may feel regarding a new learning culture, Häcker (2007) compares *self-regulated* with *self-determined* learning. Self-determined learning expresses a way of learning that includes self-reflection beyond self-promotion. It requires a learner to identify and to address not only learning opportunities but also the limitations of learning (environments), external (social, institutional) factors influencing learning goals, processes, dilemmas, and paradoxes of a learning process. In contrast, self-regulated learning is reduced to decisions by learners, which are concerned with the operative aspects of learning only, such as when and where learning takes place, which learning methods and means are used, and what pace is applied.

The comparison of the two approaches helps to address underlying fears and misunderstandings concerning the change of learning culture. It might also help those involved in rethinking the application of a new learning culture and the role of new digital media in educational organizations. Table 6.2 (Häcker, 2007) illustrates the differences of the two approaches and their attributes, conditions, and underlying organizational as well as social models. The focus on the differences comes with a

Table 6.2 Self-Determination and Self-Regulation of Learning

Criteria of Comparison	Self-determination of Learning	Self-regulation of Learning
Underlying organizational, model and idea of man	"Complex Man"—an organization consists of complex individuals und supports their autonomy, which is mutually respected (subject theoretical approach based on Hegel)	"Homo Oeconomicus"— Individuals are aiming to be part of a self-regulating systems for maximum benefits (system theoretic approach)
Social objective	— Humanisation of learning — Promotion of equal opportunities/solidarity — Influence on social framework conditions	— Development of human capital — Promotion of competition — Optimisation of socio-economic position of individuals making use of social framework conditions
Freedom of decision by learners	— Subjects and objectives of learning i.e., meaning of learning for the life-perspective of learners — Operational aspects such as time, location, media, methods, partner, form, methods	— Operational aspects such as time, location, media, methods, partner, form, methods — Outcomes and goals of learning are predetermined by qualification frameworks and given learning objectives
Preconditions	— Self-regulation competences must exist/be trained — Knowledge of limitations of room for manoeuvre — Promotion of (self-)reflection about learning/teaching behaviour and institutional/social context — Support system provided by educational organizations (consultancy, certification, provision of means and places for learning)	— Self-discipline in the framework of social and systemic rules — Knowledge of "rules of the game" — Training and development of (self-) competences — self reflection in form of self-promotion of own competences — Support system provided by educational organizations (consultancy, certification, provision of means and places for learning)
Organizational change in educational organizations (Kil, 2003)	Turnaround on the basis of learning processes by means of deutero/Meta Learning (change is a result of reflective learning of members of an organization) (Honegger, 2009) in a Learning Organization	Restructuring to increase efficiency and effectiveness by means of double-loop learning (change is a result of feed-back control loops) in a Learning Organization

simplification that aims to facilitate the understanding, although in real life, self-regulation and self-determination might be less clearly divided.

When asking about the role of new media in educational organizations, the question might be simplified to: "Do we want to do the same as before but more efficiently or can we dare do something new, exploiting the added value of the new digital technologies?" Table 6.2 illustrates that promoting self-determined learning by implementing new media would require something new and daring. Furthermore Table 6.2 shows that both learning forms still have something in common and that both require a support system (e.g., educational organizations and educators) although their role changes. Moreover, it emphasizes that self-regulation competences are required to learn in a self-determined way but that self-regulation needs to be expanded by the principle described in German as *Widerstaendigkeit* (Bernhard, 2007), meaning an understanding of learning based on *resistance* against "the world" (learning objectives, requirement, conditions, and environments).

How is the process of changing the learning culture in an educational organization related to resistance?

Change in educational organizations can only happen when it is supported by all members, including educational managers, instructors, and administrators. It is natural to assume, however, that change processes will encounter resistance. This is especially true of educational organizations. The structure of educational organizations is one of the main reasons for resistance to change. Most educational organizations are "expert organizations" in that trainers or teachers have a high degree of autonomy in carrying out their work. However, even in other educational organizations, the work of trainers and teachers requires autonomy concerning the methods and the tools used. Furthermore, teachers and trainers often identify more with their community of peers or their discipline than with their organization as a result. Teachers in adult education often have freelance status and work for more than one employer or in the case of higher education, recognition of a national or international expert community is more important than recognition within the parameters of one's own institution.

This means that a change to the learning and teaching culture within an organization can easily be undermined by trainers and teachers. Indeed, there is a general impression that many educational organizations have a good ICT infrastructure but most of the teachers and trainers are not using it as expected (by learners, politicians, and educational experts). In this respect, Stang (2003) came to the following conclusion based on empirical research at German *Volkshochschulen* (adult education centers). Although these organizations usually have a good technical infrastructure and show a general openness to new technologies while also adhering to traditional forms of learning, they are often associated with resistance to change vis-à-vis organizational structures. Stang identified a number of reasons for this resistance (e.g., lack of personnel, financial resources, skepticism concerning new media, and lack of orientation to innovation at management level). On the other hand, if the implementation of a new learning culture is reduced to merely technical and didactic aspects, the management level often does not see the need to become fully involved.

How can we deal with resistance within a change management process of an educational organization?

The implementation of a new learning culture is a change management process on an organizational level leading to the question that forms the heading of this section. While there is agreement about the idea that resistance is part of every change management process, there are different perspectives about how to deal with it (Cacaci, 2006; Doppler, 2005; Kühl, 2000; Thiel, 2000). The majority of definitions of resistance in change processes imply that resistance is disturbing to the change process and has therefore to be overcome. On the other hand, there is some agreement about the fact that it is better to work with resistance than against it. If the latter dictum is true, it can be helpful to change the perspective slightly and to ask if there are ways of resignifying resistance in productive terms?

From this perspective, the definition of resistance would be associated with the following points:

- A natural reaction to a change process
- An indicator for being affected (as a member of an organization) on an emotional, material, social, political, and cultural level
- An indicator for potential contradictions and dilemmas within the change process itself
- Questions about its legitimacy and potential consequences on an organizational level.

According to this definition of learning culture, then, it is important to take both the personal and the organizational levels into account.

On the basis of this definition, it is possible to derive an analytical tool to examine resistance productively. This analytical tool can be used in preparation of the implementation of a change process (such as the implementation of the VITAE model), which is targeted at trainers and managers in educational organizations. It aims to detect potential resistance in advance and use the results to further develop change

Table 6.3 A Tool for Analysing Resistance in Change Processes

Level of Reflection	Guiding questions of analysis of resistance in change processes
Awareness level	Am I aware that, — resistance is a natural reaction to change? — resistance is an indicator of members of an organization being affected by the change process? — resistance can be an indicator for contradictions, dilemmas and other discrepancies of the change process itself? — I have to ask for the legitimacy of resistance and am I prepared to deal with consequences on the level of persons, organizational structure or on the level of design of the change process itself?
Discovery level	What kind of symptoms of resistance have I observed / do I have to look for?
Analysis on an emotional and personal level	To what extent will the expectations of members of the organization concerning goals, objectives and forms of cooperation of working in the organization be disappointed? Does the change result in an increased or decreased burden? To what extent do those concerned by the change get support and experience acceptance and mutual trust?
Analysis on an emotional and organizational level	Does/did the organization allow members to experience change as something positive? How does the organization deal with critique (change is regarded as critique to the status quo)? To what extent does/did the organization respect existing agreements with colleagues and deal with changes to them openly?
Analysis on a material and personal level	To what extent do colleagues regard the change as a material risk?
Analysis on material and organizational level	To what extent are potential changes transparent to colleagues? Does/did the organization make it clear to what extent existing material agreements, work load, and career opportunities are affected by the change?
Analysis on a social and personal level	Do colleagues fear a loss of status? Do colleagues fear that existing promises and informal agreements are no longer valid?
Analysis on a social and organizational level	To what extent is participation of colleagues in the change process possible? To what extent can colleagues contribute their own expectations and ideas?
Analysis on a political and personal level	To what extent might colleagues fear the loss of power or the loss of autonomy? To what extent are factual arguments contra the change rooted in contents or in political interests?
Analysis on a cultural and personal level	To what extent are personal norms and values of colleagues concerned by the change?

Continued

Table 6.3 Continued

Level of Reflection	Guiding questions of analysis of resistance in change processes
Analysis on cultural and organizational level	To what extent does the change process provide a vision colleagues can identify with? To what extent does the style of communication and leadership allow participation and open criticism?
Analysis on mode of change and personal level	Might colleagues feel taken by surprise or feel forced into the change process? How have/will colleagues experience decision taking concerning the change process?
Analysis on mode of change and organizational level	Does the organization provide the necessary resources (personnel, time, technological infrastructure) to implement the change process? Which modus shall be followed—revolutionary, evolutionary, incremental change? Is the need for change plausible? Is the dissatisfaction with the status quo obvious? Do colleagues have the chance (and enough time) to acquire the necessary skills and competences to implement the change? Does the organization have the ability to collect, process and distribute knowledge about itself and its environment/stakeholders?
Action	Based on the analysis, do I regard resistance as legitimate? Do I see potential for productive use? To what extent can: — the conditions of the change process be changed? — interventions turn colleagues from persons concerned with change to active participants in a change process? — inconsistencies, antagonism and dilemmas of a change process be discussed openly? — the analysis help to discover "blind spots" of the change process and alternative approaches?
Reflection	To what extent am I aware of reverse feedback effects i.e., that the analysis of resistance might make resistance "attractive," "interesting" or a "fashion"? Am I aware that resistance is dynamic and the results of analysis will change over time and together with a change of factors outside the organization (technological and pedagogical progress, job market situation etc.)? What about the limits and side effects of methods used to deal with resistance? Do I want to/Can I evaluate the use of methods dealing with resistance?

management strategies. However, it also helps during the implementation of the change management process (as resistance cannot be fully prevented) to find strategies for working with the points of resistance that emerge.

Table 6.4 Examples of the VITAE Model and Technology Integration

Level of Reflection	Examples
Awareness level	On this level it has been important to develop the awareness that the implementation of the VITAE model is subject to organizational development and consists of a change management process. According to our perspective resistance is something to be expected but we try to see it as productive as possible.
Discovery level	Examples for potential symptoms of resistance are lack of motivation to use new tools, aggressive behaviour, repression of the topic, verbal resistance, etc.
Analysis on an emotional and personal level	A change of learning culture implies change on different levels at the same time. Introducing the different elements of the VITAE model and furthermore numerous Web tools can easily lead to a mental overload. In our example leaving room for discussions about the added value of using certain tools has helped to keep those "on board," who are rather focused on teaching methods, organizational implementation etc.
Analysis on an emotional and organizational level	Almost all VITAE project members experienced that the change of learning culture does not result in a reduction of efforts in teaching; in most cases it even comes with an increased workload. The idea that new technologies save time is an illusion one should be open about it. Nevertheless it is important to create room for positive experiences and "celebrate" those.
Analysis on a material and personal level	The change of learning culture will most probably not save time on the side of trainers. While for a period of time extra efforts are tolerable, the impression that the change of learning culture will lead to more work for the same salary can undermine the change process.
Analysis on a material and organizational level	The change of learning culture according to the VITAE model allows for more flexibility regarding working hours and the location of trainers as a number of training/learning activities can and have to be done online. Flexibility of tele-working however comes with potential risks, such as blurring the lines between private and professional life and potential fears concerning career opportunities, when one is less attendant (and visible) at the organization.
Analysis on a social and personal level	The VITAE model can touch a number of status positions. In many educational organizations some lecturers are early adopters of technology and new learning methods and thus achieve "expert status." Sometimes this status is even connected to special software (e.g., a learning management system). If the change implies the use of new tools and reduces the importance of the old ones, resistance can be expected. Mentoring might be furthermore seen in general as a reduction of the expert's status, when through the mentoring process others turn to "experts" as well. A way to get those colleagues concerned about their expert status involved could be to provide alternative forms of status to them, e.g., through early involvement in planning of the change process, which allows them to develop their status position in a new direction (e.g., as "change management experts").
Analysis on a social and organizational level	The VITAE model foresees participation at different levels as this is one of the key elements of a change process. For example, the mentoring process itself requires the participation of colleagues. Being a mentor/mentee requires participation in a change process. This way being mentored can be seen as a facilitator for participative change/development processes within an organization. While the meaningful use of Web 2.0 tools can be promoted as part of a new learning culture it helps to support the change process by documenting the process using participative Web 2.0 tools such as a blog or podcast for example. Of course this will not replace the face-to-face activities but might provide a useful follow-up to allow for even more channels of participation.

Continued

Table 6.4 Continued

Level of Reflection	Examples
Analysis on a political and personal level	Every organizational development process results also in a change of micro politics and the distribution of power in an organization. If, for example, the importance of an LMS is reduced in favour of more flexible arrangements of web-tools this concerns not only the status but also the question of budgets and access. This means resistance can be expected from those who seem to lose power in the process.
Analysis on a cultural and personal level	The introduction of a "new" learning culture means that we ourselves have mostly experienced traditional learning cultures in our life so far. Although we are aware, for example, of the advantages of a learner-centric approach, one can easily fall back on a teacher-centric way of thinking.
Analysis on a cultural and organizational level	The VITAE model makes use of the "intercultural story metaphor" to provide a potential basis of identification. This is reflected in the title and introductory sentences to the different modules of the VITAE template. The model of the acculturation process for a new cultural environment has a number of analogies with the change process model. By involving other areas of life experience the vision of the change management process can be communicated more effectively.
Analysis on mode of change and personal level	Every kind of "pro forma" participation in a decision-making procedure should be avoided as it will (sooner or later) cause resistance.
Analysis on mode of change and organizational level	The result of this analysis might uncover "blind spots" in the change process. In adult education organizations, developments concerned with learner independence, self-reflective learning and the development of personal learning environments, are often regarded as a positive and almost "natural" process (Schaffert & Hilzensauer, 2008). Such a learning culture comes with requirements concerning the "learning abilities" of learners and not all learners are able to deal with this.
Action	Especially in the (micro-) political realm it has to be noted that not all forms of resistance can be used productively. In a change process there might be actors who use it as an opportunity to gain power at the expense of the aims of the change process and the performance of the organization. Such a resistance would be regarded as illegitimate from the perspective of change management and in such cases a decision to overcome such a resistance might become necessary.
Reflection	The very analytical approach of self-reflection presented here has of course its limits. Some sources and reasons for resistance can only be revealed with the help of experts and the use of less analytical methods such as "constellation work" and psychodrama activities. However most organizations have little experience with such methods and such methods can cause resistance themselves.

The analytical tool consists of guiding questions divided into different "levels of reflection," starting from a level of awareness, followed by a level of discovery—the central analysis level, a level of action, and finally by a level of (meta-)reflection. The different points of the definition of resistance are the source for defining the different levels and sublevels. Table 6.3 provides an overview of those guiding questions of "self reflection" for each level.

This is followed by practical examples illustrating the potential use of the tool in relation to technology integration (see Table 6.4). While the primary area of application is the planning of the implementation of the VITAE model as a change management process, many of the guiding questions are also helpful in terms of planning a mentoring process—as mentoring can also be seen as a "mini-change management process" in itself. It is a snapshot of an analysis done toward the end of the projects and is provided as a support to the guiding questions of Table 6.3. Those examples also motivate participants to see the guiding questions as a starting point for further development based on experience gained when dealing with resistance in a concrete change management process.

The model can be used to make better decisions in (planning) a change management process by identifying the issues and questions that need to be addressed. It allows trainers as well as managers to regard resistance as an integral element of change and encourages them to rethink the methods used and the provision of resources provided to implement learning technologies as part of a new learning culture and organizational development.

Conclusion

The VITAE model requires management support in order to promote a new learning culture. The implementation of a new learning culture will not be successful when it is merely reduced to a technological or pedagogical perspective. It is in fact an organizational development process and requires an holistic approach. However, such an organizational change process will always encounter resistance. Analytical tools such as those presented in this chapter can help to develop a productive counterperspective to resistance to technology integration, and in turn provide indicators for frictions and discrepancies in the change process, thus helping to make the change process more sustainable. This model is highly applicable to contemporary learning environments in which Web-based and digital technologies are being integrated.

References

Bennett, S., Maton, K., & Kervin, L. (2008). The 'digital natives' debate: A critical review of the evidence. *British Journal of Educational Technology, 39*(5), 775–786.

Bernhard, A. (2007). Simplify your life—Die Infantilisierung der gesellschaftlichen Lernräume und die Vermüllung des Bewusstseins als pädagogische Herausforderungen. In D. Kirchhöfer & G. Steffens (Ed.), *Infantilisierung des Lernens?—Neue Lernkulturen—ein Streitfall* (pp. 59–73). Frankfurt: Lang.

Bingimlas, K. A. (2009). Barriers to the successful integration of ICT in teaching and learning environments: A review of the literature. *Eurasia Journal of Mathematics, Science & Technology Education, 5*(3), 235–245.

Cacaci, A. (2006). *Change management—Widerstande gegen Wandel Plädoyer für ein System der Prävention.* Wiesbaden: Deutscher Universitäts-Verlag.

CEDFOP – European Centre for the Development of Vocational Training (2008). The shift to learning outcomes—Conceptual, political and practical developments in Europe. Luxembourg: Office for Official Publications of the European Community.

Cuban, L. (1986). *Teachers and machines: The classroom use of technology since 1920.* New York: Teachers College Press.

Doppler K., & Lauterburg C. (2005). *Change management—Den Unternehmenswandel gestalten.* Frankfurt: Campus-Verlag.

ECDL Foundation (2010). Website. Retrieved May 10, 2010, from http://www.ecdl.org

European Commission (2010). *The European Credit System for Vocational Education and Training (ECVET).* Retrieved May 10, 2010, from http://ec.europa.eu/education/lifelong-learning-policy/doc50_en.htm

Fisch, M., & Gscheidle, C. (2008). Mitmachnetz Web 2.0: Rege Beteiligung nur in Communities. Media Perspektiven 7/2008. Retrieved May 10, 2010, from http://www.daserste.de/service/studie08_4.pdf

Gonella, L., & Pantò, E. (2008). Didactic architectures and organization models: A process of mutual adaptation. Retrieved May 10, 2010, from http://www.elearningeuropa.info/files/media/media15973.pdf

Häcker, T. (2007). *Portfolio: ein Entwicklungsinstrument für selbstbestimmtes Lernen. Eine explorative Studie zur Arbeit mit Portfolios in der Sekundarstufe 1.* Hohengehren: Baltmannsweiler: Schneider Verlag.

Honegger, B. D. (2009). Willkommen in Beats Biblionetz!. Retrieved May 10, 2010, from http://beat.doebe.li/bibliothek/w00497.html

JISC (2008). *Great expectations of ICT: How higher education institutions are measuring up.* Research Study Conducted for the Joint Information Systems Committee (JISC). Retrieved May 10, 2010, from http://www.jisc.ac.uk/publications/research/2008/greatexpectations.aspx

Kil, M. (2003). *Organisationsveränderungen in Weiterbildungseinrichtungen: Empirische Analysen und Ansatzpunkte für Entwicklung und Forschung.* Bielefeld: Bertelsmann.

Kirchhöfer, D. (2004). *Lernkultur Kompetenzentwicklung: Begriffliche Grundlagen.* Berlin: Arbeitsgemeinschaft Betriebliche Weiterbildungsforschung.

Kirchhöfer, D. (2007). Neue Lernkultur und Infantilisierung. In D. Kirchhöfer & G. Steffens (Eds.), *Infantilisierung des Lernens?—Neue Lernkulturen—ein Streitfall* (pp. 17–42). Frankfurt: Lang.

Kühl, S. (2000). *Das Regenmacher-Phänomen: Widersprüche und Aberglaube im Konzept lernender Organization*. Frankfurt/Main: Campus-Verl.

Lankshear, C., & Knobel, M. (2007). *Digital literacies: Concepts, policies and practices*. Frankfurt: Lang.

Mediascope Europe (2008). *EIAA Mediascope Europe 2008: Executive summary*. Retrieved May 10, 2010, from http://eiaa.net/Ftp/casestudiesppt/EIAA_Mediascope_Europe_2008_PanEuropean_Executive_Summary.pdf

Miller, D., & Glover, D. (2010). Interactive whiteboards: A literature survey. In M. Thomas & E. Cutrim Schmid (Eds.), *Interactive whiteboards for education: Theory, research and practice*. Hershey, PA: IGI Global.

Nielsen J. (2006). *Participation inequality: Encouraging more users to contribute*. Retrieved May 10, 2010, from http://www.useit.com/alertbox/participation_inequality.html

O'Reilly T. (2005). *What is web 2.0? Design patterns and business models for the next generation of software*. Retrieved May 10, 2010, from http://www.oreilly.de/artikel/web20.html

Parker, N. K. (2004). The quality dilemma of online-education. In A. Terry & F. Elloumi (Eds.), *Theory and practice of online learning* (pp. 385–409). Edmonton: AU Press, Athabasca University.

Prensky, M. (2001). Digital natives, digital immigrants. *On the Horizon, 9*(5), 1–6.

Redecker, C. (2009). *Review of learning 2.0 practices: Study on the impact of Web 2.0 innovation son education and training in Europe*. European Commission, Joint Research Centre. Retrieved May 10, 2010, from http://ftp.jrc.es/EURdoc/JRC49108.pdf

Reputation Defender (2010). Website. Retrieved May 10, 2010, from http://www.reputationdefender.com/?lang=en

Rheingold, H. (2000). Community development in the cybersociety of the future. In D. Gauntlett (Ed.), *Web studies: Rewiring media studies for the digital age* (pp. 170–178). London: Arnold.

Schulmeister, R. (2008). Gibt es eine »Net Generation«? Work in Progress. Retrieved May 10, 2010, from http://www.zhw.uni-hamburg.de/pdfs/Schulmeister_Netzgeneration.pdf

Schawbel, D. (2009). *Me 2.0: Build a powerful brand to achieve career success*. New York, NY: Kaplan.

Siemens, G. (2005). Connectivism: A learning theory for the digital age. *In International Journal of Instructional Technology & Distance Learning, 2*(1). Retrieved May 10, 2010, from http://www.itdl.org/journal/jan_05/Jan_05.pdf#page=7.

Sindler, A. (2004). *Etablierung einer neuen Lernkultur—Modelle medienbasierter Lernarrangements zur Förderung selbstregulierten Lernens im Kontext der Organization*. Wien: Lit-Verlag.

Stang, R. (2003). Neue Medien in Organizationen der Weiterbildung—Empirische Befunde am Beispiel der Volkshochschulen, online (DIE). In E. Nuissl,

C. Schiersmann & H. Siebert (Eds.) *Erfahrungen mit Neuen Medien*. Bielefeld: Bertelsmann.

Tapscott, D. (1998). *Growing up digital: The rise of the net generation*. New York: McGraw-Hill.

Tapscott, D. (2009). *Grown up digital: How the Net generation is changing your world*. New York: McGraw-Hill.

Taylor, F. W (2006). *The principles of scientific management*. New York: Cosimo.

Thiel, H-U. (2000). Widerstand gegen Veränderungen in Supervision und Organizationsberatung. In H. Pühl (Ed.), *Supervision und Organizationsentwicklung*, (pp. 228–245). Wiesbaden: VS, Verlag für Sozialwiss.

UNESCO [United Nations Educational, Scientific and Cultural Organization] (2008). ICT competency standards for teachers: Implementation guidelines, Version 1.0. Retrieved May 10, 2010, from http://cst.unesco-ci.org/sites/projects/cst/The%20Standards/ICT-CSTImplementation%20Guidelines.pdf

VITAE Project Page (2008). We want to empower vocational teachers to mentor their students and colleagues to work competently in the digital world. Retrieved May 10, 2010, from http://www.vitae-project.eu

PART II

Applying Digital Education

CHAPTER 7

Virtual Learning Environments: Personalizing Learning or Managing Learners?

Philip Banyard, Jean Underwood, Lianne Kerlin, and James Stiller

Introduction

Over the past 15 years, the Technology and Learning Team at Nottingham Trent University has conducted a range of national research projects in schools and colleges across the UK. This first decade of the new century has seen significant changes in both the capacity and functionality of the digital technologies available to managers, teachers, and learners in schools. These technological developments have the potential to support innovative ways of learning and teaching as well as of managing educational information. Where these opportunities have been taken up, new ways of processing and owning information have occurred, leading to changes in the relationships between teachers and learners. This chapter looks at the key messages from this program of research and considers how to increase the benefits accruing from technology-enhanced learning environments and also explores their limitations for learners and teachers.

Our research has identified major changes in pedagogy, management, and learners' approaches to learning. These have led to teachers and learners developing new ways of working, which in turn create greater engagement and enhance motivation. Digital technologies have facilitated the tracking of the performance of individual learners and given teachers more information from which to develop individual learning programs. In UK schools, teachers now routinely have online access to student attendance, conduct and achievement (Smith, Rudd & Coghlan 2008). Some schools have pioneered and promoted new techniques for achieving this, for example a secondary school in the east of England has cooperated with a software company to produce a system for monitoring conduct of learners across the school (Underwood et al., 2009a). The *ibehave* (ISIS Software, 2010) system allows teachers to record and access the incidents of good and bad behavior by the learners and the system also generates automatic feedback to parents about their children at the school. The *ibehave* system has been marketed to local schools and the income from these sales is helping to fund other IT initiatives in the school. This facility and similar systems are transforming the management of information in schools and offer the potential to transform the relationship between the teacher and the learner (Underwood et al., 2009a).

The key question to consider concerns the impact of individual technologies on teaching and learning and how this technology can be used to greatest effect. Sometimes a technological innovation appears to be an excellent idea but fails to deliver, and sometimes a major impact can come from an apparently minor technological innovation. Wikis appeal to teachers and lecturers as an ideal medium to create class projects but despite their apparent usefulness the facility has not been effective at the learner level as it is not commonly used by the student body. This is mirrored in the development and use of the microblogging site Twitter. This facility also appeals to managers and teachers but the demographic of Twitter users is skewed away from young people. The most recent data from the United States (Quantcast, 2010) shows that nearly 90% of Twitter users are aged 18 years or above. It also shows a steady decline in Twitter posts over the last six months.

The political context

The technology rhetoric

The work carried out by the research team and discussed in this chapter is set in the context of major UK government investment in educational technology. This investment comes with an expectation, and maybe a demand, that the technology will bring measurable improvements in educational performance. Each new major initiative, such as the roll out of broadband connectivity in the early part of the decade, was seen as providing the "silver bullet," namely, that it will stimulate major improvements in performance. In a keynote speech the UK Secretary of State for Education and Skills at the time underlined this emphasis, arguing that the government saw "ICT and its potential to transform how we teach, learn and communicate as crucial to our drive to raise standards" (Kelly, 2005, p. 4).

On the basis of these presumptions about the value of ICT in UK schools, substantial investment was made in the infrastructure of educational technology. The mean ratio of pupils to computers dropped dramatically in the period from 1998 to 2004 from 17.6:1 to 7.6:1 in primary and 8.7:1 to 4.9:1 in secondary schools. Interactive whiteboards became ubiquitous in UK primary schools and the majority of secondary schools were providing all of their pupils with an email account (Prior & Hall, 2005).

Technology targets are having significant impacts on schools (Smith, Rudd & Coghlan 2008). For example, there has been an active policy to encourage the embedding of virtual learning environments (VLEs) in UK schools; a policy outlined in the UK government's 2005 strategy paper "Harnessing technology—transforming learning and children's services." Our understanding of what constitutes a learning environment has evolved from small-scale highly specific educational packages though large-scale multifunctional VLEs, to personalized learning environments (PLEs). The latter adds individual configurability to peer-to-peer learning, community of practices (CoP), and the VLE. It would be fair to say that mainstream UK schools are currently at the VLE stage of development integrating their management systems with content delivery and a hint of learner personalization (Ofsted, 2009b). The VLE is the common term used in the UK to describe the organization of data in schools and the interface between the learner and the school. Elsewhere it is referred to differently, for example as a content management system (CMS).

The move to personalization

Alongside the belief in the efficacy of technology in education there has been a drive toward personalizing learning, which also comes with a political rhetoric. In 2005 the then UK government asserted: "Personalisation is the key to tackling the persistent achievement gaps between different social and ethnic groups. It means a tailored education for every child and young person, that gives them strength in the basics, stretches their aspirations, and builds their life chances. It will create opportunity for every child, regardless of their background" (HM Government, 2005 p. 2).

Personalized learning is understood in different ways by managers, teachers, and learners (Banyard & Underwood, 2008). Our analyses confirm the fractured nature of different stakeholders' understanding of this core educational concept: while both staff and pupils may see the personalizing of learning as good practice and a goal to be strived for, pupils often do not recognize staff efforts to deliver on this concept. This perceptual discontinuity can in part be explained by pupils equating personalization with "me time" but we also have evidence that some teachers, while accepting the personalization agenda, are still operating a controlling model of education. There are those teachers, however, who equate personalizing learning with pupil voice and choice. They also link this to the need for a curriculum that engages pupils, and for many teachers, this is not a national curriculum with set activities and limiting goals (Underwood et al., 2009a; Underwood et al., 2010).

The vision presented by the UK government is one of radical change, not just a matter of readjustments to curricula or pedagogic practice, important though these maybe, but a shift in the social dynamics and practices of all partners including learners so that the individual needs of each child can be met (see Pollard & James, 2004). This would appear to match the potentialities provided by technology-enhanced learning environments. Indeed Green et al. (2005) argue that the Gilbert Review vision of Teaching and Learning in 2020 (Gilbert et al., 2006) and the challenges posed by the personalizing learning agenda may prove difficult to meet without digital technologies as there will be a specific requirement for "the communication, archiving and multimedia affordances of digital resources" (Green et al., 2005 p. 5).

The need to identify and evaluate the role of digital technologies in supporting a more personalized learning experience is stimulated both by concerns about the performance of the current educational system but also an awareness that many learners today are already creating their personalized learning environments outside school using digital resources. For most young people, technology is part of their daily lives. Those young people with access to digital technologies are already using such resources to tailor their informal learning to their own interests (Underwood et al., 2009a; Underwood et al., 2010).

The caveat we would inject into this account of personalized learning concerns the way that the term is defined and operationalized in education. The issue is not about how learners organize their learning focused as it is on the end results of that learning. One view of a personalized education would see learners as defining at least some of their own goals. For example, Charles Leadbeater writes: "The foundation of a personalised education system would be to encourage children, from an early age and across all backgrounds, to become more involved in making decisions about what they would like to learn and how" (Leadbeater, 2004, p. 16). This is not the view that is pursued in UK schools where the goals of learning are clearly defined in the context of the National Curriculum and the related performance in national academic tests. It is the route to this performance that is seen as the opportunity for personalizing learning, but not the goals themselves.

What has been the impact of the VLE?

From our own and other surveys, the impact of VLEs at school level has been mixed (Becta, 2004, 2007; Ofsted, 2009a; Underwood et al., 2010). Good stories abound, like that of secondary school learner Nathan (described on Becta's website), who really appreciated the efficiency gains of being able to upload and download work without the bother of carrying things between home and school (Becta, 2009). These small changes in the working practice of students on the surface appear trivial but to the user are life-enhancing if not life-changing. Another example is reported by Clarke and Abbott (2008) who present evidence of reflective practice of trainee teachers being supported through the functionality of the VLE. At this level, a VLE can have a dramatic impact on learners and teachers to the point that the change is taken for granted within a short space of time. On the other hand there are numerous stories of abortive attempts to install a working VLE which illustrate the frustration of embedding large scale technology innovations into an institution (Underwood et al., 2010).

Despite financial support, many schools are still in the first throws of implementing this key government policy. The UK government's quality assurance agency's (Ofsted) 2007/8 survey of a sample of educational institutions found that schools were mostly falling behind the national timescales for installing a VLE. Even the minority of schools that had achieved a working VLE were at the stage of thinking through how it might improve learning. With newer ways of working with the technology emerging, principally provided by the potentialities of Web 2.0, Ofsted (2009a, pp. 34–35) has questioned whether this technology may become redundant even before it is fully embedded.

Web 2.0 is a fashionable expression that describes a new generation of websites. The term itself implies that the early Internet should be thought of as "Web 1.0"—a first edition, or first version. It is argued that this initial version of the Web was primarily for static information: material to be downloaded or delivered to the Internet user. Web 2.0 is different as it is a more participatory, dynamic, and social place. It is more about uploading, especially uploading for communication and collaboration (Sharples, 2010). This rapid change in technology and the way it is used develops faster than policy can deal with and makes it difficult for education authorities to plan with any confidence for future resource expenditure.

The report from Ofsted is an example of the widespread concern that technology is unable to meet people's expectations. The report states: "The vast majority of the schools visited had yet to identify how they would use the VLE that the government expects them to have in action in the next few years. At the time of their visit, only one primary school in the sample had a functioning virtual learning environment" (Ofsted, 2009a, p. 14).

Some schools, as exemplified by the following secondary school, have resisted the call to implement their VLE policy because of this perceived bias toward teachers rather than students:

> One of our case study reports records: The school does not have a VLE at the moment because the ones that were piloted still seem teacher driven and not focussed on student learning. They do not include social networking opportunities, and Web 2.0 technologies. VLE's tend to be rather static and should be focussed on student engagement and learning. (Interview with Secondary School teacher: Underwood et al., 2010)

The focus on the individual, including their personal characteristics, and on personal choice has been shown to increase learner motivation and may in turn lead to improved performance (Chen & Liu, 2008; Chou & Wang, 2000; Larkin-Hein & Budney, 2001). However, there are schools that have successfully embedded the technology into their practice as is articulated by this primary headteacher from our own, as yet unpublished, work:

> The VLE has been a major influence in developing the personalisation agenda. Teachers can tailor materials for small groups of pupils. The parents are involved therefore there is a holistic approach to learning, and it helps parents to understand where the pupils are. The teachers planning and assessment has always been good, but the VLE has focused

the mind and sharpened the offerings. (Interview with Primary School headteacher, ongoing research project)

There will be individual differences in responses to all technologies. Ofsted report that: "We found no direct correlation between computer expertise and VLE development; rather it was the more skilled and confident teachers and tutors who treated the VLE as an extension of their normal work. A manager at one college with a well-used VLE said: "A VLE is just another tool in a good teacher's repertoire; it is not an end in itself" (Ofsted, 2009b, p. 12).

The VLE appears self-evidently to be a good idea but does it deliver as much as it promises and what are the key benefits and barriers to success? One perceived benefit is the possibility of predicting student performance from the large body of log file and other data concerning student activity through the application of data mining methods to discover hidden patterns, associations, and anomalies (Superby, Vandamme & Meskens, 2006; Nagi & Suesawaluk, 2008). However, perceived disadvantages often relate to the entry level skills required to take advantage of the system (Underwood et al., 2010). Our research over the last ten years (Underwood et al., 2004; Underwood et al., 2006, 2010) has witnessed the initial stuttering introduction of VLEs before the current mass roll-out and we are well-placed to comment on how schools have worked with this technology to create workable and bespoke systems for their particular needs.

One school that highlights the potential of the VLE as well as the incipient problems surrounding the technology is a secondary school in a UK provincial town. This school has been very proactive in developing bespoke technology and currently gains significant income from licensing its software to other schools. The school had two false starts with VLEs from which it was unable to gain much benefit despite substantial technical expertise and support within the school. Finally, like many other schools with embedded technical support, it has migrated to building its own Moodle. Interestingly, the teaching staff do not have a clear understanding of the Moodle platform but this lack of understanding does not inhibit their use of the system. To the average user, Moodle is perceived as an extension of the web and for many teachers at this school, the terms Moodle and website are synonymous.

The VLE is currently used mainly as a repository for information although there are plans to extend usage and exploit more of the functionality of the system. Will this happen? Such innovative use usually starts with the more technologically savvy individuals but in this school the innovation leaders are already looking elsewhere for increased functionality. These staff see that greater benefits are to be had by using facilities outside the VLE such as blogs, social networking sites (e.g., Ning), course developments software (e.g., Hot Potatoes), and other Web 2.0 tools. It was suggested that the VLE was frustrating for the IT literate. This frustration is mirrored by many IT literate students who prefer Google to a library interface when searching for learning resources.

The VLE is perhaps not the most effective way of creating a PLE for learners. The rise of social software (McLoughline & Lee, 2007) means that learners are able to personalize their learning outside of the structures of their schools and colleges. The technology affordances offered by Web 2.0 digital technologies have been grasped by many learners as well as some teachers (Holah & Davies, 2009), as they find new ways to excite and encourage their students.

While the school network provides a valuable data resource for teachers and managers, the utility of these data is enhanced though the activities of a dedicated data manager. Teachers are confident with this aspect of the network and appreciative of the gains it provides. The usefulness of network facilities as an aid to pedagogy is less developed, which is a common observation in schools. Could it be that the VLE provides a basic resource for teachers for them to build their teaching on? This can work well for teachers who can use it as foundation for their teaching, but the perceived value of the VLE is such that many teachers and managers see it as a sufficient teaching resource rather than a starting point.

Joint Assessment System software (JAS)

One particular innovation in this school came from an identified deficit in the reports it was producing for pupils. The school framed the task as being to address "now and next"—identifying what level the student is at now and what they need to do next to move on. The ICT and systems manager was asked to develop an on-line self-assessment facility. The self-assessment software is now marketed as a joint assessment tool (ISIS Software, 2010) and licensed to other schools. The pupils are reported to like the system because of the instant feedback coupled with details on what they need to do next. They are currently creating subject packs, for example in maths, and hope to use the system as a means of getting ICT across the whole curriculum. There are currently 300 schools that have purchased a license for this facility.

JAS gives pupils access to a list of competency statements set at a number of levels that they can review and endorse. When they have reviewed their performance, the system generates a report summarizing where they are now and what they need to do next. On one level, it resembles an individual maturity model and the same system could be used to deliver an institutional e-maturity model. The pupil's review can be viewed by the teacher, who is able to amend any response they do not agree with. JAS has a number of other facilities including simple quizzes and tests that again can be reviewed by the teacher at an individual and class level. All of these activities are appreciated within the school because they support current pedagogic practice. One might say they are just innovative enough although, as we now go on to show, an element of the teaching profession does want more than efficiency from VLE usage.

Teacher perceptions of the VLE

In our interviews and focus groups with school managers and teachers (Underwood et al., 2004; Underwood et al., 2005; Underwood & Banyard, 2006, 2008) we have recorded a marked and consistent ambivalence to the VLE. This ambivalence is not the case of a luddite profession unwilling to respond to new technology as teacher assessments of the VLE concept were largely positive. Teachers recognized the potential of the VLE to contribute to their professional practice and (when successfully embedded into the curriculum) to greatly enrich learning. This is not achieved, however, when the chosen system is not compatible with the school and teaching practices in place.

In those focus groups and interviews, teachers outlined the key characteristics of a functional VLE. They identified key features in the way the VLE needs to be set up, the way that learners experience it, and also the way that teachers are able to use it. In the first place, it is clear that when the VLE is introduced, it needs to be effective and supported. Although this would seem an obvious point, it is one that is difficult to enact because it requires the early identification of a fit-for-purpose system. Many schools have reported trialing VLEs that failed to offer the attributes of a VLE identified here. Negative experiences of VLEs resulted in a level of disillusionment and recovery of goodwill often proved difficult. Early identification of a usable platform maintained enthusiasm among staff and pupils. It is also necessary to have good support from the local authority (LA). The majority of schools with fully functioning VLEs had knowledgeable LA support in the choice and implementation of their VLE policy. However, not all LAs had effectively operationalized their VLE policy. Initial delays in selecting a system, often followed by decisions to change, meant that schools were unsure as to whether to wait for the LA's decision or independently determine a suitable system to invest in. While educational independence can be a boon, the cost in time, money, and goodwill of such aborted implementations is a concern. A further issue concerns maintenance and whether it is carried out by a technician in the school, ICT coordinator, the head teacher, the LA, or by the company providing the portal. A reliable and maintained system is essential to maintaining effective learning and positive attitudes toward the VLE. Finally, there is the issue of remote access. If the system is being used to provide and store work, it needs to be accessible at home. This also provides the opportunity for families to become involved in the child's learning.

A number of surveys have found that staff value the VLE for its covert rather than overt impact on learning, namely, they appreciated the administrative functions that allowed them to track learner progress and so make informed judgments of how to support those students (Ellis, 2001; European Schoolnet, 2003).

When we consider the way that learners experience their VLE, then, the system needs to be easy-to-negotiate, reliable, and intuitive. It was clear that VLEs deemed user-friendly and which provided the support demanded of it had a higher rate of use within the schools. They also need to be interactive so that teachers and learners are able to upload, mark, and provide feedback to work online. Other necessary facilities include forums, email, and social networking. It is also important that the VLE is pupil-centered and it was a common complaint of rejected VLEs that they were teacher-oriented. Although such VLEs facilitate planning and delivering lessons, teachers felt that such tools were in conflict with the personalizing learning agenda. It was argued that there should be the opportunity for learners to set their own targets and workloads and use the VLE to organize their learning effectively.

So for many, but not all, teachers it is important that the VLE works with and not against current pedagogic practice and that that chosen VLE supports the working practices within the school. It is also clear that VLEs cannot be introduced quickly and we identified a need for a three- or four-year program of implementation. This needs to be accompanied by appropriate and extensive staff training, and alongside the training, the schools have to offer time to develop VLE materials. One headteacher was building time into the staff schedules to update and maintain their areas on the VLE, without this, workloads may be increased greatly.

This long, and not exclusive, list of requirements raises issues about the ambition of introducing VLE as the key driver of educational change. Are we asking too much of this technology and have we fully framed our expectations of this facility?

The gap between potential and use

As part of our most recent project (Underwood et al., 2009b), we explored the gap between the perceived potential of technology and its actual use. We drew on our past research (Becta, 2004; Underwood et al., 2004, 2005, 2009a, 2010) and used interviews with teachers to devise an instrument to capture this gap. We identified three main fields of use for the VLE; curriculum development, communication, and administration, and further identified some key functions under each of these headings. The list of key functions was the stimulus for discussion with teachers, who were asked to identify the potential uses of a VLE with the help of the list but with the clear understanding they could add further functions should they wish to. Once they had identified the potential uses that their school's VLE was able to support, they were asked to provide a statement of which of these functions they actually used. This research is on-going but in this chapter we include the contrasting responses of two technology-savvy teachers. Teacher 1 is a senior manager with responsibility for ICT in the school (Figure 7.1, Teacher 1) while teacher 2 is head of a subject department but also has responsibility for e-learning in the school (Figure 7.1, Teacher 2). We make no claim that these are representative of teachers in general but the similarities in their understanding of the functions of an VLE compared to the disparity in their actual use of the system is illuminating.

Teacher 2 identified 20 potential functions of the VLE, four more than teacher 1. There was a core of 13 functions which both teachers recognized; external communication and curriculum development were not seen as key functions of the VLE by either teacher. The use of the VLE to host job specifications was an interesting additional function raised by teacher 2. On the curriculum side, teacher 1 saw hosting individual learning plans (ILPs) as a noteworthy function.

Both teachers used a reduced set of the known functions in their own practice. However, teacher 1 reported using 12 of the 16 functions identified. These occurred across the three identified areas of administration, curriculum development, and external communication. Use of

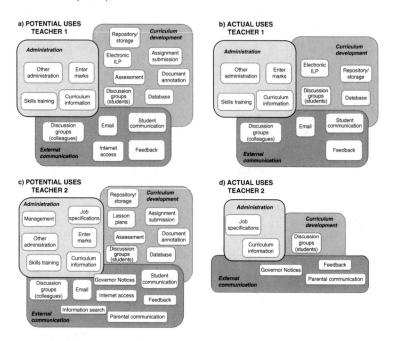

Figure 7.1 Potential VLE use and actual VLE use for Teacher 1 and Teacher 2.

the VLE to support assessment is possibly the most surprising admission from this activity. Teacher 2, on the other hand, identified using a much-reduced subset of only 7 out of 20 functions, the majority of which had administrative or communicative roles rather than tools to support pedagogic practice. This lack of focus on the learner is in sharp contrast to the interviews we conducted under Impact 2008 (Underwood et al., 2010). When we asked schools who rejected a specific VLE why they had taken that decision, the most common reason was that they were teacher-oriented. Although such VLEs facilitate planning and delivering lessons, teachers felt that they were in conflict with the personalizing learning agenda. It was argued that there should be an opportunity for learners to set their own targets and workloads and use the VLE to organize their learning effectively.

We alluded to ease of use earlier in this paper. Research on the student use of the Internet, in particular, search engines provide some insight into the failure to fully engage with the VLE. Brophy and Bawden (2005) found that students were more likely to use Google than their library's customized database even though the latter provided better quality, that is more targeted, searches. However, Google was more accessible and less opaque and, even though it gave poorer quality outputs, it was the preferred tool for students. As in many other areas of their lives, these students are operating under the satificer principle (Simon, 1983). Software developers should be concerned that so little of what they are offering is being adopted by target users. School managers should be questioning whether they have bought an overspecified system with all the ensuing costs that implies, or whether they need to increase the quality and quantity of training of staff in order to get the best out of such an expensive purchase. We would suggest the latter is the case. In schools where some form of VLE has become embedded in practice, it is not unknown to find two VLEs being used, each supporting essential but different activities within the school.

The impact of personalized learning

In our Impact 2008 project, we surveyed over 330 teachers. We achieved this through personal contact with selected schools and collected the data via an Internet questionnaire. This questionnaire covered issues of personalized learning, the impact of technology on teaching as well as questions about the use of ICT. Of interest to our argument about the VLE was the open response question that invited our teachers to name their most important pieces of technology. Over half identified their Interactive Whiteboard as their "must have" technology and a further quarter chose their laptop. There were mentions for Google, YouTube, and datasticks but very few for the VLE. This may be an artifact of the question and teachers' perception of what constitutes technology or it may show that teachers are not enthused by this facility. A further question about online resource received more endorsements for the VLE but even for this question the endorsements were minimal.

Stiles (2007), we suggest, would view these findings as unsurprising as he questions whether the VLE can remain the core of any institution's e-learning strategy. He has argued that although many institutions have built their ICT strategy round the concept of the VLE, the technology has proved to be incapable of delivering the flexibility required for the lifelong learner to become reality. This is because the functionality of the VLE is more supportive of a transmission mode of education rather than a more tailored, flexible, and personalized experience required for lifelong learners. Stiles's argument, based on tertiary distance education, can be extended to mainstream education and it would appear the students in our studies concur with his analysis.

If not the VLE, then what?

Phipps, Cormier, and Stiles (2008) argue that while the VLE has an important role in the student experience, making it a safe and sensible option from the perspective of the institution, it is a solution to an old problem, which may have lost its relevance in a world of continuous change that requires a continual re-skilling of the population. In particular they question the appropriateness of the VLE as a tool to encapsulate the full sum of a student's educational experiences. With this they are highlighting the need for enhanced e-portfolios, which may be held across a range of tools and platforms.

In addition, our own work has shown that learners can be ambivalent toward the VLE. In focus groups with primary and secondary pupils (Underwood et al., 2009a), we explored their technology use and their attitudes toward it. One group of year 9 learners (aged 13 years) identified their favorite technologies as iPods, laptops, phones, Sky, MSN, and most surprising, datasticks. The pupil who chose the datastick explained his choice as being because the "school can't steal it." By this, he meant that he could bring material to and from school without it being tracked and this made the datastick preferable to the VLE because of the privacy it provided. In a truly personal learning environment, then, some parts of it will be private but a VLE will not offer this facility.

The VLE is able to provide access to a range of learning resources and also to inform about courses and assessments (see Weller (2010) and Sclater (2010) for a more in-depth discussion of these points). It is also able to facilitate interaction between users but this facility does not appear to be well-developed or used. Learners and teachers prefer to use facilities outside of the VLE and outside of the school. It is argued that the VLE is not able to create a truly personal learning environment (Holah & Davies, 2009). The VLE does not reflect how learners interact with new technologies and restricts their learning journey. It is also in danger of deskilling teachers by providing a routine and limiting structure within which to teach. The question, as identified by Holah and Davies, is whether one size fits all? As the VLE effectively defines a limited path through the new digital technologies and does not empower learners to facilitate their own learning using the new technologies, it would suggest that the system can only be an "everyman" technology at a very basic level.

This gap between the learning and formal educational technology is also noted in the Harnessing Technology Report (Becta, 2008): "Levels of access to and use of technology are high among young learners—especially out of school. However, their experience of technology in formal education generally differs from that at home and there are increasing indications that learners' expectations of technology, and, as a result, of learning, are not being met. Learners commonly report that they enjoy learning with technology, and increasingly use a range of tools and approaches to support their learning, including the use of Web 2.0 technologies, which may not be recognized and supported in formal settings" (p. 23).

The answer proposed and enacted by Holah and Davies is to use the range of opportunities provided by Web 2.0 digital applications. The many interactive sites and facilities that can be found in cyberspace allow learners to share, create, and broadcast. An example of the power of this approach is a facility created by Holah and Davies for teachers of psychology. Psychexchange (www.psychexchange.co.uk) allows teachers to upload and comment on teaching resources, ideas, and videos. Since it was created in 2008, it has created a large and active community of psychology teachers. It has over 21,700 users, of which 5,000 have been active in the last month (accessed May 2010). There are 3,700 files uploaded and these have been downloaded over 800,000 times. A community of practice in the Wengerian (1998) sense, that is a group of people who share a concern or a passion for something they do and learn how to do it better as they interact regularly, has been created within a short time that allows teachers to share resources and good practice.

Conclusions

The emergence of new digital services and tools on the Web, developments in interoperability, and changing demands pose significant issues but also opportunities for the educational system as a whole. The ambitions for the PLE are immense and the expectation is high. This latter is based on the notion that teaching and learning are relatively well understood and can be enhanced by the addition of a single innovation. This single innovation is tasked with creating personalized and engaging learning environments for learners, for encouraging interaction between learners, for providing an anyplace, anywhere, anytime resource, and for providing tracking information for teachers and school managers.

We ask whether this ambition is achievable. Is it possible to produce a "one-size-fits-all" facility that provides a personalized experience for learners? And is it possible to create a top down system that learners can take ownership of?

Our research shows the benefits of the PLE for schools and for learners. We have found numerous examples of how individual teachers have gained great benefit from the school-wide systems. But we have found little evidence of general principles that can be applied to all, or even most schools. We argue that we have evidence for the benefits of personalized learning and also for the use of PLEs, but we observe that there is a need for a clearer focus on what each of these educational projects is aiming to achieve.

References

Banyard, P., & Underwood, J. (2008). Understanding the learning space. *eLearning Papers, 1*(9), 1–12.

Becta (2004). What the research says about Virtual learning Environments in teaching and learning. Retrieved September 22, 2008, from http://publications.teachernet.gov.uk/default.aspx?PageFunction=productdetails&PageMode=publications&ProductId=15003&

Becta (2007). Harnessing technology schools survey 2007. Retrieved May 31, 2010, from www.schools.becta.org.uk/uploaddir/

Becta (2008). Harnessing technology: Next generation learning. Retrieved May 31, 2010, from http://publications.becta.org.uk/download.cfm?resID=37348

Becta (2009). Harnessing technology: The learner and their context increasingly autonomous: Learners using technology in the context of their family lives and beyond. Retrieved May 31, 2010, from http://research.becta.org.uk/index.php?section=rh&catcode=_re_rp_02&rid=17242

Brophy, J., & Bawden, D. (2005). "Is Google enough? Comparison of an internet search engine with academic library resources." *Aslib Proceedings, 57*(6), 498–512.

Chen, S. Y., & Liu, X. (2008). An integrated approach to modelling learning patterns of students in web-based instruction: A cognitive style perspective. *ACM Transactions on Computer Interactions, 15*(1), 1–28.

Chou, H., & Wang, T. (2000). The influence of learning style and training method on self-efficacy and learning performance in WWW homepage design training. *International Journal of Information Management, 20*(6), 455–472.

Clarke, L., & Abbott, C. (2008). Put posters over the glass bit on the door and disappear: Tutor perspectives on the use of VLEs to support pre-service teachers. *Teaching in Higher Education 13*(2), 169–181.

Ellis, A. B. (2001) Improving undergraduate education in the mathematical and physical sciences through the use of technology. Report to the National Science Foundation. Retrieved May 31, 2010, from http://www.wcer.wisc.edu/archive/teched99/Tech_Ed_Final.pdf

European Schoolnet (2003). *Virtual Learning Environments for European Schools: A survey and commentary.* Brussels, EUN.

Gilbert, C., August, K., Brooks, R., Hancock, D., Hargreaves, D., Pearce, N., Roberts, J., Rose, J., & Wise, D. (2006). *2020 Vision: Report of the teaching and learning by 2020 review group.* Nottingham: DfES publications.

Green, H., Facer, K., & Rudd, T., with Dillon, P., & Humphreys P (2005). *Personalisation and digital technologies.* Bristol: Futurelab.

HM Government (2005). *Higher standards, better schools for all, more choice for parents and pupils.* Retrieved May 31, 2010, from http://www.thedlc.org/resources/personalised_learning/higher_standards_better_schools_for_all%20chapter4.pdf

Holah, M., & Davies, J. (2009). Delivering personalised learning through technology: The teachers' perspective. *CAL09,* Brighton, UK

ISIS Software (2010). www.isissoftware.net

Kelly, R. (2005). UK Secretary of State for Education and Skills, BETT 2005 Keynote address, January, 5, 2005. Retrieved May 31, 2010, from http://www.dfes.gov.uk/speeches/search_detail.cfm?ID=177

Larkin-Hein, T., & Budney, D. D. (2001). Research on learning style: Application in the Physics and engineering classrooms. *IEEE Transactions on Education, 44*(3), 276–281.

Leadbeater, C. (2004). Learning about personalisation. Retrieved May 31, 2010, from http://www.demos.co.uk/files/learningaboutpersonalisation.pdf?1240939425

McLoughlin, C., & Lee, M. J. W. (2007). Social software and participatory learning: Pedagogical choices with technology affordances in the Web 2.0 era. In ICT: Providing choices for learners and learning. *Proceedings Ascilite Singapore 2007.* Retrieved May 31, 2010, from http://www.ascilite.org.au/conferences/singapore07/procs/mcloughlin.pdf

Nagi, K., & Suesawaluk, P. (2008). Research analysis of Moodle reports to gauge the level of interactivity in elearning courses at assumption university. ICCN"08: *Proceedings of the 18th International Conference on Computer and Communication Engineering,* Kuala Lumpur, Malaysia, pp. 772–776.

Ofsted (2009a). The importance of ICT, Information and communication technology in primary and secondary schools, 2005/2008. Reference no: 070035. Retrieved May 31, 2010, from http://www.ofsted.gov.uk/content/download/8797/95679/file/VLE%20: An evaluation %20of%20their%20development.pdf

Ofsted (2009b). Virtual learning environments: An evaluation of their development in a sample of educational settings. Retrieved May 31, 2010, from www.ofsted.gov.uk/publications/070251

Phipps, L., Cormier, D., & Stiles M. J. (2008). Reflecting on the virtual learning systems – extinction or evolution? *Educational Developments, 9*(2), 1–4.

Pollard, A., & James, M. (2004). *Personalised learning: A commentary by the teaching and learning research programme.* London: TLRP.

Prior, G., & Hall, L. (2005). *ICT in schools survey 2004: ICT in schools research and evaluation series 22.* London: DfES.

Quantcast (2010). Retrieved February 10, 2010, from http://www.quantcast.com/twitter.com#summary

Sclater, N. (2010). eLearning in the Cloud. *International Journal of Virtual and Personal Learning Environments. 1*(1), 10–19.

Sharples, M. (2010). Web 2.0 technologies for learning at key stages 3 and 4. Learning Sciences Research Institute. Retrieved May 31, 2010, from http://www.lsri.nottingham.ac.uk/web2.0/

Simon, H. A. (1983). *Reason in human affairs.* Stanford, CA: Stanford University Press.

Smith, P., Rudd, P., & Coghlan, M. (2008). Harnessing technology: Schools survey 2008. Retrieved May 31, 2010, from http://research.becta.org.uk/index.php?section=rh&catcode=_re_rp_02&rid=15952

Stiles M. (2007). Death of the VLE? A challenge to a new orthodoxy. *Serials, the Journal for the International Serials Community 20*(1), 31–36.

Superby, J., Vandamme, J., & Meskens, N. (2006). Determination of factors influencing the achievement of the first-year university students using data mining methods. In *EDM'06: Workshop on Educational Data Mining* (pp. 37–44). Hong Kong, China.

Underwood J., Baguley, T., Banyard, P. Dillon, Farrington-Flint, L., Hayes, M., Le Geyt, G., Murphy, J., & Selwood, I. (2010). *Understanding the impact of technology: Learner and school-level factors.* Coventry: Becta. Retrieved May 31, 2010, from http://research.becta.org.uk/upload-dir/downloads/page_documents/research/understanding_impact_technology_learner_school_level_factors.pdf

Underwood, J., Baguley, T., Banyard, P. Dillon, G., Farrington-Flint, L. Hayes, M., Le Geyt, G., Murphy, J., & Selwood, I. (2009a). *Personalising learning.* Coventry, Becta. Retrieved May 31, 2010, from http://partners.becta.org.uk/page_documents/research/reports/personalised_learning.pdf accessed February 2010.

Underwood, J., & Banyard, P. (2006). Learning and technology: A happy conjunction? In K. Steffans, R. Carneiro & J. Underwood (Eds.), *Self-regulated learning and technology enhanced learning environments* (pp. 64–71). Aachen: Shaker Verlag.

Underwood, J., & Banyard, P. (2008). Managers,' teachers' and learners' perceptions of personalised learning: Evidence from impact 2007. *Technology, Pedagogy & Education. 17*(3), 233–246.

Underwood, J., Ault, A., Banyard, P., Durbin, C., Hayes, M., Selwood, I., Derrick Golland, D. Hayes, M., Selwood, I. Somekh, B., Twining, P. & Woodrow, D. (2004). Connecting with broadband: Evidence from the field. Coventry: Final project report for Becta. Retrieved May 31, 2010, from http://research.becta.org.uk/upload-dir/downloads/page_documents/research/connecting_with_broadband_summary.pdf

Underwood, J., Banyard, P., Betts, L., Farrington-Flint, L., Kerlin, L., Stiller, J. & Yeomans, S. (2009b). Narrowing the gap: An exploration of the ways technology can support approaches to narrowing the gap for under and low-achieving learners in secondary schools. Coventry: Becta. Retrieved May 31, 2010, from http://research.becta.org.uk/index.php?section=rh&catcode=_re_rp_02&rid=17439

Underwood, J., Banyard, P., Bird, K., Dillon, G., Hayes, M., Selwood, I. Somekh, B., Twining, P. & Woodrow, D Ault, A. (2005). The impact of broadband in schools. Coventry: Final report for Becta. Retrieved May 31, 2010, from http://research.becta.org.uk/index.php?section=rh&catcode=_re_rp_02&rid=13662

Weller, M. (2010) The centralisation dilemma in educational IT. *International Journal of Virtual and Personal Learning Environments. 1*(1), 1–9.

Wenger, E. (1998). *Communities of practice, learning, meaning and identity.* Cambridge: Cambridge University Press.

CHAPTER 8

Teaching Spanish in Second Life

Dafne González, Cristina Palomeque, and Paul Sweeney

Introduction

Multiuser virtual environments (MUVEs) are becoming increasingly popular within the educational community as a 3D immersive platform for experimentation and innovation (Molka-Danielsen & Deutschmann, 2009; Wankel & Kingsley, 2009). One of the most popular MUVEs is Second Life (SL) given its widespread availability and low entry costs. The successful integration of synchronous voice into Second Life provides an enormous potential for foreign language learning (Silva, 2008).

This chapter is a case study of the action research process involved in the development of a Spanish course for tourism aimed at beginners in Second Life. This course derives from a project developed under the auspices of Languagelab.com, a private organization that offers courses of English and Spanish as a foreign language in Second Life. The Spanish project was conceived in 2007 and its aim was to develop a 10-week course for complete beginners to equip them with basic linguistic skills and competencies to survive when traveling to Spanish-speaking countries. The first public commercial run of the Spanish course started in July 2008. The course was entirely designed and delivered within Second Life with students from different countries from around the world such as the UK, the United States, Finland, Slovenia, and Belgium, and ages ranged from 20 to 55. Most of the participants had not met before starting the course. When interviewed before the course, all students reported to be complete beginners of Spanish and to be fluent in English. All students were fairly competent in ICT; however, their level of experience and competence with Second Life varied.

Project rationale

The course was designed and implemented by certified English and Spanish teachers. Their aim, as researchers, was to study the interactive, social, and learning potential of MUVEs for language learning in order to successfully design a Spanish for beginners course around a holiday theme. Whereas the English courses offered by the same institution were at intermediate level and above, research showed that those interested in taking a Spanish course in Second Life were mostly real or false beginners. Thus, the Spanish project dealt with a new challenge: teaching a foreign language to beginners in a 3D MUVE environment.

Teaching a language to beginners poses a number of challenges, especially if done solely or mainly through the target language (Antes, 2008). In a best practice, real life classroom, teachers must make use of nonverbal language such as gesture and facial expression to communicate meaning, something which becomes more complex in a MUVE context where many of these options are not available (Sherblom, Withers & Leonard, 2009). Other teaching strategies must therefore be found to teach beginners in a MUVE.

In the initial stages of this study (2007), we could find very little research related to teaching foreign languages to beginners in Second Life. In practice, there were some spaces where English and Spanish were being taught, but apart from the recording of experiences carried out by a few educators and institutions such as Penn State University (2007), there was a lack of research on teaching foreign languages at beginner levels in MUVEs. However, there is a growing body of research on general learning experiences in MUVEs. Svensson (2003) reports using the MUVE Active Worlds with his students to deliver presentations. Toyoda and Harrison (2002) portrayed a virtual version of the University of Nagoya, which they developed for students of Japanese. Campbell (2003) described a course for Japanese learners of English using Active Worlds with the aim of fostering collaboration and cultural awareness. Koenraad (2008) reported on an increase in user-perceived learning, especially vocabulary and functional language, in the Virtual Language project (ViTAAL).

Subsequent to the completion of this project, two significant works were published on learning and teaching in virtual worlds—Molka-Danielsen and Deutschmann (2009) and Wankel and Kingsley (2009). In their intro-duction, Wankel and Kingsley (2009) emphasize the exploratory nature of many training and development activities taking place in virtual worlds, namely, that Second Life is in integral part of their working life for very few language learners and that many learners have no previous experience of Second Life.

Dudeney and Ramsey (2009) list a number of "entry barriers" for using Second Life in Higher Education: variable quality of the syn-chronous voice feature and the difficulty of configuring this; confus-ing interface design; above average hardware demands for nongamers; and lack of appropriate "orientation spaces." In common with almost every other Second Life project the researchers have seen reported on, this results in lower than expected uptake and/or a significant drop-out rate early in the program. Because this project was taking place on a private SIM or region in Second Life, there were no recorded "griefing" incidents or other e-safety issues, though of course learners may have encountered these in their wider use of the 3D world.

Supporting this, Deutschmann and Panichi (2009) note a range of important factors in preparing faculty and students for Second Life including prior attitudes and expectations. Sherblom et al. (2009) point out that many of the positive effects of computer-mediated communica-tion (CMC), which facilitate group communication and participation, are likely to be applicable to Second Life and in fact the virtual environ-ment offers more "interpersonal uncertainty reduction strategies espe-cially when its presentation of a virtual space is similar to a physical space" (p. 34). The design of the space was an integral part of our pro-gram, not only from the perspective of pedagogic design efficiency, but also to encourage recognition and empathy on the part of the learners.

Sherblom et al. (2009) differentiate between generic challenges to interpersonal communication posed by using virtual worlds and the spe-cific issue of the loss of nonverbal cues. They note that the former poses a greater challenge for learners than the latter. The issue of the loss of non-verbal clues and paralinguistics is something which the researchers were very conscious of in exploring ways of applying best practice classroom approaches to virtual worlds. This is a key aspect of developing any type of program for real and false beginners because the learners do not have sufficient language skills to talk about or clarify what they are doing. Such concerns were central to the researcher's project design and a range of mitigating and supporting practices were developed in response.

Given the likelihood that the novelty of the medium for many stu-dents would lead to steep learning curves, the researchers were convinced of the importance of the role of the teacher as a point of reassurance and familiarity as well as of instructional input. Anderson (2009) found in a study of voice based courses in Second Life that, "similar to research results from studies of face-to-face classroom interactions, instructors in Second Life can and do portray nonverbal immediacy behaviours (use of avatar gestures and non-linguistic clues)" (p. 108) and that these "positively influence some student outcomes" (p. 108). However, she also noted that while her results mirror other studies in establishing a link between instructors' nonverbal immediacy and students' *affect* (i.e., liking) for the instructor, unlike other studies they did not also have a corresponding *affect* for their course—and that this may be due to technology barriers or learning curves.

Research questions

In order to guide the research toward the teachers'/researchers' objectives, the following four research questions were identified:

1. How can languages be taught in Second Life?
   —Is it possible to teach beginners?
2. How can we design a course to be delivered in Second Life?
3. Which language approach to teaching is the most appropriate for Second Life?
   —What resources will be needed?
   —How is student learning going to be assessed?
   —What teaching skills are needed to successfully teach a foreign language to beginners in a MUVE?
4. How do the affordances of Second Life impact on all of the above?

These questions were only our starting point but were not viewed as a rigid framework for the research. The researchers maintained an open mind in approaching this new context and were sure that more questions and doubts would emerge in the process. The main objectives agreed for the research were

1. to design a course of Spanish for beginners in Second Life
2. to implement the course
3. to analyze all the components of the course and its appropriateness in Second Life
4. to reflect on the interactive, social, and language learning potential of Second Life.

Research methodology

This study involved collaborative research carried out in Second Life, and qualitative strategies were used for data collection. Burns (1999) states that the objective of taking a qualitative approach is to offer descriptions, interpretations, and clarifications of natural contexts. She also adds that qualitative research is based on the data collected by the researcher in order to give sense to human behavior in the context of the research.

The methodological approach for this research is a case study. Yin (1989) suggests that a case study is the most adequate strategy to tackle questions or problems that reply to the question "How?" similar to those posed in the study. A case study does not need direct and exhaustive control of behavior, which was also a condition of this research, since we were not selecting our subjects and previous hypotheses had not been established. Yin adds that this methodology only focuses on contemporary issues, something which was also a characteristic of our study. Finally, Yin points out that for case studies researchers collect different sources of evidence, to achieve triangulation (Lincoln & Guba, 1985). In this study, evidence was collected from the teachers/researchers and students through reflective journals, interviews, and online questionnaires.

Furthermore, the research took an action research approach. Wallace (1988) defines action research as the systematic collection of data for the improvement of aspects related to professional praxis. Since this study collected information from both students and teachers (who were also the researchers), this study is an example of collaborative or participatory Action Research (Burns, 1999; Kemmis & McTaggart, 1988). In this respect, the phases suggested by Kemmis and McTaggart (1988) have been followed to establish the cycles of Action Research:

- The plan
- The action, that is the implementation or intervention
- The observation of the effects of the action
- Reflection, which is the base for future actions or cycles of the research.

In this way, our case study is a macrovision of all the processes in the action research cycle.

Overview of the project

This action research project started with a first cycle in which a "beta" course was run with other teachers and staff members. Through the participants' feedback, adjustments were made to the course and the second cycle started with the implementation of the first public course.

The design/planning phase

As stated in the previous section, the resulting course was a product of meetings and discussions with the peer teachers and coordinator of the project and of a beta session with staff from Languagelab. Planning meetings with the coordinator and teachers provided valuable insights into the pedagogy of course design and materials creation for the development of the lesson plans for a beta course. Lesson plans for each class were designed and materials created during the planning phase. Prior to trialing, the material was subjected to a step-by-step review or rehearsal, which resulted in frequent adjustments. Each class was then closely piloted with the participation of the teachers/researchers.

The implementation phase

A 10-week beta course was delivered to a group of 8 volunteer students. Students attended two 90-minute sessions each week. Students were asked to fill in an online survey of their impressions on the course every week. Moreover, the teachers/researchers kept a field journal to record their impressions and observations of the classes delivered.

The observation phase

Weekly teacher meetings were held to discuss pedagogical aspects of the course in general and reflections on the most recent classes. Two of the researchers were the teachers; the other researcher took the role of observer, and also participated in these teacher meetings. During the implementation of the beta course, feedback was gathered from students through several means:

- In course and postcourse questionnaires
- Online focus group sessions
- In-depth interviews with individual students

The reflection phase

The delivery of the beta course, the student feedback, and the teachers' journals and discussions together provided valuable information on the feasibility of the course and highlighted changes that needed to be made for the final product. These included

- the use of team teaching (main teacher and helper) specifically to facilitate the teaching of beginners
- change of approach from aural approach to whole language /four-skill approach
- inclusion of a Second Life skills session for the students prior to course start
- the creation of a virtual city specially designed for this course, and
- the use of Web-based support resources (wiki, recordings, interactive exercises).

The first actual course was also delivered in 10 weeks, but with a 2-hour session and another, practice-based, session of 60 minutes every week. In the following section, the elements involved in the course design, implementation, and evaluation will be seen in detail.

Design and implementation issues

This section provides an overview of the main program design issues during the planning phase and what other issues became apparent during the various cycles of development and implementation.

Key issues which informed the program design

Course objectives were very specific and tied to successful completion of real-world tasks. The commercial scope of the course was, over 10 weeks, to equip real and false beginners with basic competence in everyday tasks preparing them for a potential visit to a Spanish-speaking country.

It is generally agreed that the main aspects of successful language learning are interaction, varied input, authentic tasks, real audiences, and a positive classroom atmosphere (Egbert, Hanson-Smith & Chao, 2007). Thus, the course was designed under the communicative paradigm and took on a number of approaches. Communicative approaches such as the whole language approach (Goodman, 1986) and the task-based approach (Nunan, 2004) were considered for the design of the course. Also, given the immersive potential of the MUVE, issues from the functional-notional approach (Wilkins, 1976) were considered.

Thus, the goals for each class were linked to real-life tasks (e.g., checking in at a hotel, buying clothes, ordering food in a restaurant, buying food in a supermarket), which were accomplished through different enabling activities (role plays, guessing games, information gap, and memory games). The course offered two weekly sessions for 10 weeks. The first session of the week was devoted to presenting the new language and practicing it through enabling tasks and the second session consisted in putting the language presented in the previous session into practice through a task linked to real life and to build on what was presented the day before, depending on the task requirements and on student response.

Student MUVE skills and relationship to confidence

Learning to use a MUVE commonly involves regular challenges and frustration. The teachers/researchers were aware that some students would be experiencing this to a greater or lesser extent and were concerned about its impact on the affective filter (Krashen, 1987). Therefore, one of the priorities was to create a warm, supportive atmosphere. This is also related to what Sherblom et al. (2009) refer to as successful uncertainty reduction strategies for learners.

Teacher MUVE skills

The teachers who carried out the project were experienced and certified foreign language teachers both in face-to-face and online contexts. However, none of them had delivered a language course in a MUVE so a number of steps were taken to ensure the success of the course.

The teachers undertook a teacher-training course to acquire the necessary skills (related to general MUVE competencies and those specifically to support teaching within a MUVE) and practice to plan and deliver a class in Second Life. Also, the lessons were planned in great detail and were discussed with the rest of the members of the team. There were two beta classes delivered prior to the course. Teamwork was a key element in this study as the lessons were planned and delivered by two teachers.

Classroom management

Group management is a crucial factor in group facilitation of language learners at all levels of competency. Harmer (2007) links effective classrooms to the management of a range of variables. These include: management of the classroom space; use of voice; proximity to students; lesson staging; setting student expectations; and handling difficult and unforeseen situations. Researchers felt some knowledge could be transferred from our virtual English language praxis, but it was apparent that, at beginner level, a systematic approach was required for rules to give and check instructions; to monitor student activity; to correct and provide feedback as well as to provide students with communication strategies. Thus, a "class 0" was included in the course to go over the basic Second Life skills needed to undertake the course and the classes had a teacher helper (apart from the leading teacher) for prompting dialogues and to support students when needed.

Environment design

Normally of secondary importance, the role of the environment was foundational in this case study due to the "realistic" and immersive nature of the course. The researchers' previous work on embodiment as a key feature of language learning in 3D MUVE environments supported this (Sweeney et al., in press). Sweeney et al. argue that interactions through an avatar offer a way of identifying speakers and of assigning different messages to different participant-avatars. The absence of an embodied agent like an avatar would increase the aural load for the student, making it more difficult to distinguish voices and thus adding a further obstacle to the comprehension of the target language. Moreover, this embodied environment allows users to engage with it in a meaningful way constructing a projected and personalized identity and conforming to social norms to interact with others.

The program needed to avail itself of a sufficient variety of situational spaces—hotels, restaurants, banks, bus and train stations, retail and leisure spaces—to support its learning aims. The choice was between a series of holodecks (a tool which allows a variety of virtual rooms or 3D scenes to be created instantly when needed) or to build dedicated, permanent context for the course (i.e., a Spanish town). In choosing the latter route—named *Ciudad Bonita*—there was also a conscious attempt to make it as "real" as possible. Individual locations were often modeled, externally at least, on real locations such as the marketplace or train station of Valencia, in Spain (see Figure 8.1). A great effort was made to provide a logical sense to how these were

Figure 8.1 Scenes from the Spanish course in Ciudad Bonita (© 2009, Languagelab.com. Used with permission).

placed and linked up. Although a considerable portion of the city was invented, the designers were provided with substantial photographic evidence on which to build streets and plazas. Finally, and no less importantly, a number of fun, unusual, and informal elements were included to provide a sense of character and uniqueness so as to make the setting as welcoming as possible. The function of any given space had to be sufficiently clear at first glance and yet suggestive and engaging (for a broader discussion see Sweeney et al., 2010).

Each individual space was designed so as to "build in" task potential (e.g., restaurant tables able to accommodate anticipated class sizes) (see Figure 8.2). There also needed to be sufficient space for the teacher to deploy one-off, class-specific props in the spaces available.

Issues with real and "false" beginner levels of competency

Issues related to real and "false" beginners were a special concern in this course because teaching beginners in a MUVE was a novelty

Figure 8.2 Scenes from the Spanish course in Ciudad Bonita (© 2009, Languagelab.com. Used with permission).

for the researchers. The following concerns were shared by the researchers:

- Students may be unfamiliar with Latin script (e.g., those from an Arabic linguistic background).
- Students may be unfamiliar with communicative modern foreign language (MFL) teaching methods and have different expectations of the teacher's role.
- Students need to be become familiar with group learning behavior and the language needed to carry these out as well as become aware of the active role that is expected from them.
- There is little or no redundancy in students' use of the target language (i.e., the teacher cannot use the target language to clarify learning or procedural issues).
- Overload factor: the sheer amount of the new input (learning content, methodology) creates considerable stress on learners and may create an *affective* barrier for learning (Krashen, 1987).

- False beginner jagged learning profiles: many people at false beginner level may have had considerable prior exposure to the target language via formal, less communicative methodology (e.g., high school) so they may possess receptive skills beyond their productive level or be able to write but are less capable of oral production. Helgesen (1987) states that false beginners can engage in controlled tasks that are focused on form but their skills are limited when they engage in meaning-focused, fluency.
- Beginner vs. false beginner: although apparently a similar level, the contrast between people with very little knowledge in total and more substantial passive knowledge may create extra pressure on real beginners, as Frantzen and Sieloff (2008) report in their study of true and false beginners of French and Spanish.

As can be seen above, teaching beginners has some idiosyncrasies of its own which are not shared with teaching other levels of foreign languages in a MUVE.

Implementation

As the course to date has been run four times, the major changes occurred during or following the first two cycles with some ongoing adjustments for every subsequent implementation. As has been stated above, the Spanish courses were able to draw to a certain extent on lessons learned developing English language programs. However, this was limited by the fact that lessons for beginner level programs present a number of challenges that had not been experienced previously by any of the practitioners involved.

As this process represented a learning experience for the teachers, they kept a journal of the classes (see "Progress and Evaluation" section) and also took pictures and made recordings. They also met weekly to discuss the running of the previous class and the planning or changes that needed to be done for the next class. The students' feedback together with the instructors' experience proved valuable to introduce some changes to the course. Based on the implementation of the course, the following were observed:

- Reinforcing one of the many parallels with good practice face-to-face communicative teaching, it was found that groups of 8 to 12 were an ideal number. Going beyond that quickly had a disproportionate effect on the organizational efficacy.

- Activities which involved a bodily (or avatar) response were useful to boost the students' confidence.
- It was important to provide technical support to ensure students have no audio problems as these problems can hinder the class.
- There was a shift from an emphasis on oral production to a more rounded, whole-language approach. The initial cycles of the course had been concerned to keep a focus on form (grammar and written record of vocabulary) to a minimum so as not to distract too much attention from the immersive aspect of developing competence in tourist situations. However, feedback from learners indicated a greater need for focus on form. This was incorporated along with the development of materials for other skills (reading and listening), which were added to the course but accessed mainly via the course wiki.
- There was a need for more visual aids to be added to the environment to support the students' learning. The teachers added these visuals through 2D illustrations (e.g., image illustrating a learning point) or 3D "rezzableobjects" (3D objects that can be loaded into the Second Life environment such as a bowl of fruit or a street sign, again, in support of a learning point).
- There was a need for self-access materials to reinforce class sessions.
- Establishing a good atmosphere with students proved important for the well-running of the course. If a student did not feel a bond with the rest of the group, it was likely that he or she would not finish the course.

Progress and evaluation

To carry out our study, different kinds of data were collected from the teacher-researchers, teacher-observer, and students in order to achieve the triangulation needed in qualitative research. Stake (1995) points out that case studies with a qualitative approach should emphasize the quality of the activities and the processes. Observation and reflection were the main means to assess our research in each of the phases. However, some data collection instruments for systematization such as online surveys were used.

Interaction is one of the fundamental principles to promote language acquisition (Pica, 1996; Long, 1996; Gass, 1997; Burton & Clennell, 2003) and this is even more important when we are dealing with online learning. Wagner (1994) points out that interactions are reciprocal events that require at least two objects and two actions, and the interaction occurs when these objects and events influence each other mutually. Moore (1989) categorized three kinds of interactions: learner-content, learner-instructor, and learner-learner. Hillman, Willis and Gunawardena (1994) add a fourth element, the interaction learner-interface, which occurs when the student uses technology to communicate about the content of instruction.

Thus, we used a rubric to assess the interactive qualities of our course entitled "How Interactive are YOUR Distance Courses? A Rubric for Assessing Interaction in Distance Learning" (Roblyer & Ekhaml, 2000). This instrument measures interaction for four different aspects of the process:

- Social rapport-building activities created by the instructor
- Instructional designs for learning created by the instructor
- Levels of interactivity of technology resources
- Impact of interactive qualities as reflected in learner response

The first three aspects were considered by the researchers in the planning phase, and the fourth, was analyzed during the implementation and evaluation phases. In the four elements, we achieved a high level of interactive qualities as described in the rubric:

1. In addition to providing for exchanges of personal information among students, the instructor offers a variety of in-class and outside-class activities designed to increase social rapport among students.
2. In addition to communicating with the instructor, instructional activities require students to work with one another (e.g., in pairs or small groups) as well as with outside experts in order to share results with one another and the rest of the class.
3. In addition to technologies allowing two-way exchanges of text information, visual technologies such as two-way video or video-conferencing technologies permit synchronous voice and visual communications between instructor and students and among students.
4. By the end of the course, over 75% of students in the class had initiated interaction with the instructor and other students on a voluntary basis (i.e., other than when required for the class).

Researchers were also interested in valuing student engagement as a measure of success of the course. For this, the instrument "Indicators of Engaged Learning" (see Jones, Valdez, Nowakowski, & Rasumssen, 1995) was used. This instrument was also used by the researchers during the planning phase to guide our design, during the implementation phase, to observe student performance against the different variables of engagement, and finally, when analyzing student feedback of the course.

Throughout the different phases of our research, each of the researchers kept a reflective diary where we took notes about the process we saw. The instruments mentioned above were very helpful guides to keep the teachers/researchers focused during the process. The following are excerpts of the researchers' diary illustrating some of the issues and problems encountered during the implementation of the course (see Boxes 8.1–8.3).

Box 8.1   Journal entry 1

First day of the first commercially run Spanish course

One of the students, LU, is one-day old in SL and is really struggling in SL. There is a big difference between LU and the rest of the class. On many occasions, the rest of the group has to wait for her. We need to find a way to help newbies without disrupting the rest of the class. Nevertheless, it is important that students don't feel frustrated the first day or they won't come back. At the end of the session, we offered to meet with LU before the next class and go to the English orientation part of the city for her to practice ("English Orientation" is a space built in an area of the English city designed specifically to help newbies acquire basic SL skills). It's possible that we find ourselves with more students like LU who saw the advert on the Web and decided to sign up for the course with no previous knowledge of SL so we have to be ready to provide technical support.

Box 8.2   Journal entry 2

Second week of the Spanish course

I was concerned about the length of the classes because the first session is a two-hour class but students haven't complained about feeling tired or becoming boring; on the contrary, they say that they really enjoy the classes because they are fun and it is easier for them to remember everything because they're playing and because of the situational nature of the course.

Box 8.3   Journal entry 3

Sixth week of the Spanish course

Today we had prepared a treasure hunt as we are halfway through the course. The treasure hunt was designed to be carried out in teams and have the teams find clues and get to the treasure. We were going to be there to monitor the process. Unfortunately, SL wasn't working well and there was a lot of lag. Because of that, the objects we had set up to give out note cards and pictures weren't working so we had to read the clues out loud to the students. It was a shame because we had put in a lot of effort in that treasure hunt. You always need a plan B when dealing with ICT!

As can be seen from the journal entries, the courses were also a learning process for the teachers involved, as they highlighted aspects such as differing levels of proficiency, length of the classes, and problems with the Second Life environment. A great deal of planning was involved before the course, nevertheless, a lot of decisions had to be made on the spot, especially when the Second Life program was not responding.

During the planning phase, Bloom's Taxonomy (Bloom, 1956) was also considered to make sure the objectives of the course and each of the classes covered the different learning domains (cognitive, affective and psychomotor), as well as the categories within each domain. The cognitive domain is particularly important to develop the course content. Molka-Danielsen and Linneman (2009) make the case for inclusion of the affective domain. We take this further asserting that the psychomotor domain cannot be neglected in a course in Second Life, as students should be able to master Second Life skills in order to successfully participate and complete any interactive course in this environment. Furthermore, one of our methodological approaches to teaching is Total Physical Response (Asher, 1981), which is intimately related to psychomotor skills. Later, in 2008, Bloom's Digital Taxonomy (Churches, 2008) was also considered.

In order to collect data from our students, during the beta course, they completed a weekly feedback survey created using a Web questionnaire tool. The questions for this survey were taken from the "Indicators of Engaged Learning" instrument (see Jones, Valdez, Nowakowski, & Rasumssen, 1995). Also, for the beta and the first course, we held individual meetings with students throughout the sessions and a group meeting at the end of the course.

In this survey, participants were asked to rate (very appropriate, appropriate, somewhat appropriate, barely appropriate, and not appropriate), different aspects of the course (location, vocabulary teaching, repetition, activities, pace, resources, teaching approach, atmosphere, teacher support, Second Life self-access materials, and course wiki).

For analysis, the ratings were divided into a binary mode, the first three as positive (appropriate), and the last two as negative (not appropriate). All the aspects were considered in a positive way, that is, none of the aspects were rated neither "barely appropriate" nor "not appropriate." The teaching approach, teacher support, vocabulary teaching, and resources were very highly rated (95% of the time they were considered very appropriate and 5% appropriate). The only aspect that was rated "somewhat appropriate" during one of the weeks was Second Life self-access materials.

This feedback gave us weekly input to rethink our next steps. For example, in the first week the rating of pace was 40% very appropriate and 60% appropriate. With this information, we revised the number of activities we were introducing each week. There were two other statements to rate in the survey:

1. I think this is as good as or better than a real life class.
2. I feel satisfied with what I learnt.

During the 10 weeks, all the students selected the choice "I completely agree" for both statements.

In the individual and group meetings, participants expressed their opinions about the course. The first group meeting was videoed for further analysis. During the other meetings, the researchers took individual notes and then compared them. This is a summary of the comments made by the students in those meetings:

• The input used from one class to the next one was excellent.
• Having a wiki was a real plus to support the Second Life course.
• Different learning styles are well integrated.
• Interest is kept along the class.
• Visual aids are very well used and created.
• Learning vocabulary was good when the written form had audio (e.g., numbers).
• Correcting from teachers was well carried out.
• Team-teaching was wonderful, another plus of the course.
• It was a great idea to identify the CB buildings (or places) with their names.
• The incorporation of old vocabulary and phrases to the new ones is a great way to improve our learning.

- The sequencing of the lessons from simple to complex made me feel confident in every class.
- The classes are so fun that the time passes too quickly.
- Each class is different, with new resources and places. This variety kept me interested during the whole course.
- I loved the dynamic nature of each class.
- Without even noticing, I was learning how to read, speak, write, and understand what the teachers and others were saying.

Suggestions

- It would be a great idea to have real world interaction with videos in Spanish.
- It would be great to watch TV or to listen to the radio from real broadcasting to pull out words to increase vocabulary and the understanding of Spanish (translation or words could also be a good exercise).

After going through two cycles of Action Research, the questions that guided our study have broadly been answered. In fact, it was possible to design a course for beginners, create the necessary resources and activities to promote interaction and learner autonomy using a combination of teaching approaches, and according to our observations and feedback received, students accomplished the course objectives. Moreover, through the teachers' own experience, it was possible to design a teacher training workshop. After the first commercially launched course, a teacher training course containing the Second Life skills a teacher needs to master in order to teach in Second Life was offered. This workshop also included activities to make teachers aware of what it takes to adopt and adapt language teaching methodologies to Second Life. The course culminated in teachers designing minilessons and implementing them. This last activity was very revealing of which of those teachers were really ready to start teaching a Spanish for beginners course in Second Life. At the time of writing, four courses have been delivered, and each time adjustments were made in order to cater to the different characteristics of each group of students.

On the other hand, lessons have been learned from the harmful effects of unstable technologies in Second Life while delivering a class. Audio issues (not being able to talk, listen, having background noise) can make students restless, which can lead to lack of concentration. Other examples of problems faced when teaching or learning in Second

Life are temporary unavailability of the Second Life platform, system slowdown or "lag," which hinders movements, and an inability to view class images and objects. However, the positive aspects of the experience have outgrown any of the encountered technological problems.

Conclusions and future implications

The results obtained in case studies cannot be generalized from a statistical point of view to other populations (Wallace, 1998). However, the results are important, in the first place, for the researchers involved in the study; and in the second place, because many questions can be generated from the results for further research. In our case, we have learned that it is possible to teach a course of Spanish for beginners. However, having scaled one peak, we are now able to pose the next series of challenges.

Supporting technologies

- Technology has more usually been associated with the distance or non face-to-face, asynchronous element in course design. As it is clearly possible to create an engaging, face-to-face, embodied language learning experience in Second Life, should we reconsider our traditional paradigm of blended learning to allow for the "face-to-face" component to be delivered via a MUVE?
- Are there other voice enabled MUVEs which have similar affordances to Second Life for delivering this type of course or language learning in general?
- Encouragement for those working on enabling virtual learning environments (VLEs) to interface with Second Life. Sloodle (2009), the open source project which integrates the multiuser virtual environment of Second Life with the Moodle learning management system, is probably the leader in this field to date.

Design issues

- Can we use the same design procedure for more advanced levels? Could the results be extrapolated?
- How would classes be carried out if all the participants did not share a common proficiency in English?
- Could this methodology and course framework be used for any language beginners course in Second Life or indeed in another voice enabled MUVE?

- Was the fact of having a city for the course fundamental for its success?

Skills and resources for teaching a course in Second Life

- This course was delivered by a core team of researchers, two of whom were also highly skilled in Second Life and were the main program authors. What is the minimum level of skills and resources necessary for a course such as this to be delivered "out of the box"?

- Does the demanding learning curve for practitioners to become proficient users and teachers in Second Life (30–40 hours), with considerably more for competent material design, hinder its potential as a widespread educational tool?

- There is a learning curve for students: Second Life is essentially an authoring platform which potentially enables any user to completely customize their environment. However, the learning curve and likely skill level of students restricts in many cases what can be attempted in task design. Could it also hinder the mainstream potential of a language course in a 3D MUVE?

- Are there technological "fixes" for some of the above issues? This is relevant to both design and skill perspectives. The launch (February 2010) of a new beta version of the Second Life programme or "viewer" has greatly enhanced the ability of Second Life to handle Web-created content such as Google docs and video. Unlocking the Web as a source of instructional content is essential for its wider uptake and integration with other e-learning tools.

Final remarks

This case study provides some promising insights for foreign language learning in digitalized virtual worlds like Second Life. It also raises important issues related to MUVE technology and MUVE skills as well as pedagogical language-related aspects such as course design and materials creation. This study has focused on beginner levels in MUVEs and the special teaching approaches and resources used. There are clearly many promising fields of research in exploring further the areas of instructional design in virtual worlds, teaching skills, and appropriate use resources.

At the point of this project's inception in 2007, presence-based virtual worlds such as Second Life were considered by many to be the next phase for Web usage and that mass subscription to such virtual worlds and the use of avatars would become widespread. At the time of writing in early 2010, this predicted uptake has not materialised. Instead, many educators have shifted their attention to social networking platforms such as Facebook and Twitter and the increasing affordances of so-called SmartPhones. Meanwhile 3D gaming worlds are very solidly established and their content is becoming ever more mainstream. Many technology trend watchers now believe that social virtual worlds will blend with social networking platforms in the near future and that these will act as a portal for a combination of immersive and augmented reality experiences via PC, tablet, or mobile (Sweeney, 2010).

As such, the authors are confident that teaching and learning experiences in MUVEs will become more appealing and accessible as virtual worlds gain wider acceptance whether in themselves or linked with other digital technologies. The recent relative boom in research on education in virtual worlds should in turn lead to the emergence of models of good practice across a range of disciplines (Sweeney, 2010). It is hoped that this work will contribute to ongoing exploration in this field.

References

Anderson, T. (2009). Online instructor immediacy and instructor-student relationships. In C. Wankel & J. Kingsley (Eds.), *Higher education in virtual worlds: Teaching and learning in Second Life* (pp. 101–114). Bingley, UK: Emerald Group Publishing.

Antes, T. A. (2008). Kinesics: The value of gesture in language and in the language classroom. *Foreign Language Annals, 29*(3), 439–448. Retrieved May 10, 2010, from http://www3.interscience.wiley.com/journal/121508391/abstract?CRETRY=1&SRETRY=0

Asher, J. J. (1981). The total physical response: Theory and practice. In H. Winitz (Ed.), *Native language and foreign language acquisition* (pp. 324–331). New York, New York: Academy of Sciences.

Bloom, B. S. (1956). *Taxonomy of educational objectives, Handbook I: The cognitive domain.* New York: David McKay Co. Inc.

Burns, A. (1999). *Collaborative action research for English language teachers.* New York: Cambridge University Press.

Burton, J., & Clennell, C. (2003). Interaction as the way and means of language learning. In B. Jill & C. Charles (Eds.), *Interaction and language learning.* Alexandria, VA: TESOL Publications.

Campbell, A. (2003). *Foreign language exchange in a virtual world: An intercultural task-based learning event.* Unpublished paper written in partial fulfillment of an

MEd in e-learning at the University of Sheffield, U.K. Retrieved May 10, 2010, from http://e-poche.net/files/flevw.html

Churches, A. (2008). *Bloom's digital taxonomy*. Retrieved May 10, 2010, from http://www.scribd.com/doc/8000050/Blooms-Digital-Taxonomy-v212

Deutschmann, M., & Panichi, L. (2009). Instructional design, teacher practice and learner autonomy. In J. Molka-Danielsen & M. Deutschmann (Eds.), *Learning and teaching in the virtual world of Second Life* (pp. 27–41). Trondheim: Tapir Academic Press.

Dudeney, G., & Ramsay, H, (2009). Overcoming the entry barriers to Second Life in higher education. In C. Wankel & J. Kingsley (Eds.), *Higher education in virtual worlds: Teaching and learning in Second Life* (pp. 11–28). Bingley, UK: Emerald Group Publishing.

Egbert, J., Hanson-Smith, E., & Chao, C. (2007). Introduction: Foundations for teaching and learning. In J. Egbert & E. Hanson-Smith (Eds.), *CALL environments: Research, practice and critical issues* (2nd ed., pp. 1–15). Alexandria, VA: TESOL Publications.

Frantzen, D., & Sieloff, S. (2008). Anxiety and the true beginner—False beginner dynamic in beginning French and Spanish classes. *Foreign Language Annals, 38*(2), 171–186.

Gass, S. (1997). *Input, interaction and the second language learner*. Mahwah, NJ: Lawrence Erlbaum Associates.

Goodman, K. (1986). *What's whole in whole language? A parent/teacher guide to children's learning*. Portsmouth, NH: Heinemann Educational Books, ED 300 777.

Harmer, J. (2007). *How to teach English* (3rd ed.). Harlow: Pearson Longman.

Helgesen, M. (1987). False beginners: Activating language for Accuracy and fluency. *The Language Teacher, 11*(14), 23–29.

Hillman, D. C., Willis, D. J., & Gunawardena, C. N. (1994). Learner-interface interaction in distance education: An extension of contemporary models and strategies for practitioners. *The American Journal of Distance Education, 9*(2), 1–4.

Jones, B. F., Valdez, G., Nowakowski, J., & Rasumssen, C. (1995). Plugging in: Choosing and using educational technology. Council for Educational Development and Research, *NCREL*. Retrieved May 10, 2010, from https://docs.google.com/Doc?docid=0AUruA4hUH3iwZDZ3c2huZ183Z3puMmN4ZjY&hl=en

Kemmis, S., & McTaggart, R. (1988). *The action research planner* (3rd ed.). Geelong: Deakin University.

Koenraad, T. (2008). How can 3D virtual worlds contribute to language education? Paper presented at WorldCALL 2008. Retrieved May 10, 2010, from http://www.callinpractice.net/koenraad/publications/worldcallpdf-2.pdf/at_download/file

Krashen, S. D. (1987). *Principles and practice in second language acquisition*. New York: Prentice-Hall International.

Lincoln, Y., & Guba, E.G. (1985). *Naturalistic inquiry*. Newbury Park, CA: Sage Publications.

Long, M. (1996). The role of the linguistic environment in second language acquisition. In W. Ritchie & T. Bhatia (Eds.), *Handbook of second language acquisition* (pp. 413–468). San Diego, CA: Academic Press.

Molka-Danielsen, J., & Deutschmann, M. (Eds.). (2009). *Learning and teaching in the virtual world of Second Life*. Trondheim: Tapir Academic Press.

Molka-Danielsen, J., & Linneman, L., (2009). Sim creation and management for learning environments. In J. Molka-Danielsen & M. Deutschmann (Eds.), *Learning and teaching in the virtual world of Second Life* (pp. 61–76). Trondheim: Tapir Academic Press.

Moore, M.G. (1989). Three types of interaction. *American Journal of Distance Education, 3*(2), 1–6.

Nunan, D. (2004). *Task-based language teaching*. Cambridge: Cambridge University Press.

Penn State University. (2007). Student comments from Professor Gloria Clark's Fall 2007, Spanish 1 course at Penn State University. *The Language Educator*. ACTFL. Retrieved May 10, 2010, from http://www.actfl.org/i4a/pages/index.cfm?pageid=4801

Pica, T. (1996). Second language learning through interaction: Multiple perspectives. *Working papers in educational linguistics, 12*(1), pp. 1–22, ERIC ED401756.

Roblyer, M. D., & Ekhaml, L. (2000). *How interactive are YOUR distance courses? A Rubric for Assessing Interaction in Distance Learning*. DLA 2000 proceedings. Retrieved May 10, 2010, from http://www.westga.edu/~distance/roblyer32.html

Sloodle (Simulation Linked Object Oriented Dynamic Learning Environment) (2009). Retrieved November 28, 2009, from http://www.sloodle.org/blog/?page_id=2

Sherblom, J., Withers, L., & Leonard, L. (2009). Communication, challenges and opportunities for educators using Second Life relationships. In C. Wankel & J. Kingsley (Eds.), *Higher education in virtual worlds. Teaching and learning in Second Life* (pp. 29–46). Bingley, UK: Emerald Group Publishing.

Silva, K. (2008). Second Life. *TESL-EJ, 12*(1). Retrieved May 10, 2010, from http://tesl-ej.org/ej45/m1.pdf

Sweeney, P. (2010, June 18). *Virtual worlds: Now what?* Retrieved May 10, 2010, from http://www.eduworlds.co.uk/2010/06/virtual-worlds-now-what/

Sweeney, P., Palomeque, C., González, D., Speck, C., Canfield, D., Guerrero, S., & Mackichan, P. (2010). Task design for language learning in an embodied environment. In G. Vincenti & J. Braman (Eds.), *Teaching through multi-user virtual environments: Applying dynamic elements to the modern classroom*. Hershey, PA.: IGI Global.

Stake, R. E. (1995). *The art of case study research*. Thousand Oaks, CA: Sage.

Svensson, P. (2003). Virtual worlds as arenas for language learning. In U. Felix (Ed.), *Language learning online: Towards best practice*. Lisse: Swets & Zeitlinger.

Toyoda, E., & Harrison, R. (2002). Categorization of text chat communication between learners and native speakers of Japanese. *Language Learning & Technology, 6*, 82–99.

Wankel, C., & Kingsley, J. (Eds.). (2009). *Higher education in virtual worlds: Teaching and learning in Second Life*. Bingley, UK: Emerald Group Publishing.

Wagner, E. D. (1994). In support of a functional definition of interaction. *The American Journal of Distance Education, 8*(2), 6–29.

Wallace, M. (1998). *Action research for language teachers*. Cambridge, UK: Cambridge University Press.

Wilkins, D. A. (1976). *Notional syllabuses*. Oxford: Oxford University Press.

Yin, R. (1989). *Case study research: Design and methods* (revised edition). Newbury Park, CA: Sage Publishing.

CHAPTER 9

"The Wisdom of Practice": Web 2.0 as a Cognitive and Community-Building Tool in Indonesia

Mary Burns and Petra Wiyakti Bodrogini

Introduction

The use of Web 2.0—the so-called read/write web (DiNucci, 1999; O'Reilly, 2005)—has increasingly found a home in the developed world as a vehicle for teacher and student learning. In much of the developing world, however, Web 2.0 applications remain little known and rarely used in teacher professional development and educational capacity building (Lim et al., 2003). In 2009–2010, Education Development Center (EDC) introduced a suite of Web 2.0 applications as part of an online professional development program for 60 technology trainers in six Indonesian provinces. The goal of this program was to help these technology trainers become effective school-based coaches who could then help teachers integrate classroom technology to support learner-centered instruction.

Despite their lack of familiarity with Web 2.0 tools and the novelty of online learning, coaches benefitted greatly from the peer learning afforded by the online course in general and Web 2.0 applications in particular. This benefit had two immediately observable outcomes. First, coaches' conversations and exchanges exhibited more higher-order thinking skills than was the case either in the learning management system (LMS), Moodle, or in face-to-face professional development settings. Second, the ongoing use of Web 2.0 applications resulted in the types of interaction with knowledge, practice, and online colleagues that Wenger (2006) has identified as critical to the formation of communities of practice.

Many Asian university and workplace distance learning programs have yet to capitalize on the peer-based learning capacities of online learning (Lim, 2007). Indeed, much research has argued that the participatory nature of online learning in general and Web 2.0 technologies in particular contravenes Asian styles of learning (Hofstede, 1997; Moran & Myringer, 1999). While further research on the synergy between Web 2.0 technologies and teaching and learning within an Asian context is warranted, our experience suggests that the use of Web 2.0 applications, as part of a deliberately fashioned instructional approach focusing on collaborative learning, can enhance the critical thinking and collaboration skills of online learners. Further, we contend that the use of Web 2.0 applications complements, rather than contradicts, Asian styles of learning and working.

This chapter provides an overview of EDC's coaching program in Indonesia; discusses current trends of Web 2.0 technologies in the Asian/Indonesian context; documents coaches' uses of Web 2.0 technologies, and postulates how Web 2.0 tools can support higher-order learning and community formation among learners, particularly within an Asian context.

Building capacity for teacher trainers: EDC's coaching program in Indonesia

Like many Asian nations, Indonesia is seeking to refashion its educational system from one focused on "lower-order" thinking skills and learning as a solo endeavor to more "twenty-first century" learning—collaboration, higher-order thinking, and technology use. Several impediments stand in the way of such ambitions. First, traditional "stand and deliver" instruction is still the norm in Indonesia—among teachers and among those responsible for teacher formation. Next, Indonesia has one of the lowest Internet penetration rates (10.5 percent) and one of the highest Internet costs in Asia (Latchem & Jung, 2010). Indeed, the Economist Intelligence Unit (2008) ranks Indonesia 68th in a list of 70 Asian nations in terms of e-readiness. Such realities are particularly grave as Indonesia must upgrade the basic qualifications of 1.6 million primary school teachers and has identified online learning as one way to do so.

In 2009, USAID asked EDC to develop a nationwide pilot to examine how online learning could upgrade the knowledge and skills of

Indonesian primary school teachers. Given the existing weaknesses of current professional development, EDC focused on developing a new model of capacity building—a school-based coaching program to provide the continuous place-based teacher professional development and support so critical to teacher learning.

This pilot, five months in length, was launched in six provinces. Sixty educators were recruited to serve as school-based coaches. To help them, EDC provided three weeks of face-to-face instruction in such areas as using technology to promote learner-centered instruction, facilitation techniques, and school-based classroom observations and feedback. Coaching candidates then continued with their coaching formation by participating in a ten-session (21-week) coaching course, "Strategies and Techniques in School-based Coaching," via Moodle.

The online coaching course was explicitly designed to incorporate the characteristics of collaborative learning (Johnson & Johnson, 1988). Each of the ten sessions scaffolded the coaching trajectory—helping coaches work with the teacher to adapt and implement a model lesson; coteach a lesson with teachers; and observe and provide feedback to teachers in their solo teaching of this lesson. As coaches learned a particular technique via the online course (e.g., assessing teachers' needs or helping teachers plan a lesson), they consulted with their online colleagues and deployed this technique in schools with teachers. Upon implementation, they "returned" to their online environment, primarily now using Web 2.0 applications to discuss, evaluate, share, and document their practice.

In addition to Moodle, coaches used some form of a Web 2.0 application on an almost weekly basis. Web 2.0 applications were purposefully selected and incorporated so coaches could share information and resources; informally communicate with colleagues and their online mentor (an online instructor who had previously been a school-based coach); plan school-based coaching activities; discuss and reflect on coaching activities and their work with teachers; and conduct self- and peer-assessments of a particular school-based activity with teachers.

Web 2.0 in Asia

Internet use has a firm foothold in many Asian nations, but Web 2.0 applications are much less commonly used. Indeed, only Japan and South Korea reside within the top 10 list of Web 2.0-using nations (*The Economist*, 2010). The use of Web 2.0 in education, though modest relative to other sectors (Selwyn, 2005), is increasing worldwide (Demirel,

Duman, Incensu & Göktas, 2008). However, while the authors did uncover some examples of Web 2.0 for teacher education purposes in Asia (blogs in undergraduate education in Malaysia and the use of Nings for teacher training in the Philippines), the use of Web 2.0 as an educator capacity building tool within Asia appears to be severely limited (Oliver & Goerke, 2008).

The most prominent uses of Web 2.0 applications within Asia, and indeed within developing-country contexts, seem to fall into one of three broad categories:

- *Citizen journalism/crowdsourcing*: Citizen journalism, and its group variant, "crowdsourcing," are the individual or collective use of social media tools to broadcast the "real story" behind some event. The use of Twitter by Iranian supporters of the opposition candidate in June 2009 is one such example. Ushahidi, an open-source platform that maps text messages by time and location, is another. Ushahidi was developed to track reports of ethnic violence following Kenya's 2008 elections and documented relief efforts in Haiti's 2010 earthquake.
- *Issue-oriented social networks or "niche groups"*: These are networks of individuals or groups who coalesce around particular issues, such as environmental issues (Cormode & Krishnamurthy, 2008). Greenedia, a "green" social media site, is one example of an issue-oriented social network. It serves as a distribution channel for user-created blogs and podcasts, all focused on environmental issues, particularly within Asia.
- *Informal uses of Web 2.0*: Across Asia, informal, "personal" social networking has proved increasingly popular—particularly in Hong Kong, Taiwan, Singapore, South Korea, and Japan (*The Economist*, 2010). The use of personal social networking sites such as Facebook has increased dramatically across the continent (the travails of Twitter and Facebook in China notwithstanding). Indonesia has recently emerged as the world's third largest Facebook-using nation (Morrison, 2010) despite the novelty of social networking in Indonesia and in spite of opposition to Facebook by the Indonesian Islamic Religious Leaders Council (Republika, 2009).

Definitions of and distinctions between Web 1.0 and Web 2.0 abound (Cormode & Krishnamurthy, 2008; Hardogan, 2009). Because of its technical features—for example, a public API to allow third-party enhancements (Cormode & Krishnamurthy, 2008)—Web 2.0 has been christened as the "read/write" or "second generation" Web, while Web 1.0 has been termed the "read" or "first generation" Web (O'Reilly, 2005). Such designations aside, it can often be difficult to differentiate between the two retronyms. Table 9.1 attempts to outline these distinctions.

Our decision to utilize Web 2.0 applications as part of coaches' online learning rested on four motivations. The first was financial. Because we hoped to bequeath this program to our Indonesian counterparts, the technology tools selected needed to be low cost. Since Web 2.0 applications often mimic and augment standard office-type desktop applications, coaches could use free Web 2.0 applications—for example, Web-based word processing and concept-mapping tools—for instructional purposes.

The second was borne of a fear of attrition. Though research has found "reasonable rates of effectiveness" in distance courses (Perraton,

Table 9.1   Web 1.0 vs. Web 2.0

	Web 1.0	*Web 2.0*
General characteristics	• Proprietary • Three "Rs"—reading, receiving and researching	• Non-proprietary • Three "Cs"— contributing, collaborating, and creating
Structure	Static	Dynamic
Communication	• More passive • Hierarchical and controlled—hub and spoke communication pattern	• More active • Flat and decentralized—networked communication pattern
User interactions	May allow user-to-user connections but this is often mediated by the website itself	Allows users to form connections via links to "friends;" membership in groups; and subscriptions or RSS feeds of updates from other users
Interaction with site	Typically does not allow users to post content or do so in a restricted or single media format (e.g., text-based comments on a web site); restricted privacy controls; typically does not facilitate sharing among users	Allows users the ability to post content in many forms: photos, videos, blogs, comments on other users' content, tagging of own or others' content, and some ability to control privacy and sharing
Authorship	Closed system—content creation and consumption are carried out by two separate sets of actors (producers and consumers)	Open system—users create and modify their own personalized content for their own use. Users are both producers and consumers of content

Creed & Robinson, 2002), distance learning suffers from high attrition (Potashnik & Capper, 1998). Among Asian open universities, this attrition rate can be as high 90 percent (Latchem & Jung, 2010). This may be due to the limited ongoing support and asynchronous nature of a medium that is neither time- nor place-based. To counter the asynchronicity of Moodle-based communication, we deliberately selected a number of Web 2.0 applications, such as Skype, DimDim, and Voice Thread, to provide synchronous, ongoing "face-to-face" interaction among coaches and between coaches and instructors (Tables 9.2 and 9.3 describe these applications).

Third, while we wanted coaches to have the uniform, standardized learning experience offered by an LMS (Weller, 2010), we were sufficiently concerned about the restrictiveness, latency, and broadcast nature of an LMS and the attendant impact on coaches' interaction with one another. By embedding a suite of less bandwidth-intensive Web 2.0 applications, participants could leave the uniformity of the LMS, where interactions tend to be of a more one-to-many formalized nature, and interact instead with a variety of personalized tools that facilitate the type of educator control, flexibility, and personalization less available in learning management systems (Weller, 2010).

Finally, by relying on "the cloud" (Vaquero, Rodero-Merino, Caceres & Linder, 2009), we hoped coaches could communicate and collaborate to develop a wealth of local-language learning materials, such as audio and video, that would be disseminated broadly, thus augmenting and localizing the content and diversity of the online course (Warschauer, 2008).

Using Web 2.0 applications for school-based coaching

As they embarked on their work with teachers, our online learners first needed a general grounding in the conceptual and logistical issues involved in school-based coaching. Essentially, they had to be able to help teachers with two broad sets of classroom tasks. The first was to help teachers adapt a model, one-computer lesson for their own classroom and then support teachers through the ensuing planning, design, and practice that such adaptation entailed. Table 9.2 outlines online learners' uses of Web 2.0 applications as part of their orientation as coaches and as part of their overall task in helping teachers with instructional planning.

The second task involved "co-teaching" a model lesson with teachers. Coaches helped teachers revise the lesson, observed the teacher in her solo teaching of the lesson, and provided corrective feedback. These

Table 9.2   Web 2.0 Tools to Build Understanding of Coaching and Instructional Planning

Coaching Session (Title)	Web 2.0 Tool Utilized	Explanation of Application	Use by Coaches	Purpose
Face-to-face orientation	Etherpad	Document sharing tool that allows users to collaboratively compose, edit and revise writing	Collaboratively develop and assess written online posts	Written anchors to model appropriate and well-developed models of written communication
Session 1: Getting Started as a School-Based Coach	Mind Meister	Concept mapping application. Users co-create and edit one another's concept maps	Concept mapping and brainstorming	• Baseline assessment of coaches' understanding of coaching, the coaching process, and effective coaching practices • Repeated as part of summative assessment following course completion (Session 10)
Session 2: Assessing Teachers' Needs	Voice Thread	Multimedia space. Users upload moving and still images and hold synchronous and asynchronous text- and audio-based conversations around these media	Videotape their initial meeting with teachers and upload it to Voice Thread for peer evaluation	• Help coaches self-assess their performance in organizing and facilitating teachers' meetings • Mechanism for peer-based formative assessment and feedback
Session 3: Goal Setting with Teachers	Voice Thread	(See above)	Create PDFs of teachers' individual goal-setting rubrics and upload to Voice Thread	Peer-feedback mechanism: Coaches provide one another with feedback on teachers' goal-setting rubrics
Session 4: Planning and Adapting a Lesson	Diigo	Social bookmarking tool. Users annotate web sites through "tags," share web-based resources and communicate and form communities around such resources	Search, find, evaluate, annotate and compile lists of useful resources that could potentially help other potential and future coaches in Indonesia	• Assess coaches abilities to evaluate web-based content • Compile resources as part of a coaching handbook

Continued

Table 9.2 Continued

Coaching Session (Title)	Web 2.0 Tool Utilized	Explanation of Application	Use by Coaches	Purpose
Mid-Course Meeting	DimDim	Web-conferencing tool. Users hold live video and audio meetings	Synchronous online meeting as a mid-point check-in about their performance in the online course and school-based coaching activities	Build a sense of community— coaches meet in real time and "see" colleagues in other provinces whom they wouldn't normally see
Sessions 1–10	WordPress	Blogging tool	Develop an e-portfolio documenting what they've learned about coaching	• Synthesize best practices in coaching • Compose individual and personal reflections on their coaching journey

associated tasks—coteaching, observation, and feedback—and the Web 2.0 applications supporting such tasks, are outlined in Table 9.3. Taken together, the use of Web 2.0 applications outlined in Tables 9.2 and 9.3 reveals two broad patterns of use within this online learning experience, which are discussed in the following sections.

Knowledge generation: "The Wisdom of Practice"

First, coaching is a highly performance-based endeavor. Coaches must be able to advise teachers; help them plan effective lessons; utilize technology; model good instructional practices; assess teacher practice; and provide nonthreatening and meaningful feedback. Because of this performance-based focus and the peer-based learning design of this course, the preponderant use of Web 2.0 applications allowed coaches to view one another's practice and provide peer assessment, guidance, and feedback. As Table 9.2 illustrates, this meant the use of lesser-known, but more task-appropriate Web 2.0 tools such as Voice Thread (used in four of ten online sessions). Using Voice Thread, coaches uploaded video of their own coaching performance and received real-time, synchronous feedback and guidance from colleagues about their coaching performance. These

Table 9.3 Web 2.0 Tools Used for the Coteaching Process

Coaching Session (Title)	Web 2.0 Tool Utilized	Explanation of Application	Use by Coaches	Purpose
Session 6: Co-Teaching	Voice Thread	(See description in Table 2)	Select a 30-second video example of a co-teaching episode that did not go well for purposes of improvement	• Peer-feedback mechanism: Coaches provide one another with feedback on their co-teaching activity • Formative assessment: Online instructor sees which and where coaches need additional help or guidance
Session 7: Facilitating Teacher Conversations	Gabcast	Audio-blogging tool. Users create podcasts and audio files	Create a two-minute audio summary of benefits and challenges of an open lesson	Develop coaches' synthesizing skills
Session 9: Solo Teaching, Classroom Observations and Feedback	Ning	Social networking platform focused on building online communities who share interests/ activities. Users can post video, files and images.	Discuss teachers' solo teaching activities; coaches' roles as classroom observers; and assess their performance in providing feedback to teachers	• Provide discussion space where coaches could write at length about their experiences observing and providing feedback on teachers' instructional performance • Demonstrate to coaches a professionally (vs. personally)-based social networking site
	Voice Thread	(See description in Table 2)	Select a three-minute video segment of a teacher's solo teaching effort that best illustrates how the coach helped this teacher. Forms the basis for an online discussion with learning teams	• Visual documentation of coaches' impact on teachers' instructional practices • Form of self-assessment and reflection for the coach who "takes the measure" of his/her work

video examples served as scaffolds by which weaker coaches could structure their own interactions with teachers. This interplay among observation, scaffolding, and increasingly independent practice helped coaches develop self-monitoring and self-improvement skills needed to advance toward proficiency (Collins, Brown & Holum, 1991).

Next, the many cognitive processes supported by the variety of Web 2.0 tools outlined in Tables 9.2 and 9.3 meant that knowledge-generation was a public, collaborative, iterative, and cognitively sophisticated endeavor (Warschauer, 2008). Coaches had to externalize their internal thoughts; internalize external actions; and communicate their learning through verbal, visual, or text-based language (Vygotsky, 1978). The social interaction and collaborative knowledge generation made possible by Web 2.0 applications was critical to the development of coaches' knowledge about coaching.

Evidence of this interaction could be seen in the rich and multidimensional nature of coaching content created, four characteristics of which are briefly noted here.

- Differentiated *types* of knowledge: Coaches generated multiple types of text-based knowledge, not simply narrative or expository information, but descriptive, definition-based, and problem-solving text structures. This information served as a reference to address emergent and complex coaching-related issues.
- Hierarchy of *knowledge structures*: Associated conversations around content development seemed to reflect a hierarchy of knowledge structures and typology of ideas. Within Web 2.0 discussions, coaches generated knowledge structures that could be described as *ideological* (doctrines or beliefs that reflect the social needs and aspirations of teachers); *normative* (expressing values and associated standards of behavior); *causal* (guidelines or strategies on how to achieve objectives); *prescriptive* (suggesting norms for certain practices) and *intrapersonal* (personal reflections and exchanges about their tasks) (Tannenwald & Wohlforths, 2005).
- Variety of knowledge *formats*: Content creation assumed a variety of media formats. For example, coaches used the online concept-mapping tool, MindMeister, to develop coaching schema. They built a library of quality-controlled Web-based coaching resources via the social bookmarking site, Diigo. Using Gabcast, coaches audio-blogged the benefits and challenges of Open Lessons (where teachers view one another teaching a lesson) and posted coteaching video episodes in YouTube. Finally, through WordPress, coaches

assembled all material into a personal e-portfolio available online as a series of coaching handbooks for Indonesian educators.

• *Appropriated and remixed* knowledge creation: Coaches interacted with an established "canon" of coaching (readings by instructional coaching experts). By transferring such knowledge to real-world situations (classrooms), their theoretical knowledge was leavened by school-based experiences. Coaches further plumbed these experiences through online discussions, involving writing, a reflective and communicative act in which experiences are filtered through language. This blending of conceptual and experiential knowledge shared with online colleagues resulted in a third category of knowledge—social knowledge (Hacking, 1999). Together, these three distinct forms of knowledge—canonical, experiential, and social—served as a sort of cognitive "mash up" in which distinct forms of information combined to form a new multifaceted understanding of instructional coaching.

In short, coaches utilized the creative and communicative features of Web 2.0 applications to develop an epistemology of coaching—or what Schulman (1994) calls the "wisdom of practice."

Establishing presence

The session-specific uses of Web 2.0 tools in Tables 9.2 and 9.3 focus on knowledge about, reflection on, and evaluation of coaching practice. In Table 9.4, the nonsession-specific use of Web 2.0 tools portray a second purposeful focus of the use of Web 2.0 tools. For our novice e-learners to successfully complete their online course, they needed multiple opportunities for various forms of ongoing communication.

Continuous communication is essential for maintaining and sustaining an online community and is vital to the very success of online learning. In what is the often "lonely" experience of online learning (Prescott & Robinson, 1993), this constant stream of communication and scheduled collegiality was critical in helping coaches feel part of an online community with likeminded colleagues. We therefore deliberately designed ongoing communication opportunities in a variety of configurations (one-to-one, learning teams of four individuals, and one-to-many with the online facilitator holding whole-group synchronous meetings).

The uses of Web 2.0 tools for ongoing communication served three general purposes for online learners. First, it provided the sort

Table 9.4   Web 2.0 Applications for Ongoing Communication

Web 2.0 Tool Utilized	Explanation of Application	Use by Coaches	Purpose
Twitter	"Micro-blogging" tool: Users can compose and receive 140-character messages	Send short, whole-group updates	• Frequent, ongoing, brief communication among coaches and among online instructors and coaches • Attempt to mimic the kinds of brief, informal conversations individuals have in face-to-face settings
YouTube	Video-sharing website	Upload video examples, comment on one another's videos and include videos in e-portfolios	• Visual documentation of key coaching practices • Visually archived instructional tool for coaching procedures
Flickr	Photo-sharing site where users can upload, tag, annotate and share photos	Upload photos to Flickr for sharing, online discussion and for inclusion in their e-portfolios	• Visual documentation of key coaching practices • Alternative visual documentation tool for coaches who might have difficulty using video
Skype	Internet phone conferencing application. Users talk and text in real time (and see one via built-in or external web-cams)	Used to provide scheduled and as-needed voice and "face" support for particularly difficult coaching procedures	Allow real-time communication to lessen the latency and isolation that may occur in online courses
Gabcast	Audio-blogging tool that allows users to create podcasts	Pairs of coaches were assigned to summarize one session's readings, course assignments, coaching activities, and discussions	• Assess coaches' understandings of readings and discussions • Provide nontext summary of important content and topics related to coaching

of "high-touch" contact and sense of belonging that may be absent in online courses. Interviews with twenty-five of sixty coaches revealed that this constant communication was a major contributor to the high completion rate (90 percent) in the online course. This assertion is supported by Gorham's (1988) claim that "verbal immediacy" and "just-in-time" assistance are critical elements in the coherence of online groups and Latchem and Jung's research (2010) demonstrating that Web 2.0 applications can result in higher retention rates in online courses.

Next, blending Web 2.0 tools with Moodle's discussion forum appeared to broaden the overall communication landscape. Within the discussion forum, conversations tended to be longer, more focused on readings and assignments, more formal and more "permanent" (given the archival nature of an LMS). In contrast, the use of Web 2.0 applications for informal ad hoc communication (outlined in Table 9.4) yielded less formal and developed—but nonetheless valuable—patterns of communication. Coaches noted that Web 2.0 tools were a particularly useful means of motivation, affirmation, and quick information sharing—all important for group coherence and collegiality. Interviews with coaches suggest that the informal and ongoing communications supported by Web 2.0 applications added a spontaneity, continuity, and intimacy to conversations largely absent from those of the LMS discussion forum and that the overall complementarity of communication (formal and structured versus informal and spontaneous) resulted in a more supportive learning environment for coaches.

Finally, and cumulatively, as noted earlier, online learning can be a lonely experience. The use of Web 2.0 tools for informal, ongoing communication furnished a sense of "presence" among learners and between instructor and learners. Rourke, Anderson, Garrison, and Archer (2001) define presence as having three dimensions: cognitive (discussions of knowledge and procedures); social (emotional engagement among learners); and instructional (modeling effective pedagogical practices) and cite "presence" as critical in successful online learning experiences.

Impact of Web 2.0 tools on coaches

The previous section described coaches' uses of Web 2.0 applications as part of the coaching process. We now address the most discernible impact of the use of Web 2.0 applications on coaches—their movement toward higher-order thinking skills and the formation of an online community of practice. Each outcome is discussed below.

Higher order thinking

Bloom's Taxonomy of Educational Objectives organizes learning along a continuum—from acquisition of knowledge (recitation of information) to evaluation of information. This framework helps teachers develop, plan, execute, and evaluate different "levels" of learning. For example, in one domain of knowledge, a student may be required to "know" the dates of particular historical events, while in another he or she may need to be able to evaluate the competing claims of two nations at war. Within education, the "higher-order" thinking skills outlined by Bloom—application, analysis, synthesis, and evaluation (frequently termed "critical thinking") are the (often elusive) goal of lesson design and instruction. As any teacher or professional development provider knows, it is quite difficult to design "higher-order" activities and discussion questions where learners analyze and evaluate information—particularly in educational systems that have not emphasized these ways of thinking.

A major rationale for introducing and using technology in education is that when used appropriately, computers can serve as "mind tools" (Jonassen, 2000) resulting in the development of higher-order thinking. This has not always proved true. In our face-to-face professional development sessions with coaches, we frequently and unsuccessfully struggled to help them develop higher-order thinking skills within a certain domain. Similarly, their use of technology often reinforced versus transcended more lower-level thinking as coaches often used higher-order technology tools (e.g., spreadsheets) in lower-order cognitive ways (e.g., displaying versus analyzing information).

In contrast to these face-to-face experiences, coaches' online use of Web 2.0 applications appeared to be of a much higher cognitive caliber. Indeed, we witnessed the kinds of quality content development and particularly, critical reflection, via Web 2.0 tools not observed in face-to-face settings. Overall, their use of certain Web 2.0 technologies appeared to move coaches toward greater analysis, synthesis, and evaluation.

Table 9.5 outlines some of the ways that coaches utilized Web 2.0 applications, the activities associated with each and the specific "cognitive level" of Bloom's Taxonomy that each addressed. As illustrated in the table, both the intentional *design* of certain Web 2.0 applications and their intentional *use* as part of the online course resulted in practices that were by their very nature much more higher level—applying knowledge, analyzing practice; summarizing/synthesizing information; and evaluating their own and one another's coaching performances.

The following example may encapsulate how Web 2.0 applications helped to facilitate higher-level thinking. In one activity, coaches were required to coteach a computer-based lesson with teachers. While one coach cotaught with the teacher, his/her partner recorded the coteaching episode. Coaches then identified a coteaching episode with which

Table 9.5 Thinking Skills, Activities, and Web 2.0 Applications (Burns, 2009)

Coaches were…	Through these activities….	Using these Web 2.0 applications…	Cognitive Level (Bloom's Taxonomy)
Categorizing and classification	Tagging web-based resources	Diigo	Knowledge, comprehension, application analysis and evaluation
Soliciting and providing constructive feedback	Real-time feedback sessions on a coaching-related "problem"	Ning	Analysis, synthesis and evaluation
Summarizing session's readings and discussions	Audio summaries of weekly readings and assignments	Gabcast	Synthesis
Communicating visually	Image compilation and tagging	Flickr	Analysis
Peer-assessment	Real-time conversations around artifacts	Voice Thread	Analysis, evaluation
Creating models of good discussion posts	Collaboratively developing written anchors to serve as models for good online posts.	Etherpad	Comprehension, application analysis, synthesis and evaluation
Reflecting, self evaluating and discussing	Journal writing as part of e-portfolio	WordPress, Ning, DimDim, Skype	Application analysis, synthesis, and evaluation

they were dissatisfied and uploaded this video to Voice Thread where their colleagues assessed and provided feedback on the coteaching. In so doing, coaches had to analyze colleagues' practice; mentally compose reactions into a concise verbal message they wished to share with colleagues; and communicate in ways that were constructive, detailed and comprehensive. Such an activity touched on Bloom's cognitive domains of analysis, synthesis, and evaluation.

Community of practice

Online learning environments differ from one another along numerous dimensions (Dillemans, Lowyck, Van der Perre, Claeys & Elen, 1998)—their linearity, types of interactions, temporality (fixed time versus self-paced), models of learning (cohort-based versus solo learners), and purpose. However, research suggests that online educational initiatives geared to helping teachers learn new skills and practices are best served through a community approach (Kleiman, 2004) allowing learners to view model practices; experience using them in their particular classroom setting; reflect upon their experience with colleagues; and engage in the type of analytical and reflective discussions with peers and mentors that spreads "the wisdom of practice" (Schulman, 1994).

Community building has become synonymous with organizational and human performance improvement. Within teacher professional development, "communities of learning" and "communities of practice" are often used synonymously. However, there are multiple types of community and stages of community development (Burns & Dimock, 2007; Wenger, 2006). "Communities of interest" mark the initial stage of community development, providing the social context within which "members" connect to one another via a shared professional interest. As members become more involved in the professional endeavor, these communities of interest can evolve into communities of learning, the defining characteristic of which is communication about shared learning experiences (Burns & Dimock, 2007).

The final stage of community development is a community of practice. Within such communities, reflection and discussion are transformed into action. According to Wenger (2006), communities of practice require the three following components:

• a domain (knowledge with which a group interacts)
• a community (a group of individuals interacting with the same domain and engaged in the same practice, activities, and discussions, who help each other and share information)
• a practice (shared competence in which individuals develop a shared repertoire of resources, experiences and ways of addressing recurring problems).

Though we were not able to find comparable data for instructional coaches, Jackson and Bruegmann (2009), in their study of "knowledge spillovers" among teachers, report that new teachers benefit most from exposure to high-ability peers. Kandel and Lazear (1992) suggest that teachers with higher performing peers can be pushed toward improved performance. In their study of online learning in Asia, Dhanarajan (2005) and Leung (2007) note that peer-based online learning is "deeper and more meaningful" than nonpeer-based online learning experiences.

Within the online learning experience discussed in this chapter, coaches formed communities of practice in which collegiality and collaboration were the prime characteristics. Coaches were not simply talking about instructional ideas—they were using Web 2.0 applications to create information, share ideas, and assess one another's school-based coaching performances. Together, they were coteaching with teachers; soliciting one another's input to improve the learning process; and helping other coaches manage the logistical and conceptual challenges associated with technology—and supporting one another as they did so.

Coaches themselves reported that the use of Web 2.0 tools facilitated deep connections with colleagues around school-based practice. As Table 9.6 indicates, coaches rated Web 2.0 tools highest in allowing them to share ideas and resources (8.7 out of 10), form communities (8.3), interact with colleagues (8.2), and connect with colleagues (8.0).

This formation of a community of practice offered several benefits to coaches and to the coaching program. First, it furnished the emotional, logistical, and procedural supports for its members in the pursuit of common interests and goals, transforming an undertaking from the individual to the shared realm. Second, it resulted in

Table 9.6 Influence of Web 2.0 Tools on Coaches' Behavior

To what degree did the Web 2.0 tools you used help you attain the following outcomes? (N=60)	*Mean (1–10)*
Community formation	8.3
Interaction with my online colleagues	8.2
Connect with my online colleagues	8.0
Reciprocity (helping one another)	7.8
Group coherence	7.7
Sharing ideas and resources	8.7
Creating (ideas, tools, resources)	7.8
Critical thinking skills	8.0

Note: This information is derived from an online end-of-coaching survey containing a series of statements pertaining to Burns and Dimock's (2007) characteristics of community type (interest, learning and practice). Coaches indicate their level of agreement with each statement, ranking each from 1–10. Results were tabulated, averaged, and categorized based on a pre-developed cut score to signify community types. A minimum cut score of 7s signified a community of practice.

a purposeful educational network of professionals formed around a "joint enterprise" (Wenger, 1998)—school-based coaching—that served the larger public good (school improvement). Third, it made possible goal-oriented knowledge generation and shared learning lubricated by the trust, mutual support, and open communication that form the basis of a community and that were facilitated by technology-based opportunities to talk, write, videoconference and co-create knowledge and ideas on a continuous basis despite a lack of physical proximity.

Finally, this community of practice made public the private, embedded, and tacit professional knowledge of individuals within the group so that knowledge generation was transformed into informed practice that resulted in instructional change in classrooms. Learners were engaged in activities in a supportive environment—creating knowledge not just *in* the community but *for* the community (Holmes, Tangney, FitzGibbon, Savage & Meehan, 2001).

Why Web 2.0?

The discussions about higher-order learning and communities of practice beg some obvious questions. Could all of the above have occurred without Web 2.0 technologies? Could the desired cognitive behaviors of analysis, synthesis, and evaluation have occurred via email, chat, and a traditional online course? Could coaches have formed online communities of practice without the use of Web 2.0 tools?

The answer to these questions is possibly—but with much greater difficulty. Based on observations of and interviews with coaches, Web 2.0 applications appeared to possess a number of inherent characteristics that made them more intuitive learning tools; more suited to the promotion of higher order learning than traditional uses of the Web; more amenable to community formation; and more appropriate to our particular audience of novice technology users. We offer these observations and explanations, noting that they are exploratory and based on our own unique circumstances in Indonesia, and urging that more research on Web 2.0 tools as higher-level cognitive and community-building tools be undertaken.

First, Web 2.0 tools are dynamic. Users could constantly update and refresh their own content as well as that of others. The multitude of processes supported by a variety of Web 2.0 tools (shared concept mapping, word processing, video analysis, group conferencing, etc.) meant that learning became more public, collaborative, and iterative

(Warschauer, 2008) than it would have been without the use of Web 2.0 technologies.

Next, because they are unbounded by time (allowing for synchronous and asynchronous communication) and multichannel in nature (supporting video, audio, computer conferencing, or chat), Web 2.0 applications supported differentiated communication—one-to-one communication, many-to-many communication, and various configurations in between. Coaches reported that such variety encouraged the development of social skills, collaborative learning, and the fostering of personal relationships amongst participants as components of the learning process (Anderson, 2003).

Third, though this varies among applications, Web 2.0 tools possessed a high degree of interactivity. Sims (1999) defines "interactivity" as allowing for learner control; facilitating program adaptation based on learner input; permitting various forms of participation and communication; and aiding the development of meaningful learning. Although the design and degree of interactivity may vary, Web 2.0 applications allowed coaches to interact with content, technology tools, experiences, and most importantly—with one another.

Fourth, designed for purposes of communication and collaboration, Web 2.0 applications connected individuals to and within a larger learning community. Using Voice Thread, DimDim, and Ning for sharing, dialogue, and discussion facilitated the types of communities of practice that reduced isolation, made learning and experimentation less risky, and promoted mutuality and reciprocity. Interviews with coaches suggest two distinct advantages of Web 2.0—versus Web 1.0 applications (such as developing web sites). The first is that the duality of Web 2.0 tools—the fact that they serve as both authoring and communication tools—appeared to help coaches feel more comfortable in both creating information and communicating and collaborating around that information. Next, this duality erased the "anonymity of the commons" (Burns, 2006). The Web is a public space. Yet it is so vast and decentralized, and its audience so large and diffuse, that creative efforts, even when directed to publishing sites, may not be read, or even if read, not acknowledged. In cocreating ideas, strategies and insights as part of an overall online community, coaches had an immediate audience—one another. This larger community of peers afforded participants a familiar and targeted audience who acknowledged and honored their efforts.

Fifth, much of the use of Web 2.0 applications involves writing. The dual nature of writing—the fact that it is private and public; cognitive and sociocultural (Vygotsky, 1978); and a means of internal reflection and external communication—makes writing a particularly rich cognitive act. Through writing, coaches developed an idea or claim; supported their idea with evidence, anecdotes, experiences, and/or details; organized thinking into a logical sequence; and utilized language and text structures to communicate this thinking. This claim is supported by research at Britain's Open University in which students who participated in synchronous online peer discussions demonstrated improvements in higher-order thinking skills and collaborative knowledge development (McAlister, Ravenscroft & Scanlon, 2004).

Finally, their "hybrid" versus unitary design made such applications uniquely generative and transformative. This assertion is perhaps better illustrated within Puentedura's (2006) continuum of technology use. According to Puentedura, technology has four main affordances. It can "substitute" for a particular activity (e.g., word processing for typewriting) or it can "augment," "modify" or finally, in the highest stage, "redefine" an activity—that is, make possible the creation of previously unimaginable human endeavors. When a coach on one Indonesian island viewed a coteaching video example from a colleague on another island and offered real-time feedback to this colleague, as occurred via VoiceThread, working, learning, and collaboration were not simply augmented or modified. They were "redefined."

However, Web 2.0 applications are not without their drawbacks (Latchem & Jung, 2010; Sclater, 2008, 2010; Selwyn, 2005). Since information resides in the "cloud," content is vulnerable—subject to vandalism, Internet interruptions, loss, and discontinuity of the site (in the case of Etherpad). Web 2.0 applications are vulnerable to commoditization or commercialism as formerly free Web 2.0 applications, such as Ning, become monetized.

Further, the decentralized nature of Web 2.0 applications makes safeguarding of intellectual property, archiving conversations, and tracking utilization difficult. The simple technical structure of many Web 2.0 applications often straightjackets users from engaging in more cognitively sophisticated tasks. Finally, the use of Web 2.0 applications for content creation raises issues of quality control by undermining expertise in favor of what Keen (2007) calls "the cult of the amateur."

Web 2.0 and Indonesian culture

Much has been written about the difficulties faced by Asian learners with online learning in general and Web 2.0 in particular (Moran &

Myringer, 1999). Asian societies are generally described as "high-context" cultures in which communication is indirect and formal (Hofstede, 1997). While we certainly found evidence of high-context communication patterns in Moodle's discussion forum, we found higher levels of directness and informality in Web 2.0 applications. Our experience using Web 2.0 applications in Indonesia uncovered no evidence to support Moran and Myringer's (1999) contention that sociocultural, collaborative learning conflicts with long-held Asian learners' "reverence" for the teacher, text, and exam. On the contrary, it appeared that the group-based cultural practices of Indonesia complemented the use of Web 2.0 applications in several respects.

First, face-to-face communication and context are important in Asia (Jung & Sasaki, 2008). Many Web 2.0 applications such as VoiceThread, Skype, and DimDim support this kind of "virtualized" face-to-face, real-time communication (Zhang, 2007). Not coincidentally, these applications were the most popular among our coaches for whom synchronicity was a major benefit of Web 2.0 use.

Next, Asian cultures tend to be task oriented, intellectual, social, and participatory (Gan, 2009; Latchem & Jung, 2010). The Web 2.0 applications utilized in this online coaching course allowed for collaboration around coaching-related tasks and the generation of an epistemology of coaching. Further, Web 2.0 tools allowed for smaller, more intimate interactions and more private configurations of learner-interaction and learner-instructor interaction than the larger whole-cohort type of interaction supported by Moodle. The variety of social interactions supported by Web 2.0 tools (learner-instructor; learner-learner; learner-content) plays a fundamental role in the process of cognitive development (Vygotsky, 1978); may support deeper and more meaningful learning (Anderson, 2003); and can result in higher-quality online discussions (Marjanovic, 1999).

Third, the use of Web 2.0 applications within the online coaching course mirrored the most dominant patterns of technology use in Asia. This includes sending and receiving SMS; uploading photos and video; and talking—by cell phones (Latchem & Jung, 2010). One can plausibly argue that Web 2.0 applications appear to mimic patterns of technology use with which many Asian technology users are familiar.

Fourth, our experience indicates that Web 2.0 applications can facilitate the peer-based, collectivist cultural practices so common within Indonesia (Hofstede, 1997; Triandis, Brislin & Hui, 1988). Birnholtz (2007) suggests that online collaboration works best in cultures that are collaborative while Millambiling (2008) observes that effective instruction in Indonesia requires group-based student collaboration. The use of Web 2.0 applications accommodate this collaborative and shared learning and in so doing can support the Indonesian government's current drive toward constructivist, collaborative curriculum implementation (Ibnu, 2007). Zeeng, Robbie, Adams, and Hutchison (2009), citing their use of Web 2.0 applications in a cross-cultural setting, contend that Web 2.0 applications are not monocultural but rather multicultural.

Finally, within Indonesia, the political shift from Suharto's authoritarianism to democracy (Harris, 2009) has provided an opportunity for people to express themselves more freely in a more egalitarian manner. While Indonesia remains a high power-distance culture (Hofstede, 1997), cultural dynamics and communication patterns are changing among younger Indonesians (Mulder, 2005). While we witnessed some deference of younger coaches toward older coaches in the Moodle discussion forum and more in face-to-face settings, we saw little evidence of this type of age or class deference using Web 2.0 applications. Because of their increasing familiarity with technology, young Indonesians, like young people across Asia and across the globe, have demonstrated their enthusiastic adoption of the types of social media and technical networks that connect them to evolving, diverse, and multiple networks of peers (The Economist, 2010).

Moving forward with Web 2.0

We conclude with two recommendations for Asian-based (indeed all) institutions, individuals, and/or programs wishing to utilize Web 2.0 applications as part of an online or blended learning experience that promotes community and deep learning.

First, tools themselves do not make a community. Instructional design is critical in maximizing the creative and communicative potential of Web 2.0 applications. The online course described here was purposefully designed to build a community of practice to ensure application of learning in classrooms. We designed the course as a five-month experience where all coaches worked together on the same goals and activities. Coaches came together in three separate face-to-face workshops over a period of a year and worked together in schools with a partner. Because online discussions and shared practice are the "ties" that "bind" a collection of individuals into a collaborative community, we established continuous opportunities for communication and collaboration. Finally, we made explicit this emphasis on community. Participants understood why they needed to communicate with peers and how and why shared interactions enhanced and deepened learning. Second, the use of Web 2.0 applications must occur within a specific pedagogical framework. Our online coaching course was explicitly designed as a learner-centered experience. We developed clear tenets of what learner-centered interactions would look like in the course and helped instructors model learner-centered approaches in their online interactions with coaches (for example, open-ended questions and facilitative versus didactic instruction). We created a set of shared norms to guide all interactions and transactions. This instructional approach ensured that discussion questions built on participants' experiences; that content was targeted at participant needs; and that performance-based and collaborative assessment techniques were employed to measure coaches' progress.

Because of these explicit foci on collaboration and learner-centered instruction, we were able to help coaches understand the use of tools—Web 2.0 applications—as vehicles for community formation, knowledge generation, and learning. Coaches came to see the World Wide Web, not just as a collection of resources, but rather as a collection of human collaborative efforts with likeminded "colleagues" working together toward common goals in a common space and for a common good.

References

Anderson, T. (2003). Getting the mix right again: An updated and theoretical rationale for interaction. *The International Review of Research in Open and Distance Learning, 4*(2). Retrieved May 10, 2010, from http://www.irrodl.org/index.php/irrodl/article/view/149/230

Birnholtz, J. P. (2007). When do researchers collaborate: Toward a model of collaboration propensity. *Journal of the American Society for Information Science and Technology, 58*(14), 2226–2239.

Burns, M. (2006, February). Improving student writing through online mentoring. *Learning and Leading with Technology, 33*(5), 38–47.

Burns, M., & Dimock, K.V. (2007). *Technology as a catalyst for school communities: Beyond boxes and bandwidth.* Lanham, MD: Rowman & Littlefield.

Burns, M. (2009, June). Threading, tagging and higher order thinking: Using Web 2.0 applications with Indonesian teacher trainers. *E-Learn.* Retrieved May 10, 2010, from http://www.elearnmag.org/

Collins, A., Brown, J. S., & Holum, A. (1991, Winter). Cognitive apprenticeship: Making thinking visible. *American Educator, 15*(3), 6–11.

Cormode, G., & Krishnamurthy, B. (2008, February). *Key differences between Web 1.0 and Web 2.0* [PDF document]. Retrieved May 10, 2010, from http://www2.research.att.com/~bala/papers/web1v2.pdf

Demirel, T., Duman, D., Incensu, S., & Göktas, Y. (2008, May). Using blogs (web logs) in higher education: Toys or tools? *Proceedings of the 8th International Educational Technology Conference*, Anadolu University (pp. 1114–1117).

Dhanarajan, G. (2005, September). Sustaining knowledge societies through distance learning: The nature of the challenge. Keynote speech presented at the 19th Annual Conference of the Association of Asian Open Universities, Jakarta.

Dillemans, R., Lowyck, J., Van der Perre, G., Claeys, C., & Elen, J. (1998). *New technologies for learning: Contribution of ICT to innovation of education*. Leuven: Leuven University Press.

DiNucci, D. (1999). Fragmented future. *Print: Design & new media, 53*(4), 32. Retrieved May 10, 2010, from http://www.cdinucci.com/Darcy2/articles/Print/Printarticle7.html

Economist Intelligence Unit (2008). E-readiness rankings 2008: Maintaining momentum. A white paper from the Economist Intelligence Unit [PDF document]. Retrieved May 10, 2010, from http://a330.g.akamai.net/7/330/25828/20080331202303/graphics.eiu.com/upload/ibm_ereadiness_2008.pdf

Gan, Z. (2009, February). Asian learners re-examined: An empirical study of language learning attitudes, strategies and motivation among mainland Chinese and Hong Kong students. *Journal of Multilingual and Multicultural Development, 30*(1), 41–58.

Hacking, I. (1999). *The social construction of what?* Cambridge, MA: Harvard University Press.

Hargadon, S. (2009, December 16). Educational networking: The important role Web 2.0 will play in education. Retrieved May 10, 2010, from http://www.scribd.com/doc/24161189/Educational-Networking-The-Important-Role-Web-2-0-Will-Play-in-Education

Harris, S. (2009, June 29). Menimbang demokrasi, merajut optimism. *Kompas.* Retrieved from http://cetak.kompas.com/read/xml/2009/06/29/03324211/menimbang.demokrasi.me

Holmes, B., Tangney, B., FitzGibbon, A., Savage, T., Meehan, S. (2001, March). Communal constructivism: Students constructing learning for as well as with others [PDF document]. Retrieved May 10, 2010, from http://www.scss.tcd.ie/publications/tech-reports/reports.01/TCD-CS-2001–04.pdf

Ibnu, S. (2007, March). Menyikapi KTSP sebagai tantangan untuk menyelenggarakan pembelajaran yang lebih baik. *Jurnal Pendidikan Inovatif, 2*(2). Retrieved May 10, 2010, from http://jurnaljpi.wordpress.com/jpi-volume-2/nomor-2/suhadi-ibnu/

Jackson, C. K., & Bruegmann, E. (2009, July). Teaching students and teaching each other: The importance of peer learning for teachers. NBER working paper No. 15202. Washington, DC: National Bureau of Economic Research. Retrieved from http://www.nber.org/papers/w15202

Johnson, D., & Johnson, R. (1988). *Learning together and alone*. Englewood Cliffs, NJ: Prentice Hall.

Jonassen, D. (2000). *Computers as mindtools for schools: Engaging critical thinking.* Upper Saddle River, NJ: Merrill.

Jung, I. S., & Sasaki, T. (2008, March). Toward effective and efficient e-moderation for blended learning. *Journal of Educational Media Research, 14*(2), 55–76.

Kandel, E., & Lazear, E. (1992). Peer pressure and partnerships. *Journal of Political Economy, 100*(4), 801–817.

Keen, A. (2007). *The cult of the amateur: How blogs, MySpace, YouTube, and the rest of today's user-generated media are destroying our economy, our culture, and our values.* New York: Doubleday.

Kleiman, G. (2004). Meeting the need for high quality teachers: E-learning solutions [PDF document]. Retrieved May 10, 2010, from http://www.ed.gov/about/offices/list/os/technology/plan/2004/site/documents/Kleiman-MeetingtheNeed.pdf

Latchem, C., & Jung, I. (2010). *Distance and blended learning in Asia.* New York: Routledge.

Leung, P. W. (2007). Introducing e-learning in a traditional Chinese context. In M. J. Keppell (Ed.), *Instructional design: Case studies in communities of practice* (pp. 275–295). Hershey, Pennsylvania: Information Science Reference.

Lim, B., Leem, J. H., & Jung, I. S. (2003). Current status of cyber education in Korean higher education and quality control: The year of 2002. *Korean Journal of Educational Research, 41*(3), 541–569.

Lim, C. (2007, March). The current status and future prospects of corporate e-learning in Korea. *International Review of Research in Open and Distance Learning, 8*(1). Retrieved May 10, 2010, from http://www.irrodl.org/index.php/irrodl/article/view/376/671

Marjanovic, O. (1999). Learning and teaching in a synchronous collaborative environment. *Journal of Computer Assisted Learning, 15*(2), 129–138.

McAlister, S., Ravenscroft, A., & Scanlon, E. (2004). Combining interaction and context design to support collaborative argumentation using a tool for synchronous CMC. *Journal of Computer Assisted Learning, 20*(3), 194–204.

Millambiling, J. (2008, April 17) Making necessary adjustments: Teaching abroad in Indonesia [PDF document]. Retrieved May 10, 2010, from http://www.revistahumanidades.uda.cl/publica/010006.pdf

Moran, L., & Myringer, B. (1999). Flexible learning and university change. In K. Harry (Ed.), *Higher education through Open and distance learning* (pp. 57–71). New York: Routledge.

Morrison, C. (2010, June). Indonesia became Facebook's third largest country in May 2010. Inside Facebook. Retrieved May 10, 2010, from http://www.insidefacebook.com/2010/06/08/indonesia-became-facebooks-third-largest-country-in-may-2010

Mulder, N. (2005). *Inside Indonesian society: Cultural change in Java* (3rd ed.). Yogyakarta: Penerbit Kanisius.

Oliver, B., & Goerke, V. (2008, October 25). Undergraduate students' adoption of handheld devices and Web 2.0 applications to supplement formal learning experiences: Case studies in Australia, Ethiopia and Malaysia. *International Journal of Education and Development Using ICT, 4*(3). Retrieved May 10, 2010, from http://ijedict.dec.uwi.edu/viewarticle.php?id=522

O'Reilly, T. (2005, September 30). *What is Web 2.0? Design patterns and business models for the next generation of software.* Retrieved May 10, 2010, from http://oreilly.com/web2/archive/what-is-web-20.html

Perraton, H., Creed, C., & Robinson, B. (2002). *Teacher education guidelines: Using open and distance learning* [PDF document]. Retrieved May 10, 2010, from http://unesdoc.unesco.org/images/0012/001253/125396e.pdf

Potashnik, M., & Capper, J. (1998). Distance education: Growth and diversity. Retrieved May 10, 2010, from http://www.worldbank.org/fandd/english/0398/articles/0110398.htm

Prescott, W., & Robinson, B. (1993). Teacher education at the Open University. In H. Perraton (Ed.), Distance *education for teacher training* (pp. 287–315). London: Routledge Press.

Puentedura, R. R. (2006). Transformation, technology, and education. Retrieved May 10, 2010, from http://hippasus.com/resources/tte/

Republika (2009, May 25). PBNU: Facebook tak harus disikapi halal-haram. *Republika.* Retrieved May 10, 2010 from http://www.republika.co.id/berita/52325/pbnu-facebook-tak-harus-disikapi-halal-haram

Rourke, R., Anderson, T., Garrison, D. R., & Archer, W. (2001). Assessing social presence in asynchronous text-based computer conferencing. *Journal of Asynchronous Learning Networks, 5*(2), 1–17.

Schulman, L. (1994). *The wisdom of practice: Essays on teaching, learning, and learning to teach.* San Francisco: Jossey-Bass.

Sclater, N. (2008, June 24). Web 2.0, personal learning environments, and the future of learning management systems [PDF document]. *Research Bulletin, 2008*(13). Retrieved from http://net.educause.edu/ir/library/pdf/ERB0813.pdf

Sclater, N. (2010, January). E-learning in the cloud. *International Journal for Virtual and Personal Learning Environments, 1*(1), 10–19.

Selwyn, N. (2005, November). Web 2.0 applications as alternative environments for informal learning: A critical review [PDF document]. Paper presented at OECD-KERIS expert meeting, Florianopolis. Retrieved May 10, 2010, from http://www.oecd.org/dataoecd/32/3/39458556.pdf

Sims, R. (2003). Promises of interactivity: Aligning learner perceptions and expectations with strategies for flexible and online learning. *Distance Education, 24*(1), 87–104.

Tannenwald, N., & Wohlforths, W.C. (2005, Spring). The role of ideas and the end of the cold war. Special issue: Ideas, international relations, and the end of the cold war. *Journal of Cold War Studies, 7*(2), 13–42.

The Economist (2010, January 30). Global swap shops: Why social networks have grown so fast and why Facebook has become so dominant. A special report on social networking. *The Economist,* 5–8.

Triandis, H., Brislin, R., & Hui, C. (1988). Cross-cultural training across the individualism-collectivism divide. *International Journal of Intercultural Relations,* 12, 269–289.

Vaquero, L., Rodero-Merino, L., Caceres, J., & Linder, M. (2009). A break in the clouds: Towards a cloud definition. *Computer Communication Review, 39*(1), 50–55.

Vygotsky, L. S. (1978). *Mind and society: The development of higher mental processes.* Cambridge, MA: Harvard University Press.

Warschauer, M. (2008). Laptops and literacy: A multi-site case study. *Pedagogies: An International Journal, 3*(1), 52–67.

Weller, M. (2010, January). The centralization dilemma in IT. *International Journal for Virtual and Personal Learning Environments, 1*(1), 1–9.

Wenger, E. (1998). Communities of practice: Learning as a social system. *The Systems Thinker.* Retrieved May 10, 2010, from http://www.co-i-l.com/coil/knowledge-garden/cop/lss.shtml

Wenger, E. (2006). Communities of practice: A brief introduction. Retrieved May 10, 2010, from http://www.ewenger.com/theory/communities_of_practice_intro.htm

Zeeng, L., Robbie, D., Adams, K. M., & Hutchison C. (2009). Where's my class? Using Web 2.0 for collaboration in a design environment [PDF document]. *Proceedings from Ascilite 2009* (pp. 1140–1147). Retrieved May 10, 2010, from http://www.ascilite.org.au/conferences/auckland09/procs/zeeng.pdf

Zhang, T. (2007). A cultural look at information and communication technologies in Eastern education. *Educational Technology Research and Development, 55*(3), 301–314.

CHAPTER 10

Teaching Research Methods with Social Media

Kelli S. Burns

Introduction

Today's traditional undergraduate students have been raised in a digital world. The class of 2013 was born in approximately 1991, when the Internet was made available for commercial use and reached a penetration of one million computers, Tim Berners-Lee introduced the Web browser, and Linus Torvalds released the first version of the Linux operating system kernel. A lifetime of exposure to technology has created an influx of students to American colleges and universities who are skilled at using the Internet to communicate and access content via computers or handheld devices. As Driscoll (2007) stated:

> Today's tech-savvy student generation is actively participating in social networking and other online communities, so most students not only understand how to use Web 2.0 teaching tools, they thrive in the environment when Web communication solutions are integrated in the classroom. (p. 10)

The technological abilities of students and the technological demands of industry have created an opportunity for educators to infuse technology into the classroom to benefit students and take advantage of their abilities.

The term "Digital Natives" has been applied to today's youth, including traditional college students. As Prensky argued, "It is now clear that as a result of this ubiquitous (technological) environment and the sheer volume of their interaction with it, today's students think and process information fundamentally differently from their predecessors" (2001, p. 1). Those who have not grown up surrounded by technology, but have adopted it and adapted to it, are called "Digital Immigrants," a label that describes many current educators. Prensky stated that "the single biggest problem facing education today is that our Digital Immigrant instructors, who speak an outdated language (that of the pre-digital age), are struggling to teach a population that speaks an entirely new language" (2001, p. 2). These labels are useful in the way they highlight the potential chasm between learning styles of students and teaching methods of educators, as well as the potential opportunities to connect with students on a different level.

The EDUCAUSE Center for Applied Research's (ECAR) annual survey of undergraduate students and information technology (IT) in 2009 found that 88.3% of students surveyed own laptops, 51.2% have an Internet-capable handheld device, and almost all have high-speed Internet access (Smith, Salaway & Caruso, 2009). College students use these resources to spend an average of 19–25 hours a week on the Internet. Slightly more than 90% of those surveyed are social networking users with most (66.2%) accessing a social networking site daily. Communication via text messaging (89.8%) and instant messaging (74.0%) are also extremely prevalent among college students. Fewer students are uploading videos to video-sharing sites (44.8%), adding content to wikis (41.9%), contributing to blogs (37.3%), or downloading podcasts (35%).

A 2008 study by the technology research group CDW-G provided important insights about university technology resources (Nagle, 2008). Their survey of more than 1,000 university students, faculty, and staff found that although more than 80% of faculty members teach in a "smart classroom," only 42% use this technology during every class session. Furthermore, about 63% of students use technology every day, but only 23% have an opportunity to use it in the classroom. Another finding was that the primary perceived obstacle to expanding university technology is resistance by faculty members as a result of their lack of technological knowledge and their dissatisfaction with the training provided (Nagle, 2008).

Graduates, particularly those who enter careers in media, communications, and marketing, are not only expected to be content creators capable of producing videos and podcasts, but also content broadcasters who use the Internet and its social media applications (e.g., blogs, microblogs, video-sharing sites, wikis, and social networking profiles) as distribution mechanisms for this content. Although students may seem to be prepared to enter a technologically competitive world, they may not understand how to effectively use social media for business purposes. Peak (2009) discussed this irony after observing students talking on cell phones outside his campus building:

> This encounter reminded me of how continually amazed I am at the technological sophistication of the students that cross our university campus and enter my classroom. On the other hand, I am often equally surprised at just how little they really understand about the advanced technological devices and systems that are such an important part of their lives. (p. 1)

Scardamalia (2002) emphasized the need for educators to embrace technology to prepare students for a knowledge society that relies on the creation of knowledge over mechanical production.

Digital natives, although surrounded by technology their whole lives, may not be as sophisticated with social media tools as one would assume. Some students may need the guidance of educators to introduce them to social media, particularly as it applies to their specific field. This study explores the integration of social media skills into research methods assignments. Not only will this study present data to support the inclusion of social media skills in a course, but also ideas for specific assignments.

Existing research

Educators attempt to respond to marketplace trends in an effort to prepare graduates, and one of the most significant trends over the past 15 years has been the increased use of technology. In turn, technological advances in the industry have fueled an increased focus in the literature on technology in the classroom. One stream of research in the education literature has examined the application of technology for instructional purposes, including distance or Web-based education. The innovative technologies of 1994 were recommended as a way to improve course delivery and relevance (Roach, Johnson & Hair, 1994). In 1995, Ferrell predicted that information and technology would influence the structure of the marketing curriculum and the delivery of instruction. In 1998, Kelley, Conant, and Smart used a Delphi forecasting study to explore expectations for the first decade of the new millennium, concluding that technology was predicted by the expert panel to be used more extensively to deliver classes. In a subsequent study of marketing educators, Smart, Kelley, and Conant (1999) found that with respect to technology, educators expressed the need in the next 10 years to become more Internet-savvy, use e-mail more extensively to communicate with students, learn more about distance education, and use computer-generated graphics packages.

Another research stream has explored how lecture-based teaching—the traditional method of classroom instruction—is being replaced by interactive classrooms and computer-based learning packages. Student learning, among other benefits such as engagement and preparation for the workplace, are often considered as outcomes in these studies. Two studies that examined student learning from the early grades through college found that computer-based or technology-rich instruction resulted in a significant increase in achievement in test performance (Kulick, 1994; Sivin-Kachala, 1998). Learning style (Greenangel, 2002) as well as positive attitudes and experience with technology (Piccoli, Ahmad & Ives, 2001) have been found to be moderators of the impact of technology on student learning. Ueltschy's (2001) exploratory study found that interactive classrooms offered many benefits, including higher levels of student participation, more enjoyment of the learning process, and improved test scores. Schrand (2008) found that interactivity afforded by technology also facilitates more active student learning and has appeal to students with different learning styles.

The ECAR study serves to understand student use of technology for the purpose of informing college administrators and faculty (Smith et al., 2009). The study found that most students (59.6%) want a moderate amount of IT in their classes, a statistic that has remained relatively stable over the history of the annual survey. The study also examined three dimensions of student success including learning, student engagement, and convenience. The highest percentage agreed that IT makes doing course activities more convenient (70.4%), followed by agreement that the use of IT improves learning (49.4%), that the IT students have used will adequately prepare them for the workplace (46.8%), and that students get more actively involved in courses that involve IT (37.1%).

Clark, Flaherty, and Mottner (2001) examined the impact of 14 educational technology tools on perceptions of overall learning, ability to get a job, and expected job performance. This study extended previous research by including not just instructional or communication technologies, but also assignments that incorporate technology. Overall learning was correlated with nine of the technologies including technology lectures, online syllabus, online lecture outlines, instructor home pages, Internet projects, online student rosters, online grade pages, Web page projects, and online homework assignments. Ability to get a job was related to 10 of the technologies including all the previous technologies except for instructor Web page and Web page project and adding chat room, FAQ page, and online readings. Eight technologies correlated with job performance including technology lectures, online syllabus, online lecture outlines, online readings, Internet project, Web page project, FAQ page, and online homework assignments.

Granitz and Hugstad (2004) encouraged an expanded use of technology beyond the purposes of student–professor interaction to focus on learning activities that help meet marketing education objectives. Recommendations for assignments suggested by the authors included e-mail marketing exercises, Web page creation, data mining, and Internet penetration forecast modeling (Granitz & Hugstad, 2004). Castleberry (2001) described a secondary research assignment for a market research class that involved students searching both online and offline for data to answer research questions. Other marketing professors have applied technology to standard assignments. Gruca (2000) studied the movie box office market using the Iowa Electronic Markets. Heinrichs, Lim, and Hudspeth (2002) explored the instruction of marketing models with Web-based tools. Alon (2003) used Internet-based experiential exercises to build international business skills among students.

Educational researchers are now exploring how social media tools can be applied in educational settings to improve learning outcomes, yet more understanding is still needed. The term *social media*, which describes the collaborative process that creates meaning and community online through the exchange of text, photos, or videos, is often used interchangeably with Web 2.0, which more specifically refers to the "second generation of Internet-based services" (Beer & Burrows, 2007). Social media encompass blogs, podcasts, wikis, social networking sites, user-news sites, and video-sharing sites, among other tools. Even message boards, which predated the emergence of the World Wide Web by more than 10 years, could be placed in this category. Social media can be incorporated into the classroom in many ways. For example, Twitter can be used for staying connected between classes or for tweeting about a certain event. Blogs can replace paper journals or provide a forum for discussion. YouTube is a resource for educational videos or a home for student-created videos. Facebook can be used to connect a team or the entire class. Wikis are helpful for project collaboration. A key defining quality of Web 2.0 digital technologies is engagement, and it is thought that the integration of social media applications into a course will motivate a student to more fully engage with the content.

Krentler and Willis-Flurry (2005) assessed the relationship between message board use and student learning in a Principles of Marketing class through measures of student grades, rather than perceptions of learning, and found that technology had a significant effect on students' learning. They also examined the impact of student and course characteristics as moderators of this relationship, concluding that among those less likely to use the discussion board technology, marketing and information systems majors performed better than students in other majors. As the use of message board increased, there was little difference in performance among the different majors. Also, among those less likely to use the technology, those with high Internet usage in general performed better in the course. As use of the technology increased, there was little difference among students according to Internet use.

Hazari, North, and Moreland (2009) examined the potential of wikis for teaching and learning among the constructs of learning/pedagogy, motivation, group interaction, and technology. Wang and Braman (2009) found that the integration of Second Life into an introductory computer course improved the students' learning experience, increased their motivation levels, and improved their performance. A high percentage of students enjoyed using Second Life, believed it was useful for educational purposes, and believed they had the resources and knowledge to use Second Life (Wang & Braman, 2009). McKinney, Dyck, and Luber (2009) examined the use of podcasts in the classroom, finding that students scored highest when studying from a combination of lecture materials and podcasts rather than lecture notes or podcasts alone.

The literature supports the idea that incorporating social media into course assignments would improve student learning and attitudes about the course. One class that might benefit from assignments that are more engaging is the research methods class that is taught in a variety of disciplines, a class that is often one of the most unpopular in the curriculum (Bridges, 1999). Bridges (1999) found that for business students, a marketing or advertising class is preferred to marketing research. Suggestions for improving satisfaction with the course included hands-on activities and computer-based projects (Bridges, 1999).

The purpose of the project examined in this chapter was to explore ways to integrate digital social media into a research methods class as a way to collect data, share research, and monitor online conversations.

This study begins to fill a gap in the literature about the benefits of technology in course assignments as well as the application of social media in course assignments. The central question in this study was whether learning about research methods and social media can be enhanced through assignments that use social media. This study also examined whether the use of social media in assignments shifted student attitudes or beliefs about technology. Finally, respondents provided feedback on how the assignments impacted their assessment of the course. This research study presents the results of two sets of survey data that were collected over two consecutive semesters. Slightly different projects were assigned in each case.

Method for Study 1

Sample

Undergraduate students in a research methods course during the summer of 2009 at a large southeastern university in the United States participated in Study 1. The class included students from all sequences in a mass communications program—advertising, public relations, broadcasting, and journalism. Of the 39 students in the class, 29 completed a presurvey during the first week of class while 37 completed the postsurvey after the completion of the course. A total of 27 students completed both the presurvey and the postsurvey questionnaire. Almost 22% (8 students) of the posttest sample were men and 78.4% (29 students) were women.

At the beginning of the course, students created their own blogs using WordPress and then throughout the course, used the blogs to post reports, photos, and podcasts. Classroom instruction was provided to explain the basics of all the technology and social media tools. Some students needed additional assistance outside of class. The projects are described in the next section.

Project assignment descriptions

The three class assignments were completed in teams of three or four students. The ethnography project required students to upload photos to a photo-sharing site; the interview project required students to create an MP3 of interviews and upload as a podcast; and the survey project required students to create an online survey. Actual project descriptions are included in Boxes 10.1 to 10.3.

Box 10.1 The ethnography project

Ethnography project. Ethnographic research can help communicators better understand a target public so they will be able to construct a more appropriate and effective message.

Your assignment is to do a photo ethnography illustrating healthy (or positive) behaviors, unhealthy (or negative) behaviors, or use of a specific product/brand by college students. If you do not spend time with college students, you can look for these behaviors among your own friends, coworkers, or family members.

This assignment requires you to document ten people through photography and write a one-page analysis of your research. All photos must be taken by you during the course of this assignment. Upload your photos to a Flickr. com account and make them available to our class group. You will also need to post a PDF of your report and your photos on your blog. Use the Flickr. com widget on WordPress to display your photos.

Box 10.2 The interview project

Interview project. This assignment gives you an opportunity to learn how interviews are used in research. For this assignment, you will (1) write an interview guide of 5–8 questions, (2) conduct and record three interviews, (3) upload the podcasts to the Web, and (4) write a research report that summarizes the findings from your interviews.

When you locate your participants, ask if they have access to Skype, and if so, conduct your interview using Skype. If not, you can interview them over the phone or in person. In-person interviews can be recorded using Audacity or another audio program such as Garageband. Create an MP3 of your audio file and upload it to your blog using the Box.net widget on WordPress. Place a PDF of your interview project report on your blog.

Box 10.3 The survey project

Survey project. The purpose of the survey research project is to provide you with an opportunity to conduct a survey research study from start to finish. In doing so, you will develop a survey to address your research objectives, create an online survey using Surveymonkey, invite participation in the survey via Facebook, and write a research report to present your results. Place a PDF of your survey project report on your blog.

Measures

Both the pre- and posttests included a self-assessment of experience levels for conducting the following tasks: creating a blog, creating a podcast, conducting an online survey, uploading a document to the Web, uploading photos to the Web, and using Voice over Internet Protocol (VoIP) such as Skype.

Both tests also included measures to gauge student attitudes toward digital technology and social media. Students were asked if they felt social media tools were fun to use, whether they were skilled at using social media, and whether they were willing to work with and learn about social media. Additional items included whether they felt mass communications students should learn about social media, whether they believed knowledge of social media would help them get a job, and whether they thought knowledge of social media would help their performance on the job.

The posttest included items that reflected on the assignments of the class. Students were asked whether they recommended the instructor emphasize social media again the next semester, whether the social media tools were fun to use, and whether they felt comfortable using the social media tools, all measures adapted from Ueltschy (2001). They were also asked whether social media made the assignments more relevant and more enjoyable, whether they could easily use the technology again, and whether they were more actively involved in the course because of social media, with the last statement adapted from the ECAR study (Smith et al., 2009).

Finally, students were asked about outcomes with respect to what they learned about conducting research and what they learned about social media and technology. These same items were also asked in the context of whether this knowledge would help them get a job and benefit their performance on the job. The measures in this section were adapted from Clarke, Flaherty, and Mottner (2001).

Results for Study 1

The assignments provided ample opportunities for students to increase their experience levels with a variety of social media and online applications. At the beginning of the class, students felt they had the most experience uploading photos to the Web, uploading a document to the Web, and creating a blog. At the end of the class, students also indicated they had the most experience with these tasks in addition to conducting an online survey.

A comparison of pre- and postcourse assessments of skills found that students made significant gains in experience levels for four of the six tasks (see Table 10.1). They had the largest increase in experience levels for online surveys, t (25) = 4.63, p = .000, followed by creating a blog, t (26) = 3.90, p = .001, and a podcast, t (26) = 3.89, p = .001. Students were also more experienced at uploading documents to the Web at the conclusion of the course, t (26) = 3.74, p = .001. Not all students used VoIP to conduct interviews—opting to conduct interviews in person—which possibly explains why significant gains were not found for this skill. Students also had high levels of experience with uploading photos to the Web at the beginning of the course, making movement on this skill more difficult.

Respondents had high levels of appreciation for social media at the beginning of the class (see Table 10.2). They believed that knowledge of social media was important for getting a job, enhancing their performance on the job, and for mass communications students to learn. They also indicated they were willing to work with and learn about social media.

The perceptions and attitudes toward social media did not yield any significant differences between the beginning and the conclusion of the course, although for four of the six statements, the posttest mean was higher than the pretest mean. Overall, respondents had high levels of agreement with the statements at both the beginning and the end of the course, with the highest level of agreement for the willingness to work with and learn about social media, followed by

Table 10.1 Paired Samples t Test for Skills Acquired between the Start and Completion of the Course

Scales	Pre (n = 27)		Post (n = 27)		Paired samples t-test
	M	SD	M	SD	t (26)
Conducting an online survey	2.48	1.19	3.56	0.51	4.63**
Creating a blog	2.63	0.97	3.26	0.66	3.90**
Creating a podcast	1.70	0.91	2.59	0.97	3.89**
Uploading document to the Web	2.88	0.99	3.54	0.51	3.74**
Using VoIP	1.85	1.03	2.04	0.98	1.22
Uploading photos to the Web	3.59	0.64	3.59	0.64	.000

* $p < .05$. ** $p < .01$.

Note: Respondents were presented with a four-point scale where 4 = very experienced, 3 = somewhat experienced, 2 = not very experienced, and 1 = not at all experienced.

Table 10.2   Paired Samples *t* Test for Perception and Attitude Change between the Start and Completion of the Course

Statements	Pre (n = 27)		Post (n = 27)		Paired samples t test
	M	*SD*	*M*	*SD*	*t (26)*
I think social media tools are fun to use.	4.07	1.04	4.22	0.97	1.16
I am skilled at using social media.	3.54	1.17	3.81	1.17	1.66
I am willing to work with and learn about social media.	4.63	0.69	4.85	0.36	1.65
It is important for mass communications students to learn about social media.	4.78	0.58	4.81	0.40	0.33
Knowledge of social media will help me get a job.	4.81	0.40	4.78	0.51	−0.44
Knowledge of social media will enhance my performance on the job.	4.81	0.40	4.81	0.40	.000

* $p < .05$. ** $p < .01$.

Note: Items were rated on a five-point Likert scale.

the perception of the importance for mass communications students to learn about social media. Although not significant, the largest increase and the lowest overall means were for student perceptions of their social media skill levels (from $M = 3.54$ to $M = 3.81$ on a four-point scale).

The posttest included additional statements allowing students to reflect on the experience of using the social media tools in class (see Table 10.3). Students were most in agreement with recommending that social media be used again by the professor during the next semester ($M = 4.46$ on a five-point scale), the assignments being more relevant because of social media ($M = 4.35$), their ability to easily use the social media tools again ($M = 4.27$), and being more actively involved in the course because of the use of social media tools ($M = 4.22$).

Another posttest measure involved an assessment of learning outcomes related to conducting research and the use of social media and technology (see Table 10.4). Students expressed high levels of learning in both areas ($M = 3.76$ for research methods and $M = 3.70$ for social media and technology on a four-point scale).

Students also expressed high levels of agreement that what they learned about research methods and social media would help them land a job and enhance their performance on the job (see Table 10.5). Although not significant, students were slightly more likely to agree that the social media and technology would be more useful in landing a job and performing on the job than research methods knowledge.

Table 10.3   Means for Post-Test Assessment of Technology in Course

Course assessments	M	SD
I would recommend the instructor emphasize social media again next semester.	4.46	0.87
Social media made the assignments more relevant.	4.35	0.72
I could easily use these social media tools again.	4.27	0.65
I was more actively involved in this course because of the use of social media.	4.22	1.06
Social media made the class more enjoyable.	4.11	0.98
The social media tools were fun to use.	3.95	1.13
I felt comfortable using the social media tools.	3.72	1.28

Note: Items were rated on a five-point Likert scale.
$n = 35-37$.

Table 10.4   Learning Outcomes from Course

Learning outcomes	M	SD
How much did you learn about conducting research?	3.76	0.44
How much did you learn about social media/technology?	3.70	0.46

Note: Items were rated on a four-point scale where 4 = learned a lot, 3 = learned some, 2 = learned very little, and 1 = didn't learn anything.
$n = 35-37$.

Table 10.5   Learning Outcomes from Course for Future Job

Learning outcomes	M	SD
How much do you think your knowledge about social media and technology will help you get a job?	3.71	0.46
How much do you think your knowledge about social media and technology will benefit your performance on the job?	3.70	0.46
How much do you think your knowledge about research methods will help you get a job?	3.67	0.48
How much do you think your knowledge about research methods will benefit your performance on the job?	3.62	0.49

Note: Items were rated on a four-point scale where 4 = help a lot, 3 = help some, 2 = help very little, and 1 = won't help at all.
$n = 35-37$.

Additional analyses were conducted to determine whether attitudes that existed at the beginning of the course impacted the assessment of social media at the end. Correlation analysis (Table 10.6) demonstrated that three variables measured at the beginning of the course

Table 10.6 Correlation Analysis between Skill Level Prior to Course and Assessment of Technology at the End

	Precourse attitudes and beliefs		
	Skill level	*Fun to use*	*Knowledge will help job performance*
Postcourse assessment	R	R	R
I could easily use these social media tools again.	0.46*	0.49**	0.44*
Social media made the assignments more relevant.	0.51**	0.59**	0.47*
The social media tools were fun to use.	0.71**	0.75**	0.46*
I felt comfortable using the social media tools.	0.60**	0.64**	0.42*
I would recommend the instructor emphasize social media again next semester.	0.47*	0.55**	0.46*
I was more actively involved in this course because of the use of social media.	0.55*	0.55**	0.24
Social media made the class more enjoyable.	0.64**	0.71**	0.39

* $p < .05$. ** $p < .01$.

were positively and significantly related to at least some, if not all, the assessment variables at the end of the course: thinking social media tools are fun to use, being skilled at using social media tools, and the belief that knowledge of social media will help job performance.

Method for Study 2

Sample

Undergraduate students in a research methods course at a large southeastern university during the fall of 2009 participated in this study. The class included students from the public relations sequence in a mass communications program. All 33 students in the class completed both a presurvey during the first week of class and a postsurvey after the completion of the course. Slightly more than 21% (7 students) of the sample were men and 78.8% (26 students) were women. As in the summer semester, students created their own WordPress blogs to host all projects.

Measures

No major changes were made to the measures used in Study 1. Added to the list of skills were uploading a video to the Web and shooting and editing a video, based on the nature of the assignments. Uploading photos to the Web was deleted from the list in Study 1 because no assignment required that task. An open-ended question was also added to gather feedback from students about the experience.

Project assignment descriptions

The three class assignments were completed in teams of three or four students. The social media monitoring project required students to monitor social media sites for conversations about a client; the interview project required students to create an MP3 of their interviews and upload it as a podcast; and the survey project required students to create a video and an online survey. The social media monitoring project and survey project are included here. The interview project was identical in both semesters and will not be described again (see Boxes 10.4 and 10.5).

Box 10.4   The social media monitoring assignment

Social media monitoring assignment. This assignment gives you an opportunity to learn how to monitor blogs and other social media content in a way that provides similar insight offered by more traditional environmental scanning methods.

Many people will discuss an organization and its products/services on their own Web sites or on social media sites, outside of the realm of traditional media. For this assignment, you will (1) monitor the online conversation that has occurred about an organization or brand of your choosing, (2) create a table for your data, and (3) write an analysis of the conversation with suggestions for action.

To monitor the conversation, you might find bloggers who are blogging about your client organization or brand, people who are creating Web sites about it, message board members who are discussing it in forums, Twitter users who are tweeting about it, social networking users who are commenting about it, or online video producers who are posting YouTube videos about it. Your goal is to find 10 nuggets of information across multiple social media applications about your organization or brand. Here are some suggestions to guide your search:

- Check out Twitter and run a search for your client. IceRocket also offers a search of Twitter.
- Search Flickr groups to see if there is a group about your client. Flickr also offers a message board. Scan the photos for interesting information.
- Conduct keyword searches on various blog search engines like IceRocket, Technorati, or blogsearch.google.com for blogs about your organization or brand.

- Search the Web for Web sites about your organization or brand.
- Find Facebook and MySpace pages created by fans of your organization/ brand.
- Search message boards (http://messages.yahoo.com/) for users who post about your organization/brand or boards dedicated to your organization/brand.
- Find YouTube videos. Report the main message of the video and some of the insightful comments.
- Run a search on Addictomatic for a good summary site of social media conversation.
- Use Google Alerts, Social Mention, or Femtoo to receive updates about your organization/brand.

You are looking for information that will help your client understand its consumers better. Do not use social media channels, profiles, or boards that are sponsored by your company or brand or information from articles published by mainstream media sources. Avoid promotional messages ("Chick-fil-A is giving away free chicken sandwiches") and celebrity-related news ("Britney Spears spotted in Starbucks").

Your data table should describe every nugget of information: list the source, provide information about the source (Quantcast or Technorati can be used to provide statistics about a blog or Web site), list the date and time of the comment, and describe the nature of the comment itself. Write a report that summarizes your findings and place a PDF of your report and the data table on your blog.

Box 10.5   Online survey with video assignment

Online survey with video assignment. The purpose of the survey research project is to provide you with an opportunity to conduct a survey research study from start to finish. In doing so, you will create a video to encourage college students to get the H1N1 flu vaccination, develop an online survey to test the effectiveness of the video, and write a research report to present your results.

First, create a 1–2 minute video using your Flip camera. Your video should raise awareness of the H1N1 flu virus and the need to get the vaccine, change attitudes toward the flu/vaccine, and/or encourage students to get the vaccine.

Then, create a survey using Surveymonkey that asks questions that serve your research objectives and e-mail the survey link to your sample.

Finally, analyze your results and write your report. Your report and video should both be posted on your blog.

Results for Study 2

At the beginning of the class, students felt they had the most experience uploading a document to the Web, uploading a video, and creating a blog. At the end, students also indicated they had the most experience with these tasks in addition to conducting an online survey.

A comparison of pre- and postcourse assessments of skills found that students made significant gains in skill levels for all seven tasks (see Table 10.7). They had the largest increase in experience levels for creating a podcast, t (31) = 9.08, p = .000, followed by conducting an online survey, t (32) = 7.61, p = .001, and creating a blog, t (32) = 7.22, p = .000. Students were also more experienced at shooting and editing a video at the conclusion of the course, t (31) = 6.64, p = .000.

Once again, respondents had positive beliefs and attitudes toward social media at the beginning of the class (see Table 10.8). They believed it was important for mass communications students to learn, that they were willing to work with and learn about social media, and that it could enhance their performance on the job.

The perceptions and attitudes toward social media yielded significant differences for two items when comparing the beginning of the course to the end. Respondents had the largest increase in improving skill levels, t (32) = 5.32, p = .000, followed by their willingness to work with and learn about technology and social media, t (31) = 2.15, p = .039.

The posttest included some additional statements to assess the experience of using the technology and social media in class (see Table 10.9). Students were most in agreement with recommending that social media be used again by the professor during the next semester (M = 4.85 on a five-point scale), their ability to easily use the social media tools again (M = 4.69), the class being more enjoyable because of social media (M = 4.67), and the assignments being more relevant because of social media (M = 4.64).

Learning outcomes related to conducting research and the use of social media and technology were also assessed at the conclusion of the course (see Table 10.10). Students expressed high levels of learning in both areas (M = 3.84 for social media and technology and M = 3.72 for research methods on a four-point scale).

Students also expressed high levels of agreement that what they learned about research methods and social media would help them land a job and enhance their performance on the job (see Table 10.11).

Table 10.7 Paired Samples t Test for Skills Acquired between the Start and Completion of the Course

Scales	Pre (n = 33)		Post (n = 33)		Paired samples t test
	M	SD	M	SD	t (32)
Creating a podcast	1.53	0.67	3.00	0.51	9.08**
Conducting an online survey	2.09	0.77	3.39	0.66	7.61**
Creating a blog	2.64	0.93	3.58	0.50	7.22**
Shooting/editing a video	1.94	0.95	3.16	0.68	6.64**
Uploading a video to the Web	2.70	0.98	3.45	0.62	5.02**
Uploading document to the Web	3.06	1.00	3.61	0.50	3.46**
Using VoIP	2.24	1.12	2.76	0.87	3.15**

$^* p < .05.$ $^{**} p < .01.$

Note: Respondents were presented with a four-point scale where 4 = very skilled, 3 = somewhat skilled, 2 = not very skilled, and 1 = not at all skilled.

Table 10.8 Paired Samples t Test for Perception and Attitude Change between the Start and Completion of the Course

Statements	Pre (n = 33)		Post (n = 33)		Paired samples t test
	M	SD	M	SD	t (32)
I am skilled at using social media.	3.79	0.93	4.70	0.47	5.32**
I am willing to work with and learn about social media.	4.69	0.82	5.00	0.00	2.15*
Knowledge of social media will help me get a job.	4.58	0.90	4.88	0.42	1.83
It is important for Mass Communications students to learn about social media.	4.76	0.87	5.00	0.00	1.61
Knowledge of social media will enhance my performance on the job.	4.67	0.82	4.85	0.44	1.10
I think social media tools are fun to use.	4.58	0.71	4.70	0.64	0.73

$^* p < .05.$ $^{**} p < .01.$

Note: Items were rated on a five-point Likert scale.

Students were slightly more likely to agree that the social media and technology would be more useful in landing a job and performing on the job than research methods knowledge.

Additional analyses were conducted to determine whether attitudes that existed at the beginning of the course impacted the assessment of

Table 10.9 Means for Posttest Assessment of Technology in Course

Course assessments	M	SD
I would recommend the instructor emphasize social media again next semester.	4.85	0.57
I could easily use these social media tools again.	4.69	0.47
Social media made the class more enjoyable.	4.67	0.78
Social media made the assignments more relevant.	4.64	0.65
The social media tools were fun to use.	4.55	0.75
I was more actively involved in this course because of the use of social media .	4.51	0.71
I felt comfortable using the social media tools.	4.39	0.82

Note: Items were rated on a five-point Likert scale.
n = 32–33.

Table 10.10 Learning Outcomes from Course

Learning outcomes	M	SD
How much did you learn about social media/technology?	3.84	0.37
How much did you learn about conducting research?	3.72	0.46

Note: Items were rated on a four-point scale where 4 = learned a lot, 3 = learned some, 2 = learned very little, and 1 = didn't learn anything.
n = 32.

Table 10.11 Learning Outcomes from Course for Future Job

Learning outcomes	M	SD
How much do you think your knowledge about social media and technology will benefit your performance on the job?	3.94	0.25
How much do you think your knowledge about social media and technology will help you get a job?	3.91	.030
How much do you think your knowledge about research methods will help you get a job?	3.72	0.46
How much do you think your knowledge about research methods will benefit your performance on the job?	3.73	0.45

Note: Items were rated on a four-point scale where 4 = help a lot, 3 = help some, 2 = help very little, and 1 = won't help at all.
n = 32–33.

social media and technology at the end of the course. Correlation analysis demonstrated that the only significant relationship between any precourse attitude or perception and postcourse assessment of the use of technology in the course was that those who entered the class with more

Table 10.12 Correlation Analysis between Skill Level Prior to Course and Assessment of Technology at the End

Scales	r
I could easily use these social media tools again.	0.50**
Social media made the assignments more relevant.	0.49**
The social media tools were fun to use.	0.44*
I felt comfortable using the social media tools.	0.44*
I would recommend the instructor emphasize social media again next semester.	0.41*
I was more actively involved in this course because of the use of social media.	0.41*
Social media made the class more enjoyable.	0.38*

$^* p < .05.$ $^{**} p < .01.$

skill were significantly more likely to agree with all the postcourses assessments (see Table 10.12).

A total of 28 students responded to the open-ended question at the end of the survey to gather feedback about the experience of using social media. Every response, except one who did not see value in creating a podcast, communicated a positive attitude toward the social media tools used in the class. At the beginning of the course, some students lacked an understanding of why knowledge of social media would be necessary. Some were even resistant to the use of technology:

- I hated some of the technology I had to learn to use at first, but now that I learned how to use them, I have used them for almost every other class as well.
- I never created a podcast or blog before because I thought they were boring and unnecessary. But now after experiencing this class, I find these different types of social media fun to use. I think actually using social media and creating these tools is a fun and interactive way to learn about them.
- I thoroughly enjoyed the social media component of this class. The aspect of social media really helped me apply the material. I had fun using the Flip Cam. I really enjoyed the interview project as that enabled me to interview a professional, which provided me with solid evidence as to why social media was important. I admit, I was skeptical at first, but this project was a great intro to conducting research.

By the end, students saw the value in the course assignments, with some reaping immediate, tangible benefits and others recognizing the importance of learning about social media:

- The experience I gained using social media in this course helped me branch out and learn something that I wasn't previously comfortable with. I even got an internship developing a social media plan and monitoring social media for a company. I tell my employer all of my knowledge on social media that I have learned from this class.
- I am working with social media right now in an internship and I have referred back to information, Web sites, and all other sources I have learned about in this class countless times. I definitely think out of all my classes this semester this class has benefited me most as of now as far as social media goes.
- Before this class, I never really used social media and I thought it was more a tool for fun. Now, I think social media can be used in many situations like gathering research and communicating with people. It is important.
- I thought that it was interesting and fun to learn these different tools. I was unfamiliar with all of the tools other than Facebook and Twitter prior to this class. Having a blog assignment and having to convert things to mp3 and upload them to our blogs was a very good assignment that will be useful when we have jobs.

Conclusion

Incorporating social media and digital technologies into course assignments provides many benefits for students, which in turn may provide additional benefits to educators. Students in Study 1 increased their skill levels over the course of the semester with respect to creating blogs, podcasts, and online surveys, as well as uploading documents to the Internet. Students in Study 2 increased skill levels for all tasks required in the assignments. Public relations students are not as skilled in using social media tools as the advertising and broadcasting students who were students in the summer session, which may explain the significant movement in skill level throughout the course of the semester for Study 2.

While students in Study 1 did not exhibit significant shifts from the beginning to the end of the course in their perceptions of and attitudes toward social media, there was an insignificant but positive difference on the item related to skill level by the end of the course. Respondents in Study 2 reported a significant increase in skill level and willingness to work with social media.

Students were overwhelmingly positive about the use of social media and technology in the course by the end, exhibiting high levels of agreement that the instructor should emphasize social media again, the assignments were relevant because of social media, and students could easily use the social media tools again. Students in Study 1 were more likely to agree that they were more actively involved in the course because of social media, while students in Study 2 found the class more enjoyable because of social media. Students also expressed high levels of agreement that they learned a lot about both research methods and social media throughout the course and that the skills would help them get a job and enhance their performance on the job.

Correlation analysis revealed the variables measured at the beginning of the course that were significantly related to assessment of the use of social media at the end of the course. In Study 1, these variables were perceived skill level, the perception that social media is fun to use, and the belief this knowledge will benefit job performance. Skill level was the only variable that correlated significantly with the course assessment variables in Study 2. These findings suggest that students who enter the course more confident in their skills will have a better experience. The course, however, was successful at increasing student skill level both overall and with respect to the different social media tools, particularly in Study 2; therefore, all students should benefit from the inclusion of social media in their course assignments.

Limitations of the studies

This research should be considered an exploratory study that can provide insight to other educators about why and how social media can be incorporated into a research methods course. The primary limitation of this research is that the instrument has been tested with only two classes of students. Additionally, a control group was not employed because only one section of the course was taught each semester.

Future directions for research

Additional studies could explore and measure other methods of incorporating social media into the classroom. Researchers have only just begun to explore this topic, and to date, no studies have been conducted on some of the more recent social media applications, such as Twitter. Qualitative research could also explore student attitudes and technology acceptance in more depth.

This study is a natural extension of research that explored the use of technology to deliver instruction through Web-based courses and then the introduction of technology into the classroom to replace traditional lecture-based teaching. This study is situated among other studies, such as Krentler and Willis-Flurry (2005) and Clark, Flaherty, and Mottner (2001), which found a relationship between the integration of technology in course assignments and improved learning outcomes.

The research methods course is often an unpopular one in the curriculum and, for this reason, is a course that could benefit from creative ways to make it more interesting and relevant to students (Bridges, 1999). The use of social media alone cannot increase learning outcomes and student engagement in a course. These assignments must be supported by an instructor who embraces technology, stays current on technological changes, and can teach the technology to students. The instructor may also need to promote the importance of understanding social media, by bringing in guest speakers or using articles that support this perspective.

Incorporating social media into the existing curriculum alleviates the need to create a stand-alone course on the topic. Educators are encouraged to explore how blogs, videos, podcasts, wikis, and social networks can be integrated into the courses of their program's curriculum. Similarly, students are encouraged to embrace learning opportunities that involve social media to prepare themselves for the technological demands of the present and future. Although certain social media tools may evolve or become outdated, the only way to stay on top of technological change is to understand current tools and anticipate future developments.

References

Alon, I. (2003). Experiential learning in international business via the World Wide Web. *Journal of Teaching in International Business, 14*(2/3), 79–98.

Beer, D., & Burrows, R. (2007). Sociology and, of and in Web 2.0: Some initial considerations. *Sociological Research Online, 12*(5). Retrieved April 10, 2010, from http://www.socresonline.org.uk/12/5/17.html

Bridges, E. (1999). Experiential learning and customer needs in the undergraduate marketing research course. *Journal of Marketing Education, 21*(1), 51–59.

Castleberry, S. B. (2001). Using secondary data in marketing research: A project that melds Web and off-Web sources. *Journal of Marketing Education, 23*(3), 195–203.

Clarke, I., III, Flaherty, T. B., & Mottner, S. (2001). Student perceptions of educational technology tools. *Journal of Marketing Education, 23*(3), 169–177.

Driscoll, K. (2007). Collaboration in today's classroom: New Web tools change the game. *Multimedia & Internet @ Schools, 14*(3), 9–12.

Ferrell, O. C. (1995). Improving marketing education in the 1990s: A faculty retrospective and perspective view. *Marketing Education Review, 5*(3), 1–6.

Granitz, N., & Hugstad, P. (2004). Creating and diffusing a technology champion course. *Journal of Marketing Education, 26*(3), 208–225.

Greenangel, F. L. (2002). *The illusion of e-learning: Why we are missing out on the promise of technology.* Retrieved April 10, 2010, from http://www.guidedlearning.com/illusions.pdf

Gruca, T. S. (2000). The IEM movie box office market: Integrating marketing and finance using electronic markets. *Journal of Marketing Education, 22*(1), 5–14.

Hazari, S., North, A., & Moreland, D. (2009). Investigating pedagogical value of wiki technology. *Journal of Information Systems Education, 20*(2), 187–198.

Heinrichs, J. H., Lim, J.-S., & Hudspeth, L. J. (2002). Teaching strategic marketing models with Web-based business intelligence tools: Innovative guided marketing analysis. *Journal of Marketing Education, 24*(2), 135–142.

Kelley, C. A., Conant, J. S., & Smart, D. T. (1998). Marketing education in the 21st century. American Marketing Association Summer Marketing Educators' Conference Proceedings, 9, 204–210.

Krentler, K. A., & Willis-Flurry, L. A. (2005). Does technology enhance student learning? The case of online discussion boards. *Journal of Education for Business, 80*(6), 316–321.

Kulick, J. A. (1994). Meta-analytic studies of findings on computer-based instruction. In E. L. Baker & H. F. O'Neil, Jr. (Eds.), *Technology assessment in education and training* (pp. 9–33). Hillsdale, NJ: Erlbaum.

McKinney, D., Dyck, J., & Luber, E. (2009). iTunes University and the classroom: Can podcasts replace professors? *Computers and Education, 52*(3), 617–623.

Nagle, D. (2008). Is higher ed technology keeping up with student demand? *Campus Technology.* Retrieved April 10, 2009, from http://campustechnology.com/Articles/2008/10/Is-Higher-Ed-Technology-Keeping-Up-with-Student-Demand.aspx?Page=4&p=1

Peak, D. A. (2009). Why technology in the university classroom is necessary. *Journal of Information Technology Case and Application Research, 11*(1), 1–5.

Piccoli, G., Ahmad, R., & Ives, B. (2001). Web-based virtual learning environments: A research framework and a preliminary assessment of effectiveness in basic IT skills training. *MIS Quarterly, 25*(4), 401–427.

Prensky, M. (2001). Digital natives, digital immigrants. *On the Horizon, 9*(5), 1–6.

Roach, S. S., Johnson, M. W., & Hair, J. F., Jr. (1994). The current state of marketing education: Perceptions of marketing academicians and doctoral students. *Marketing Education Review, 4*(1), 2–9.

Scardamalia, M. (2002). Collective cognitive responsibility for the advancement of knowledge. In B. Smith (Ed.), *Liberal education in a knowledge society* (pp. 67–98). Chicago: Open Court.

Schrand, T. (2008). Tapping into active learning and multiple intelligences with interactive multimedia: A low-threshold classroom approach. *College Teaching, 56*(2), 78–84.

Sivin-Kachala, J. (1998). *Report of the effectiveness of technology in schools, 1990–1997*. Washington, DC: Software Publisher's Association.

Smart, D., Kelley, C. A., & Conant, J. S. (1999). Marketing education in the year 2000: Changes observed and challenge anticipated. *Journal of Marketing Education, 21*(3), 206–216.

Smith, S. D., Salaway, G., & Caruso, J. B. (2009). *The ECAR study of undergraduate students and information technology, 2009*. Educause Center for Applied Research.

Ueltschy, L. C. (2001). An exploratory study of integrating interactive technology into the marketing curriculum. *Journal of Marketing Education, 23*(1), 63–72.

Wang, Y., & Braman, J. (2009). Extending the classroom through Second Life. *Journal of Information Systems Education, 20*(2), 235–247.

CHAPTER 11

Deconstructing Formal and Informal Learning Spaces with Social Networking Sites

Joannah Portman Daley

Introduction

Largely due to the expansion and popularization of user-generated and immersive Web 2.0 platforms such as MySpace, Facebook, YouTube, Twitter, wikis, and other interactive digital media explorations, excitement around a new generation of learners has exploded. This generation has garnered several nicknames—the "Net Generation" and "Digital Natives," among them—based on the overwhelming integration of digital technology into many members' lives (Prensky, 2001; Tapscott, 1998). Furthermore, several scholars insist that, in part due to these technological advancements, these young users have become "exceptionally curious, self-reliant, contrarian, smart, focused, able to adapt, high in self-esteem, and have a global orientation" (Tapscott, 1998, p. 2), all qualities and skills that support professional success in our current knowledge-driven economy. Accordingly, there seems also to have been a change in the way that many of them gather, accept, and retain information, shifting the way they should be learning away from the "skills and drills" modes of older pedagogical styles, and firmly toward more interactive and creative ones.

Staking such claims on an entire generation is, of course, problematic, especially since part of the basis for these claims relies on undertheorized methods (Bennett, Maton, & Kervin, 2008, p. 776), many of which leave the "digital dissident" population—those who resist technology—as well as sufferers of the "digital divide"—those who do not have access to technology—misrepresented. Moreover, there is a large population of only moderate users who are not nearly as digitally literate as Tapscott's "Net Generation" or Prensky's "Digital Native" members are touted to be. In actuality, most of these young learners, regardless of technological expertise and/or usage levels, could benefit from guidance on how to use these technologies more safely and effectively—socially, academically, and professionally (see Pegrum, 2009, p. 56). Thus, the foundation of this chapter centers not on the fact that *everyone* in this generation uses these technologies, but rather on the fact that those who do are likely in possession of, and further refining, many of the aforementioned qualities and skills, all of which are highly prized assets in a knowledge worker's skill set—namely, creativity (see Reich, 1991; Drucker, 1994, Florida, 2003). Therefore, when viewing this generation's technological practices and potential via an economic framework, one might imagine that educators would seek to cultivate creativity in more areas of formal education.

Unfortunately, however, much pedagogy (and writing pedagogy in particular) has had a long-standing hesitancy to embrace creativity, as creativity has seemed to stand in direct opposition to the classical learning goal of correctness (see Connors, 1987; Murphy, 2001; Meyers, 2006). Because creativity can be difficult to teach, difficult to gauge, and is not thought to cater well to standardized tests, it is often disregarded in favor of memorization and regurgitation, which are easily countable and quantified. And although most education focuses on what it believes students need to be taught, "most schools do not recognize the value of many of these new [Information and Computer Technology] devices and web based environments" (Johnson, 2006, p. 4), which is where so much of this young generation's creativity appears to be at work (see Dye, 2007). Consequently, since many students are left to hone these qualities and skills via extracurricular digital engagement, the directions they take are not always productive in traditional terms, nor safe for that matter (see Pegrum, 2009, pp. 67–69), which is why many educators fail to see a link to effectiveness in the classroom. This means that students' creativity outside of school—their informal and personal learning—far exceeds their creativity in the classroom, and many of them "consider the reading and composing skills they acquired informally in the electronic environment . . . to be far more compelling, far more germane to their success than the more traditional literacy instruction they have received in school" (Selfe & Hawisher, 2004, pp. 204–205).

What arises here is a set of binary relationships whose existence may be viewed as potentially detrimental to pedagogy in general, writing pedagogy in particular, and most certainly our students' futures in a knowledge economy. The schism can be seen in Table 11.1.

As one can see from this list, students' informal and personal learning, such as the creative "play" found in the abovementioned Web 2.0 interactions, seems to stand in opposition to, and perhaps even threaten, the more formal and institutionally sanctioned pedagogical practices, or "academic" work, to which much of education may be accustomed. As this chapter will argue, this seeming schism created by the corresponding placed-based binaries of home/school and personal/institutional, and reinforced by the learning binaries of informal/formal, creativity/ correctness, gift/skill, and engagement/disengagement, when regarded in the context of the current knowledge economy, places students at a disadvantage in terms of preparing them for successful futures as potential knowledge workers. In some cases, this schism even goes as far as situating students' interactions with Web 2.0 as antiinstitutional. Thus, as Glynda Hull (2006) insisted, there is an urgent need for us to reassess our definitions of literacy in this novel era, where digital technology not only dominates, but also has great creative learning potential. Hence, it is out-of-school literacies, like those of Web 2.0 that this chapter aims to engage in its goal of making creativity a central rather than peripheral part of learning. After all, due to the ways technology is constantly shaping and reshaping future job opportunities, "*how* we educate our children may prove to be more important than *how much* we educate them" (Binder, cited in Freidman, 2005, p. 302).

This chapter, then, will examine the commodity of creativity in our knowledge economy, discussing the ways in which our past and

Table 11.1 Binary Relationships

Home	School
Engagement	Disengagement
Informal	Formal
Creativity	Correctness
Gift	Skill
Personal	Institutional
"Personal" writing	"Academic" writing
New economy	Old economy

current classroom pedagogy has misunderstood and even ignored creativity, and explain how writing pedagogy specifically can embrace the creativity that arises in the informal and personal learning spaces of Web 2.0 in ways that can help bridge the schism to more formal and institutionally governed learning. In particular, the following sections will target the ubiquitously assigned "personal narrative" and offer an upgraded version of this assignment via the use of a social networking profile page. In doing so, they will ultimately argue that both the affordances of digital technology and those of our new economy call for revised conceptions of both the personal and of creativity, ones that work to embrace and even unite some of the above binary preclusions. After all, while the primacy of a pedagogical relationship to correctness may have been permissible, and perhaps even productive, in the old economy which honored measurable value, controlled and predictable environments, and mass production, it becomes problematic in the new knowledge economy in which creativity is a precious commodity, value is emergent, the experimental is applauded, and the personal is privileged.

Rewriting "old domains of knowledge"

In our current economy, knowledge, rather than any good or service, is the chief resource for workers, something that Peter Drucker foresaw when he coined the term "knowledge worker" in 1959. Moving away from a "Fordist" (Gramsci, 1971) economy in which deskilled work generated mechanized and standardized production, Drucker's (1994) *The Age of Social Transformation* described what we have today: a postindustrial, information-driven economy in which great emphasis is placed on the worker and her ability to not only acquire knowledge but also to apply in critically innovative ways (see also Solomon & Schrum, 2007, pp. 9–12). Such innovation was a key concern for Richard Florida (2004), who, in *Rise of the Creative Class*, insisted that what actually powers our knowledge economy is, in fact, human creativity. Fortunately, in Florida's mind, this skill of creativity exists not only in the ability to literally "create" a new form of something, but also in the ability to think outside of the box. Thus, contrary to traditional notions of creativity as an innate gift (one that cannot be taught), recent thinking has embraced a more practical and accessible view of creativity, arguing that "[i]t is a mistake to think, as many do, that creativity can be reduced to the creation of new blockbuster inventions, new products and new firms" (Florida, 2004, p. 5).

Creativity, then, more simply put, is the ability to analyze and solve problems in innovative ways that require original thought. Not only has it has grown to be the "decisive source of competitive advantage" in today's workplace, but its high value, Florida claimed, is largely due to the fact that it belongs to the individual; it is not something that can be bought, traded, or sold, and wherever the individual goes, so it goes as well (2004, pp. 4–5). This portability was a principal quality for James Paul Gee, who posited that such static notions of security, like those that were perhaps sought after with regard to correctness, have ceased to exist. Instead, in the current economy, which he called "the new capitalism," security lies in one's employability rather than in employment. As he described it, a worker's employability is a matter of the diverse skills and experiences she has had in a variety of projects—both inside and outside the workplace—"a flexibly rearrangeable portfolio of skills, experiences, and achievements" (Gee, 2000, p. 61). Hence, Gee titled this kind of worker a "portfolio person." While Drucker argued that the essential skills of a knowledge worker, or Gee's "portfolio person"—innovation, critical thinking, and the original application of knowledge among them—are best cultivated in the setting of formal education (1996, p. 6), Gee contended that traditional classroom pedagogy is not geared to produce these "new kinds of people." In fact, Gee suggested that schools retain a Fordist perspective in their educational goals and that they are actually preparing students to enter the workforce as what he terms "backwater workers," or manual laborers, while it is students' creative, out-of-school literacy activities that aid in the creation of "portfolio people," thus serving as better preparation for knowledge work (2000, p. 62). Accordingly, former secretary of state Robert Reich (1991) warned us that to cultivate these skills in our students, the aims of pedagogy must change: "mastery of old domains of knowledge [aren't] nearly enough to guarantee a good income...What is much more valuable is the capacity to effectively and creatively use the knowledge" (p. 182).

To necessarily become these "portfolio people," students are entitled to what Gee termed "situated practice," which he defined as "hands-on, meaningful, embodied experiences of authentic and meaningful social practices involving talk, texts, tools, and technologies of the sort that help one to imagine contexts that render what is being taught meaningful" (2000, p. 67). While students should not only learn, and learn well, the standard genres of formal education, they should also learn how to deviate from those genres in productive and meaningful ways, as well as create new ones for their own social, political, and/or cultural purposes.

This task, obviously, privileges attention to both the personal and the creative, and this chapter argues, students' interactions with Web 2.0 work to promote this type of agency. Unfortunately, however, as such interactions are usually the province of the home and/or personal usage, they tend to be situated as anti-institutional. Consequently, to create the kind of portfolio people that this economy desires, such boundaries must be crossed. After all, as Gee posited, the vast changes that are occurring in our conceptions of literacy and learning demand "new relationships within, between, and among the spheres of family, school, business and science" (2000, p. 43).

What our students know as writing

With new values such as those of the new economy, it is no wonder that writing scholars have spent much time and debate trying to redefine what it means to write and be a writer in the electronic age. To be certain, the social media of Web 2.0 has more than multiplied our conceptions of written texts, and the term "writer" now applies to more individuals than ever before. This is particularly true as we consider Tapscott's take on the "Net Generation," as having many members "who multitask and connect with others through ongoing text, instant, voice, and video messaging... [who] are digital natives... nurtured by a world of digital technology, instant information, global communication, and individually customized environments" (Pletka, 2007, pp. 20–21). Among these particularly tech-savvy and tech-comfy students, both in high school and college, many are most comfortable in fast-paced, interactive, and visually oriented environments. Outside of school, they spend several after-school hours exploring a range of interactive media-based and popular culture-driven activities wherein they "gather, create, manipulate, and distribute information" in ways that allow them to "reshape themselves to meet the needs of changing economic conditions," which, according to Gee, is a defining characteristic of a knowledge worker (Jacobs, 2007, p. 177). Moreover, their multifaceted means of composition in digital environments suggest that those who are electronically composing are "deeply invested in writing—and expanding what we mean by 'writing' in the digital age" (Alexander, 2006, p. 383).

Consequently, the conversation on incorporating electronic texts in the classroom has endured for over twenty years now (see Manovich, 2003; Moran, 1992; Selfe & Hawisher, 2004). Scholars have argued that effective and responsible writing can no longer be taught through traditional means, and that "rhetoric theory, composition practice, and writing instruction all need to change to suit how writing is produced in digital spaces" (WIDE, 2005). Indeed, today, writing goes beyond just words, often necessitating the critical and careful selection of multimedia elements to make meaning: "[w]riting today means weaving text, images, sound, and video—working within and across multiple media, often for delivery within and across digital spaces. And, perhaps now more so than ever before, writing requires a deep attention to context, audience, and meaning-making across the multiple tools and media available to us as writers" (Digirhet.org, 2005, p. 240).

Amidst a swarm of fears and accusations that some of the new digital literacies, such as text messaging for example (see Crystal, 2008), were destroying writing, Katherine Blake Yancey showed that she had been paying attention (Selfe, 1999) to the changes in our students and their writing habits and argued instead that "we have a moment" primed for composition in a new key. Yancey cited writing outside the academy and technology as two factors that have altered the creation of literacy in positive, groundbreaking ways. She pointed out that this writing is self-sponsored: no one is making these students do it and do it with zest and enthusiasm at that. Consequently, she asked the critical question: "How is it that what we teach and what we test can be so different from what our students know as writing?" (Yancey, 2004, p. 301).

Unfortunately, many educators have considered writing *about* technology as a sufficient means to prepare students for its incorporation in their lives (see Wysocki et al., 2004). However, writing about technology is not enough. We need to *use it*. We need to write *with it*. After all, Gee argued that students "have a right to be allowed to produce and transform knowledge, not just consume it" (2000, p. 68). Which brings us to yet another learning binary that persists, and ought to be deconstructed, within writing pedagogy: analysis/production. In fact, one might argue that it is largely this binary that is responsible for the fact that, contrary to Yancey's beliefs and in spite of the all the work that educators have done to redefine writing in the digital age, our students *do not* see their online writing as real writing. Indeed, as a 2008 Pew Internet and American Life Study reported, "[a]t the core, the digital age presents a paradox. Most teenagers spend a considerable amount of their life composing texts, but they do not think that a lot of the material they create electronically is *real* writing. . . . At the same time that teens disassociate e-communication with 'writing,' they also strongly believe that good writing is a critical skill to achieving success" (Lenhart, 2008, p. 4). Apparently, we have yet another binary to bridge, and to do so we must not only engage, we must create.

What follows, then, is a look at what our students *should* know as writing in an attempt to cross these place-based and learning divides. As the next sections will argue, employing the social networking profile page as an alternative to the traditional personal narrative allows students to engage less traditional texts in creative ways, thus cultivating their rhetorical strength and more closely developing those portfolio skills that will lead to their employability as potential knowledge workers.

Upgrading the personal narrative to a social networking profile page

Creativity 1.0

Perhaps due in part to the rise of the personal that has accompanied the rise of our new economy, the last two decades have seen resurgence in the broader advantages of personal writing, as scholars have begun to rethink the postprocess accusations of solipsism aimed at process-inspired personal writing. This resurgence, for the most part, has been fueled largely by three factors: (1) student amenability: the fact that writing success often follows students' view of writing as "less of a chore, less intimidating, and something at which they can be successful (perhaps for the first time)" (Nicolini, 1994, p. 58), and that personal writing assignments tend to garner this sense of enjoyment; (2) critical engagement: the writing that occurs in personal genres is now seen as critical and complex in the ways that it encourages agency and authority: personal narratives are told by "writers who in using 'I' have agency and speak with authority, knowledge, conviction, and self-consciousness about issues that concern us all" (Danielewicz, 2008, p. 443); and (3) professional transference: learning and appreciating one's voice and personality is an essential step in entering the world of public and professional written discourse, something that personal writing assignments accomplish by asking writers to draw on their own experience and expertise in creative and innovative ways (Connors, 1987, p. 154).

While these are all worthy points that have worked to reinstate personal writing in the classroom, these points, when applied to traditionally written texts (i.e., composed via pen and paper or word processor), risk losing some of their pedagogical advantage in the digital age. While personal writing assignments drawn around these three arguments certainly do not become useless, they do become less effective when used on those students whose identity and means of expression are largely tied up in technological interaction and innovation and who have cultivated through these interactions complex, socially negotiated, and ever-changing conceptions of who they are and who they desire to be seen as. This is especially true when we consider that the traditional personal narrative is usually the writing assignment chosen to achieve these goals.

Generally speaking, when a composition teacher desires to infuse creativity into her classroom, the personal narrative is often the recipient of such aims, thus yoking creativity and the personal narrative in a way that may be viewed not only as undeserving, but also unfortunate—precisely because it still holds to certain notions of correctness: such as control, security, and standardization. In fact, often the first assignment of the semester, in some instances the traditional personal narrative assignment serves more as a course management tool that works to control the classroom than it does an actual exercise in rhetoric or a place for a student's creative practice. First, as students have yet to do much (or any) reading by that early point, writing about themselves as a subject matter provides an "easy" place to begin, immediately reinforcing the historical conception of the personal as uncritical (Connors, 1997, p. 179). Moreover, the assignment is often thought of as an "ice breaker," something to ease the students into the semester, in addition to a "getting to know you" exercise of sorts, both for the students as well as for the teacher. In this regard, it allows the teacher not only to "get to know" who the students are (albeit a narrow glimpse), but even more so, it allows her to "get to know" which students can write well and which ones cannot; it serves as a writing sample which weeds out the good from the bad. Often, however, the quickly labeled "good" writers here are the ones who tend to be more creative, a point that works to reinforce the gift/skill binary. In fact, without fail, personal experience dictates that each time a personal narrative is assigned, a handful of students will complain that they aren't creative, and thus fear that they will do poorly on the assignment. Those same students, however, tend to revel in the analysis of an argument, or the research paper, as they see those types of writing as lacking the creativity which they consider inaccessible. In actuality, however, isn't all writing inherently creative? Shouldn't the argument analysis invoke creativity in the same way that the personal narrative should? When we consider creativity as an innate gift, then the answer may be no. However, when we invoke the revised conception of creativity as a skill wherein one innovates and thinks with critical originality, the answer should be a resounding yes, especially in our creativity-driven knowledge economy.

While the narrative itself is inherently creative as a genre feature, because we have only allowed students to use themselves as story-telling fodder, we have indefinitely yoked the two (creativity/narrative features and personal experience) together. However, as the teacher generally dictates the theme of the traditional personal narrative assignment, many of which themes have, due to their ubiquity, turned cliché (the aforementioned summer vacation essay and the life-changing experience essay, for example), rather than encourage creativity via an exercise in self-representation—one that might actually enhance the students' critical understandings of their identity—the assignment often turns into the rote task of highlighting a singular moment through whatever lens the students thinks the teacher wishes to view it. In such a case, the creativity that the traditional personal narrative is thought to encourage or allow can be greatly lessened (clichéd is indeed the opposite of creative), or even divorced of any greater rhetorical purpose. In a worse case scenario, such circumstances can relegate the assignment to a static exercise in the mode of narration. After all, once completed, the student turns this "paper" into her teacher and rarely, if ever, revisits it except to see her grade. Hence, what we risk the assignment turning into is a largely predictable ("dead grandmother essays" are a common nickname for such narratives) and ultimately finite product whose value is, at best, questionable outside of the classroom.

Employing Web 2.0 in the writing classroom, however, may serve as a means for losing this perception of "narrative (only) = creative" and opening creativity to the many elements of digital writing that necessitate a writer's creative skills, as well as her multiple understandings of the personal. Here, then, we are breaking up yet another restrictive relationship: the staid traditional and limiting one of creativity = the personal narrative. In doing so, we allow creativity to be broadened across an entire semester's worth of writing assignments, while also allowing a student's personal story to be put in other contexts. As explored below, replacing the traditional personal narrative with a social networking profile page offers an excellent arena for the encouragement of such goals.

Creativity 2.0

While over 100 social networking sites now exist, today's students flock to MySpace and Facebook, as these particular sites' 160 million plus users have upgraded social networking from "niche activity" to cultural and social "phenomenon" (Lenhart, 2007). According to Stephanie Vie

(2008), the online writing that occurs in these sites provides a wealth of untapped potential for writing instruction and rhetorical learning in the composition classroom. She argued that, today, the problems with incorporating technology in the classroom have moved away from the access-oriented dilemmas of the digital divide and more toward the goal of incorporating technologies in ways that can help students to see them as critical, rhetorical, and educationally useful, rather than solely for entertainment or extracurricular purposes (p. 236). Indeed, Vie saw the social networking site, in particular, as having the ability to cross some of the place-based and learning binaries with which this chapter is concerned. By incorporating these sites into classroom pedagogy, educators not only have the opportunity to introduce cybersafety, but also make their students aware of the critical and creative possibilities inherent in the sites by redirecting the focus away from the usual paths of interest in this technological wonderland-of-a-social landscape: voyeurism, friendship connections, etc., and toward a complex and empowered understanding of their vast rhetorical potential.

More specifically, what makes these sites appropriate as an upgraded version of the personal narrative is the fact that they are "profile-centric." As danah boyd argued, "[s]ocial network sites are based around profile, a form of individual...home page, which offers a description of each member. In addition to text, images, and video created by the member, the social network site profile also contains comments from other members and a public list of the people that one identifies as Friends within the network" (2007a, p. 123). Unlike the insular and static conception of the personal that usually accompanies the traditional personal narrative assignment, the profile page offers a collaborative, socially negotiated, and continually shifting understanding of one's personhood within a larger community. In fact, boyd posited that social networking profile pages are where teens "[model] identity...so that they can write themselves and their community into being" (2007a, p. 120).

Accordingly, much of the rhetorical awareness we strive to teach in the composition classroom, and that which we often fail to see in the traditional personal narrative, seems inherent in the creation of these sites, as well as intuitive in the decision-making processes of users who at every turn are making critical decisions about their self-representation with regard to audience, aim, and meaning-making. Arguably, on these profile pages, users are not only creating their identities, but also engaging in the art of persuasion: their profile page serves as an argument for who they desire to be seen as. Students spend hours upon hours constructing their identities, creating the portal through which they desire to be viewed. Glynda Hull (2003) saw such activity as "the ability to render one's world changeable and oneself as an agent able to direct that change," and she argued that a "pictorial turn has supplanted the linguistic one, as images push the words off the page and our lives become increasingly mediated by popular culture" (p. 230). Not only is this process of identity formation reminiscent of Aristotle's traditional concept of ethos (Zappen, 2008, p. 323), but Hull and Mira-Lisa Katz argued that it is also an exercise in agency: in narrative construction, writers are crafting their "agentive selves" (2006, p. 43). Thus, the writing that occurs on a profile page is not only educational but also empowering; it allows students to engage in a critical milieu with popular culture through digital media technology. In essence, the interactive media of Web 2.0 is the language students use, and popular culture is the lexicon of that language. Which brings us to the importance of content creation.

Content is a key component in constructing one's online identity, and it is something that today's youth has become adept in creating. Indeed, The Pew Internet and American Life Project showed us that "American teenagers today are utilizing the interactive capabilities of the internet as they create and share their own media creations. Fully half of all teens and 57% of teens who use the internet could be considered Content Creator" (Lenhart, 2005). Jessica Dye (2007) agreed so firmly with the importance of content creation in digital spaces discourse that she went as far as to call the current generation "Generation C," with the C standing for "content," although she argued that it could just as easily stand for "creativity," "consumerism," or "connected." Dye posited that this generation builds relationships, networks, and their own identity through their content, and largely content that they create. Targeting Facebook in particular, Dye illustrated how self-definition can be linked directly to content creation: "On Facebook, you are defined by your content, as extensive or minimal as you want that to be. It can be as simple as a list of favorite bands or a multimedia buffet that reflects the user's creativity as well as his interests and allows him to share it with everyone in his network" (2007, par. 13).

Such self-definition as dictated by content introduces the importance of a critical digital media literacy and issues of intertexuality as applied to identity—both of which allow this upgraded version of the personal narrative assignment to escape the solipsist path that the postprocess movement attributed to it, and embrace both the traditionally critical aim of analysis and the newer, rhetorical aim of production. When one employs mainstream media and popular culture to represent oneself, she will undoubtedly engage in " 'textual poaching,' the appropriation of textual icons or images in the service of self-expression" (Alexander, 2006, p. 113). Indeed, Dan Perkel (2008) argued that "the creation of an online social networking profile is in actuality a complicated exercise in self-representation that requires a great deal of skill in composition, selection, manipulation, and appropriation" (p. 5). Thus, a critical understanding of the intertextuality of such borrowed "texts" becomes a crucial consideration for the rhetorical process of meaning-making. As boyd posited, a first step in developing a necessary critical eye is resensitizing oneself to the everyday "texts" to which he or she has grown so accustomed, and the interactive nature of social networking sites, with their ever-present audience, can encourage and expedite this process: "Learning how to manage impressions is a critical social skill that is honed through experience. Over time, we learn how to make meaning out of a situation, others' reactions, and what we are projecting of ourselves. . . . Diverse social environments help people develop these skills because they force individuals to reevaluate the signals they take for granted" (2007, p. 129).

In this regard, using the social networking site in place of the traditional personal narrative broadens a traditionally insular conception of the personal, making it a collaboration of social, cultural, and popular influence, something that is ever-changing and in flux, something that is complex and critical, and something that sounds very much like a product of the new economy. In fact, a look at Table 11.2 closely aligns the traditional personal narrative assignment, with its controlled themes, predictive outcomes, and static production with the old economy, while the social networking profile page, as just examined, with its ever-shifting incarnations, boundless creative potential, location-less

Table 11.2 Traditional Personal Narrative vs. Social Networking Profile Page

Traditional Personal Narrative	Social Networking Profile Page
Predictable and often singular themes	Varied and multiple themes
The personal is a singular conception	The personal is a collaborative construct
Controlled organization	Experimental and creative in organization and content
Focused on teacher	Focused on self in relation to a community
Text-centered	Multimedia-centered
Static, finite product, lacking much outside applicability	Continual, emergent process applicable to both personal and professional life

existence, and collaborative sense of the personal is far more in line with the qualities of the new economy.

Considering the above points, then, one might ask: why would we want to teach our students something that possesses such little usability in our current economy? Since so many members of this generations' experience and expertise lie in digital technology, having them write about themselves without using this technology seems not only anachronistic, but could actually be doing a disservice to their literacy education. Moreover, composing in a medium such as a social networking site, with which they already employ regularly to negotiate and construct their identities, and in which they already hold a personal stake, would seem to promote a view of writing as enjoyable and approachable, thus potentially making it more successful and engaging. And for those students who do not frequent the sites or use technology regularly, introducing a new lens through which to create and see themselves provides the potential opportunity for a deeper level of self-reflection. In addition, by engaging students in the critical considerations which accompany their creation of these sites, and the writing constituted therein, educators work toward allowing them not only to see these interactions as real writing, but also as productive writing. After all, social networking sites are places of public discourse which makes a rhetorical understanding of their aims, audiences, and meaning-making potential, garnered in the writing classroom, crucial to this generation's future as professional workers in a knowledge-based and creativity-driven economy.

Potential impediments to integration

While every assignment braves its fair share of obstacles, when considering the integration of social networking sites into the classroom, attention to a few potential impediments deserves at least a brief consideration. In specific, students' amenability to sharing this space and educators' capabilities for both using and assessing it are among some often-expressed concerns. Additionally, the suggestion of workplace demands dictating educational reform summons its own variety of apprehension.

As one might imagine, many students' initial reaction to an educator invading their personal social networking space may be an unenthusiastic one; after all, these spaces are primarily thought of as personal and private (see Barnes, 2006). However, having students create separate accounts and/or using class-specific social networks (customized Ning. com networks, for example) specifically for learning purposes allows them to reap the benefits of the abovementioned lessons, while still keeping their personal space secure. Indeed, after working for two weeks on a new profile page created specifically for a writing class, a former student returned to her personal Facebook profile page and drastically revised it based on her newfound understandings of audience consideration and impression management. Not only did she alter basic personal information and image choices, but she also cut her friend list from over 1,000 to fewer than 400, keeping only those to whom she spoke to or saw with some regularity, a choice she made based on newly realized safety concerns. Such "repositioning," Diane Penrod argued, "is an important unlearning process that helps students to move toward critically thinking about the rhetoric and the content of the materials they examine" (Penrod, 1998, p. 13). This act encourages the creation of new paradigms through which to understand media and self-representation, something that knowledge-based workplaces often ask their employees to do.

Next, the potential hurdles of teachers' technological literacy and their assessment capabilities. As touched upon earlier, many students complain that they are far more technologically literate than their teachers (see Selfe & Hawisher, 2004), and as many teachers did not grow up surrounded by technology in the same way today's students have, this is an understandable dilemma. To remedy this problem, ideally, administrators will first agree on the fundamental importance of technology use and then implement the necessary technological literacy education into their teacher-training programs. For this to happen, however, faculty members must agree on this importance and partake in organized efforts to enact such change (Solomon & Schrum, 2007, p. 111). Web 2.0 tools, and social networks in particular, allow for a participatory support community where learning can continue, either as an extension of training programs or, more informally, as educational spaces in and of themselves. However, if one's institution or faculty cohort is unable to invoke such standards and/or requirements, there is another option: one may choose to take matters into his or her own hands and view these potential obstacles as opportunities.

To do so, when considering assessment criteria for this particular assignment, one must remember that traditional conceptions of writing and rhetoric stand firm even when applied to digital spaces, thus creating a valuable opportunity for educators to illustrate the staying power of classical rhetorical concerns (audience, purpose, stance, and design) and appeals (ethos, pathos, and logos) while assessing the students' grasp of these concepts in a social networking site. That said, as educators may possess less experience with social networking sites than their students, they are also offered an occasion to allow students to partake in determining some additional rules and guidelines by which assessment should occur, thus making the students active and innovative participants in the pedagogical creation of this new, digital genre. After all, when "integrating new tools, you do not want to assess these outcomes with old models" (Solomon & Schrum, 2007, p. 170). Allowing students to partake in generating new assessment criteria not only works to promote agency among them, but also further decenters the classroom (see Freire, 1970). Moreover, such collaboration can provide an opportunity for students to teach educators about the technology from their personal perspectives and experiences. While far from perfect remedies for such impediments, these scenarios do offer educators the opportunity to feel more empowered in their ability to understand, use, and judge writing via new digital genres, and they offer students the opportunity to feel more empowered in their ability to enact change in their education, facts that will invariably prove advantageous for both parties in regard to their feelings of amenability toward, critical understandings of, and ultimate success with digital writing.

Finally, a brief word for those who may wonder if the goals of this chapter advocate education "selling out" to the workplace: the simple answer is that, whether one believes that education should or should not teach toward economic changes and the workplace's expectations for future employees, creativity, as a skill, is hardly restricted to business in terms of its value. Furthermore, the use of creativity and the rhetorical understandings of digital literacy and self-representation around which this chapter is centered will aid students in defending themselves against the ubiquitous corporate manipulations of our ever-more media-centered and digitized culture. After all, many young people today are exposed to digital technologies in nearly all aspects of their day-to-day existence. Therefore, being so intensely influenced by these technologies, a critical understanding of them, their uses, and their powers is vital.

Conclusion

As explored in this chapter, creativity is experiencing a surge, both in economic demand and in its popularity in the extracurricular digital media-related activities of our students. And for the first time in a long history, it is beginning to be viewed as a skill that is accessible to all. The place that creativity fails to see much, if any, increase, however, is the one place that, by harnessing it and directing it in valuable ways, could best serve as a productive conduit between many of the aforementioned binaries: our classrooms. The problems of student disengagement and lack of classroom-based creative preparation for a thriving knowledge economy are not going away. If anything, these problems are growing more complex and more embedded in our culture as well as in the lives of our students, especially as technological advancement continues to rise with such rapidity. And to make matters even worse, Richard Florida claimed that a "looming creativity crisis" threatens the United States as the strength of our economy, which has grown to hinge on creative activity, is in danger of losing its competitive edge. Indeed, this statement, made in 2004, is obviously even more prescient today, given the current economic climate. According to Florida, one remedial suggestion for this looming crisis is for the United States to "invest generously in its creative infrastructure." Education reform, he urged "must, at its core, make schools into places that cultivate creativity" (2004, p. 134). He cited the "legendary stories of young creators like Michael Dell building new businesses in dorm rooms or in garages in their spare time" and asked the crucial questions: "Why are [students] doing these things in their spare time? Isn't this the real stuff of education in the Creative Age?" (Florida, 2004, p. 134).

The incorporation of Web 2.0 offers a tangible means for making this vital skill of creativity a central rather than peripheral part of learning, and the social networking profile page as an upgraded personal narrative serves as an apt and instructive point of entry. With that in mind, it is not to be a matter of *if* we will incorporate these literacies into our classrooms, but *when* we will do so and how. So the real question becomes: if we wait, how many students will lose out on a valuable and equitable education in the meantime, and how much will both they and our economy suffer? Therefore, ultimately, as Florida suggests, "the United States must begin to think of creativity as a 'common good,' like liberty or security. It is something essential that belongs to everyone and must always be nourished, renewed, and maintained—or else it will slip away" (2004, p. 136).

References

Alexander, J. (2006). *Digital youth: Emerging literacies on the world wide web.* Creskill, NJ.: Hampton Press.

Barnes, S. B. (2006). A privacy paradox: Social networking in the United States. *First Monday, 11*(9). Retrieved April 15, 2009, from http://firstmonday.org/htbin/cgiwrap/bin/ojs/index.php/fm/article/view/1394/1312

Bennett, S., Maton, K., & Kervin, L. (2008). The "digital natives" debate: A critical review of the evidence. *British Journal of Educational Technology, 39*(5), 775–786.

boyd, d. (2007a). Why youth (heart) social network sites: The role of networked publics in teenage social life. In D. Buckingham (Ed.), *Youth, identity, and digital media* (pp. 119–142). Cambridge, MA: MIT Press.

boyd, d., & Ellison, N.B. (2007b). Social network sites: Definition, history, and scholarship. *Journal of Computer-Mediated Communication, 13*(1). Retrieved April 15, 2009, from http://jcmc.indiana.edu/vol13/issue1/boyd.ellison.html

Connors, R. (1987). Personal writing assignments. *College Composition and Communication, 38*(2), 166–183.

Crystal, D. (2008). *Txtng: The Gr8 Db8.* Oxford: Oxford University Press.

Danielewicz, J. (2008). Personal genres, public voices. *College Composition and Communication, 59*(3), 420–450.

DigiRhet.org (2006). Teaching digital rhetoric: Community, critical engagement, and application. *Pedagogy: Critical Approaches to Teaching Literature, Language, Composition, and Culture, 6*(2), 231–259.

Drucker, P. F. (1994, Nov.). The age of social transformation. *The Atlantic Monthly, 274*(5), 53–80. Retrieved April 19, 2006, from http://www.theatlantic.com/issues/95dec/chilearn/drucker.htm

Dye, J. (2007). Meet generation C: Creatively connecting through content. *eContent, 30*(4). Retrieved April 19, 2009, from http://goliath.ecnext.com/coms2/gi_0199–6764528/Meet-generation-C-creatively-connecting.html

Florida, R. (2003). *Rise of the creative class.* New York.: Basic Books.

Florida, R. (2004). America's looming creativity crisis. *Harvard Business Review.* October, 122–136.

Friedman, T. (2005). *The world is flat: A brief history of the twenty-first century.* New York: Farrar, Straus & Giroux.

Freire, P. (1970). *Pedagogy of the oppressed.* London: Penguin.

Gee, J. P. (2004). New people in new worlds: Networks, the new capitalism and schools. In B. Cope & M. Kalantzis (Eds.), *Multiliteracies: Literacy learning and the design of social futures* (pp. 43–68). New York: Routledge.

Gramsci, A. (1971). *Selections from the prison notebooks.* eds. Q. Hoare & G. N. Smith. New York: International Publishers.

Hull, G. A. (2006). Youth culture and digital media: New literacies for new times. *Research in the Teaching of English, 38*(2), 229–233.

Hull, G. A., & Katz, L. (2005). Crafting an agentive self: Case studies of digital storytelling. *Research in the Teaching of English, 41*(1), 43–81.

Jacobs, G. (2006). Fast times and digital literacy: Participation roles and portfolio construction within instant messaging. *Journal of Literacy Research, 38*(2), 171–196.

Johnson, J., Chapman, C., & Dyer, J. (2006). Pedagogy and innovation in education with digital technologies. Paper presented at the Fourth International Conference on Multimedia and Information and Communication Technologies in Education (m-ICTE). Retrieved April 19, 2009, from http://www.formatex. org/micte2006/pdf/135–139.pdf

Lenhart, A., & Madden, M. (2005). *Teen content creators and consumers*. Pew Internet and American Life Project. Retrieved April 19, 2009, from www. pewinternet.org/PPF/r/166/report_display.asp.

Lenhart, A., & Madden, M. (2007). *Social networking and teens*. Pew Internet and American Life Project. Retrieved April 19, 2009, from www.pewinternet.org/ PPF/r/198/report_display.asp

Lenhart, A., et al. (2008). Writing, technology and teens. *Pew Internet and American Life Project*. Retrieved April 19, 2009, from http://www.pewinternet. org/PPF/r/247/report_display.asp

Manovich, L. (2003). *The language of new media*. Cambridge, MA: MIT Press.

Meyers, D.G. (2006). *The elephants teach: Creative writing since 1880*. Chicago, IL: University of Chicago Press.

Moran, C. (1992). Computers and the writing classroom: A look to the future. In G. E. Hawisher & P. J. LeBlanc (Eds.), *Re-imagining computers and composition* (pp. 7–23). Portsmouth, NH: Boynton/Cook-Heinemann.

Murphy, J. (2001). *A short history of writing instruction: From ancient Greece to modern America*. Mahwah, NJ: Lawrence Erlbaum Associates, Inc.

Nicolini, M. (1994). Stories can save us: A defense of narrative writing. *English Journal*, *3*(2), 56–61.

Perkel, D. (2006). Copy and paste literacy: Literacy practices in the production of a MySpace profile. *Informal Learning and Digital Media*. Retrieved April 19, 2007, from http://www.dream.dk/uploads/files/perkel%2020Dan.pdf

Pegrum, M. (2009). *From blogs to bombs: The future of digital technologies in education*. Crawley, Western Australia: UWA Publishing.

Penrod, D. (1997). *Miss Grundy doesn't teach here anymore: Popular culture and the composition classroom*. Portsmouth, NH: Boynton/Cook.

Pletka, B. (2007). *Educating the net generation: How to engage students in the 21st century*. Santa Monica, CA: Santa Monica Press.

Prensky, M. (2001). Digital natives, digital immigrants. *On the Horizon*, *9*(5), 1–6.

Reich, R. B. (1991). *The work of nations: Preparing ourselves for 21st century capitalism*. New York: A.A. Knopf.

Selfe, C. L. (1999). *Technology and literacy in the twenty-first century: The importance of paying attention*. Carbondale, IL: Southern Illinois University Press.

Selfe, C.L., & Hawisher, G. E. (Eds.) (2004). *Literate lives in the information age: Narratives of literacy from the United States*. Mahwah, NJ: Lawrence Erlbaum.

Solomon, G., & Schrum, L. (2007). *Web 2.0: New tools, new schools*. Eugene, OR: ISTE.

Tapscott, D. (1998). *Growing up digital: The rise of the net generation*. New York: McGraw-Hill.

Vie, S. (2008). Digital divide 2.0: Generation M and online social networking sites in the composition classroom. *Computers and Composition*, *25*(1), 9–23.

Writing in Digital Environments Research Center (WIDE) (2005). Why teach digital writing? *Kairos: A Journal of Rhetoric, Technology, and Pedagogy, 10*(1), Retrieved April, 9, 2008, from englishttu.edu/kairos/10.1/binder2. html?coverWeb/wide/index.html

Wysocki, A. F., et al. (2004). *Writing new media: Theory and applications for expanding the teaching of composition.* Logan, UT: Utah State University Press.

Yancey, K. B. (2004). Made not only in words: Composition in a new key. *College Composition and Communication, 56*(2), 297–328.

Zappen, J. P. (2008). Digital rhetoric: Toward an integrated theory. *Technical Communication Quarterly, 14*(3), 319–325.

CHAPTER 12

Digital Education: Beyond the "Wow" Factor

Stephen Bax

Introduction

My intention in this final chapter is to address two central questions: in the light of the issues and themes raised by other contributors throughout this book, where do we stand with digital education today? Secondly, what are the prospects, roles, and concerns for digital educators in the future? My starting point will be three educational cameos, two imaginary and one real, each designed to illuminate the subsequent discussion about the nature of learning and the role of digital education.

As we consider each of these cameos, we could perhaps reflect not only on the behavior of the learners in each case, but also on the role of the educators. What precise role do the three educators here play in the process of learning?

Three educational cameos

Lecture/seminar: The first cameo is set in a Western university:

> The lecturer has a class of around 30 undergraduate students, who are in groups, all facing towards a screen. The lecturer starts by presenting a topic from the field of study, starting with a short PowerPoint presentation, linked to video clips on the Web, websites with academic articles, and also additional resources on the university's virtual learning environment (VLE). Students, who are supposed to have read a core text in

advance of the session, are invited to discuss an issue arising from the presentation in groups and to agree on a common position. After this, they are asked to participate in a class debate about the topic. Meanwhile the lecturer moderates, disagrees, and challenges any statement that is unsubstantiated, cites evidence, brings in other speakers, and refers learners to other pieces of reading. At the end of the session, the class leaves, buzzing with discussion and motivation.

Cut-and-paste essays: The second cameo could be in either a school or university:

An intelligent overseas student, new to the institution, sits down at his computer to write an essay. Feeling ignorant about the topic, he first goes to Google and types in the topic, and then clicks on the link to Wikipedia. Delighted to read an authoritative-looking entry, he cuts and pastes parts of it, with his confidence rising. Clicking on another link he finds more ideas and information, so he cuts and pastes those too. His essay is starting to look good. He remembers what his tutors told him, so he diligently copies the Web references and puts them in the references at the end of his essay. He feels he really knows something more about the topic and submits the work proudly for marking.

On receiving the essay, his tutor immediately spots the chunks from Wikipedia, and estimates that 80% of the essay is cut and pasted from the Web. He calls the student to his office and explains why this is not acceptable, and helps the student step-by-step to see how to make proper use of the information on the Internet, critically and academically, and reference it appropriately, how to get other information and ideas from resources in the library, and how to set out his own views and ideas through the essay.

Analyzing websites: The third cameo is summarized from a genuine lesson, the video of which can be found at Teachers TV (2006):

A group of 14-year-old pupils in a school in Leeds, England, are asked to examine three websites, concerning Martin Luther King, the holocaust, and Victorian robots, respectively. However, the three websites are not as they seem. The Martin Luther King site presents him from a racist perspective, and was set up by a racist organization; the second site is an elaborate attempt to deny the existence of the holocaust; the third is a clever and humorous spoof presenting a fictional story about a Victorian robot as if it were true.

However, the pupils in the study accept all three sites at face value, failing to notice anything suspicious. They treat them all as factual and reliable, and say they would happily copy and use views from them in their work. As the video commentary says, "the pupils are completely taken in by all three sites, failing to question their validity or their reliability, despite what they have been taught."

In the second half of the lesson, the teacher explains that the sites have fooled them all. He then uses the rest of the lesson to work through some useful ways of investigating such sites to check their sources of information, their reliability, and their real intentions. Through this process, the pupils come to realize that they need to be more critical and aware when dealing with Web resources. One of them comments after the lesson: "It's taught me to look behind the site and see what's there…I am really surprised at what happened today. I couldn't believe it. I've really learnt something today."

These accounts are intended to illustrate and exemplify a set of five elements, all of which, I suggest, contribute to effective educational practice. Learners in each cameo have the benefit of the following, which will be discussed in more detail in the remainder of the chapter.

Five elements of effective educational practice

Access and participation

1. *Access* to and interaction with sources of prior knowledge or information.
2. *Participation and interaction* with others, which includes a social and even an emotional dimension.

Expert intervention

1. Expert scaffolding: interaction with an expert, who actively scaffolds the experience, through planning, feedback and advice, constantly checking that learning is taking place.
2. Expert modeling: the example of an expert, who exemplifies in his or her own behavior.
   a. a set of approaches to knowledge and learning, including a criticality and rigor in dealing with sources of knowledge, and
   b. a methodical and cautious mode of expression in communicating ideas and information to others, and who models this behavior to the learner.

3. Challenge and contradiction from an expert, and from other learners.

The first two of these elements have been grouped for ease of discussion under the heading of *access and participation*. The remaining three are characterized by the inclusion of *expert intervention* in various ways, an "expert" being defined here simply as someone who is relatively more knowledgeable or experienced than the learner in the chosen field of study.

Of course, it may be that none of these five factors are in themselves indispensable to learning—learning could arguably take place without one or other of these ingredients. However, I would argue that in education, defined as the more formal process of offering structured support to learning and learners, all of these elements have important contributions to make.

The question to which we can now turn is whether digital education, as typified by the technologies popularly grouped under the Web 2.0 umbrella, currently offers these elements to learners, or might do so in the future.

The promises of Web 2.0

Web 2.0 tools are at the cutting edge of digital education. The term Web 2.0 rose to prominence when John Battelle and Tim O'Reilly debated the term at the 2004 O'Reilly Media Web 2.0 conference (Strickland, 2007; Spivack, 2007; O'Reilly & Battelle, 2009). Its definition has been debated and critiqued, but Strickland offers a useful working summary:

- The ability for visitors to make changes to Web pages [for example product reviews on www.amazon.com]
- Using Web pages to link people to other users [on social networking sites, such as www.facebook.com]
- Fast and efficient ways to share content [on www.youtube.com for example]
- New ways to get information [using, for example Really Simple Syndication (RSS) feeds]
- Expanding access to the Internet beyond the computer: Many people access the Internet through devices like cell phones or video game consoles; before long, some experts expect that consumers will access the Internet through television sets and other devices. (adapted from Strickland, 2007)

Through such resources, Web 2.0 promised a revolution in educational practice. But have these promises been fulfilled in practice?

It appears at first sight that students have indeed taken up the possibilities offered by these new resources. Lorenzo et al. (2007) offer a vivid depiction of the apparent habits and attitudes of "net generation" learners when interacting with these resources.

> Constantly connected to information and each other, students don't just consume information. They create—and re-create—it. With a do-it-yourself, open source approach to material, students often take existing material, add their own touches, and republish it. Bypassing traditional authority channels, self-publishing—in print, image, video, or audio—is common. (Lorenzo et. al., 2007, p. 2, as cited in Kennedy et al., 2007, p. 519)

The tone is breathless and optimistic, typical of much writing about digital education, appearing to admire such activity without pausing to critique it. Learners are depicted in a flurry of ecstatic interaction: "[c]onstantly connected to information and each other." They are not hindered by old thinking, as they "bypass" "traditional authority channels" with a "do-it-yourself" approach. They are themselves highly creative and multi-skilled "self-publishing—in print, image, video, or audio" in a confident fun-filled rush through the digital universe (Lorenzo et. al., 2007, p. 2, as cited in Kennedy et al., 2007, p. 519).

Kennedy et al., in research to be considered in more detail below, paint a similar picture, noting that net generation students "are also said to expect immediate answers, fast access to information, and to be assertive information seekers and adept at multitasking" (Kennedy et al., 2007, p. 517).

It is worth noting that the focus in these accounts is sharply on the first two of the five elements identified in my introduction, namely access and participation. But if net generation students in fact behave like this, what is the role for digital educators?

The role of the teacher

One influential view is that educators should *accommodate* as much as possible to such behavior, changing our practice to suit them, or else we will cease to educate effectively. For example, it is suggested that educators, who are "Digital Immigrants," are simply outdated in comparison with these modern "Digital Natives" (Prensky, 2001, p. 2). In Prensky's view, technology has the whole answer.

> My own preference for teaching Digital Natives is to invent computer games to do the job, even for the most serious content. After all, it's an idiom with which most of them are totally familiar. (Prensky, 2001, p. 4)

In this view, educators simply have to change—and should stop complaining so much in the process:

> So if Digital Immigrant educators really want to reach Digital Natives— i.e. all their students—they will have to change. It's high time for them to stop their grousing, and as the Nike motto of the Digital Native generation says, "Just do it!" They will succeed in the long run. (Prensky 2001, p. 6)

This kind of analysis is characteristic, then, of what we could call the accommodation approach to digital education, in which we educators must "accommodate" to our learners in every possible way (and stop grousing while we are at it). Our key role will be to act as "facilitators"— literally "making everything easy" for them. It will work, apparently, if we follow a Nike philosophy.

But will it? Is this really the way forward for a successful digital education?

Normalization

In previous papers, I discussed the concept of the "normalization" of technologies in education (Bax, 2003; Bax, 2010; Chambers & Bax, 2006), which I described as the stage at which a technology becomes so "normal" in the service of learning as to be invisible to its users. For example, a book and a pen are technologies which are so normalized in education, invisible yet essential, that we cease even to think of them as technologies, whereas electronic whiteboards by contrast have not generally reached that stage in most contexts (Bax, 2010). In those earlier discussions, I proposed that this concept of normalization might be helpful in understanding how technologies succeed or fail to become valuable tools in education, and in the investigation and explanation of the processes by which they succeed or fail. The concept of educational normalization has since been taken up by other researchers in various learning domains (e.g., Hansson, 2008; Allford & Pachler, 2007).

The literature on normalization and sociotechnical innovation in general suggests that a new technology often goes through a number of stages before it reaches normalization—that final point at which it becomes fully useful. When it is normalized it is often so integrated into our daily lives that it is "invisible" to its users, like the glasses on my nose or the socks on my feet. But before that it frequently goes through a number of steps we can briefly summarize as follows (cf. Rogers, 1995; Bax, 2003; Chambers & Bax, 2006; Bax, 2010; cf. Bijker, 1997).

1. Early Adopters

A few users adopt the technology out of curiosity or obsession.

2. Try once

People try it out but reject it because of early problems. They cannot see its value.
  They are skeptical or uncertain.

3. Fear—the "Ow" stage

Sometimes with a new technology we get nervous. With many innovations scare stories begin to circulate which cause users to be nervous (Appleyard, 2008).

4. Try again

We see others using the new technology and we gradually start to believe that it can indeed help us in one way or other. We try it again. We see its "relative advantage" for ourselves (Rogers, 1995).

5. Awe—the "Wow" stage

In the normalizing process, we also frequently encounter a stage of high enthusiasm, at which we start to have exaggerated expectations of what the technology can do for us.

6. Normalizing and normalization

We start to see the technology as a natural part of our lives or activity, not the center of what we do, but a useful tool, in its place, alongside other useful tools. It comes to be seen as something normal.

This informal characterization of a typical process should not lead us to assume that normalization always happens, nor that it always happens in this order or in these ways, but I suggest that this is a useful general characterization of a process which successful technologies and innovations of various kinds frequently go through.

In this light, would it then be accurate to suggest that the net generation learners whose activities were described above are using digital resources in a "normalized" way? At first glance, it would appear so—they seem to use their mobile telephones as blithely and unconsciously as earlier generations used a pen or pencil. Perhaps they tweet on Twitter without a second thought throughout the day, and update their personal Web page or blog regularly as a matter of course. The technologies seem normalized.

However, the concept of normalization in education requires that a technology be used seamlessly and in an integrated way in the service of learning (Bax, 2003). This means that active use of the technology does not in itself mean that the stage of educational normalization has been reached. In this light, it is more probable that with Web 2.0 technologies we are still at or around the "Wow" stage, still enthralled by and in thrall to the glitter of the new technologies, but not yet at the stage where we have fully integrated their potentialities into the service of real learning. Part of this "Wow" stage is that we still mistakenly believe that these technologies could do everything in education for us—a classic "technicist" mistake.

How could we move beyond that stage, toward real educational normalization? Before we can be sure that any technology has become fully normalized in any particular educational setting, we need first to research whether the resource is in fact serving the ends of learning in a fully integrated and therefore seamless, normalized way. This in turn often implies close attention to the micro- and macro-social settings in which the technology is being employed (Bax, 2010).

For this reason, the observance of merely frequent or enthusiastic use of a technology is not enough. It is important to insist that although net generation learners may be "constantly connected" or may "gather information more frequently," this alone cannot be sufficient to establish whether their use of the technology is properly normalized and therefore of maximal educational benefit to them. We need to get beyond the "Wow" stage. We need to consider the impact not on learners' routines and timetables, but on their actual learning.

Rejecting simplistic assumptions

The result of this is that while discussions of net generation learners often focus on the two areas where digital education is undoubtedly strong, namely access and participation, educators must not simply accept these activities at face value. We must ask not only "are my students using digital resources to access information, and to interact and participate?" but "how effective are these activities in engendering and promoting learning?"

Too often it is supposed that a positive answer to the first of these questions automatically means a positive answer to the second. But just as chatting in a traditional classroom does not necessarily equate with education, neither does access to information and frequent interaction in digital domains mean that any learning is necessarily taking place, and it is dangerous to assume otherwise. For this reason, researchers need to look beyond the sound, hype, and fury, and must investigate instead, critically and soberly, whether or not these technologies are genuinely operating in the service of learning.

Several chapters in this book aim to do precisely that. Costa, for example, discusses the networking practices of academic researchers, arguing that it should not be taken for granted. In terms of student use of Web 2.0 resources, González, Palomeque, and Sweeney examine the benefits of using a virtual world, Second Life, as a tool for encouraging participation and interaction in the teaching of Spanish, and again recommend going beyond the superficial aspect of use of the resources in itself. Burns offers further evidence of the value of incorporating social media into course assignments, to the benefit and greater motivation of both students and educators. Banyard et al. discuss another Web 2.0 resource designed to assist access to information, and to give opportunities for participation, namely the VLE and personalized learning environments (PLE). In their analysis they too go beyond the hype and offer a thorough, critical examination of these tools, showing how they can be of value to both learners and educators. However, they also offer a note of caution, arguing that "we have evidence for the benefits of personalised learning and also for the use of PLEs, but we observe that there is a need for a clearer focus on what each of these educational projects is aiming to achieve" (Banyard et al., this volume).

These chapters emphasize the fact, therefore, that although these technologies offer great potential to teachers and learners in terms of allowing greater access to resources and more dynamic opportunities for interaction and communication, their benefits in terms of genuine learning must not be taken for granted. The potential role of each technology in each setting needs to be researched in detail; when it comes to implementation, each resource needs to be carefully managed and "scaffolded" to ensure that it can become properly normalized in the service of learning.

This alerts us once again to the danger of looking only at the superficial use of any technology, and failing to look at the educational benefits in depth. As Pegrum (this volume) put it, "we should not be duped by the sight of fingers flying across keypads or keyboards." Chaka, in another chapter, also looks critically beneath the superficial use of six Web 2.0 technologies, remarking specifically that they need to demonstrate their "value-added" dimension—a task that requires more longitudinal studies.

Social context and culture

Chaka in the same chapter cites the importance of taking into account the social context, a point essential to the normalization of any technology (Bijker, 1997; Bax, 2003). Berger and Thomas too, in their discussion of change and resistance to technological innovation in an educational setting, also in this volume, offers an intriguing discussion of the importance of the learning culture within which an innovation is supposed to take root, noting again the limitations of any narrow or reductive concept of technological innovation at the expense of a pedagogical rationale.

This approach is precisely what underpins research into normalization in other contexts (Bax, 2010), and it is interesting to see that this emphasis on the importance of the social and cultural is no less central to Burns and Bodrigini's discussion of Web 2.0 resources in Indonesia. What is impressive about their chapter, in turn, is the means by which they take careful account of a wide range of local factors in preparing for the use of their chosen Web 2.0 technology. This attention to detail reflects their rejection of simplistic assumptions—the same assumptions which Berger and Thomas rejected—regarding the success of any of the various Web 2.0 technologies in their project. It also demonstrates an important awareness of the complexity surrounding any attempt to normalize technological innovations in new and perhaps alien contexts.

Norms and standards

To return to the five elements which I identified at the beginning of the chapter, we have noted above that the first two, namely access and participation, appear to be those most emphasized in discussions of the role of the Web in education. The point has now been made that is it important to look beyond the flurry of these features, beyond the communication, access and interaction elements, in order to examine the actual impact on learning underneath, as indeed some chapters in this volume have attempted to do.

This note of caution is important in principle because we need resolutely to keep our eyes on the ultimate aim—learning—and not be seduced by superficial activity alone. Another reason to be wary is because recent research evidence suggests that the net generation might not in fact be as digitally capable and knowledgeable of Web 2.0 technologies as the hype indicates. Kennedy et al. (2007, p. 522), for example, in a study of over 2000 first year students at three Australian universities, found that only "a relatively small proportion of students" actually used blogs, wikis, podcasts, or social bookmarking sites, and that some were not even familiar with the meaning of the terms.

This is of course only one study, but it must cause us at least to question the assumption that all young people are perfectly at home with Web 2.0 technologies. It also throws doubt on some of the more dramatic claims in the literature, such as Prensky's earlier statement that "today's students *think and process information fundamentally differently* from their predecessors" (Prensky, 2001, p. 1; emphasis in original). More importantly, it should make us question whether these young people are in fact using these technologies for any sort of genuine learning, as opposed to socializing.

To put it another way, if we are to build a stronger future for digital education we need first to be wary of any loud claims about what "all students" are doing. Secondly, it is crucial to look well beyond the two questions of access and participation. As we do so, I suggest that we should consider aspects of the educational process that have been relatively neglected in the debate, such as the last three elements on my list, the ones which in various ways involve expert intervention.

Expert intervention as an educational strategy

Characterizations of the use of the Web in education, focusing as they tend to do on issues of access to information, interaction, and participation, arguably either ignore the role of expertise in the educational process, or by implication denigrate and belittle it. We recall the depiction of the net generation learners in one quotation above as "bypassing traditional authority channels" (Lorenzo et al., op cit.) as if these authorities were no more than a hindrance. Learners were even said to be taking a "do-it-yourself" approach—and no teacher was apparently necessary here. Prensky characterized traditional educators as old-fashioned, out of touch, stuck in old thinking. Such accounts treat learning as if it involves nothing more than personal creativity and invention, which can derive no substantial or fundamental benefit of any sort from input from anyone else, least of all from "old" knowledge. In this way expertise of all kinds, especially that embodied by teachers and mentors, is debased, devalued, and treated as some sort of optional extra.

The contrast between this picture of learning and the picture painted in my three cameos is a stark one. In all of my three cameos, there is the strong presence of "someone who knows better," an expert of some sort, who has several clear roles and intervenes in various ways, not as an optional extra but at the heart of the process. One of these roles is to organize and prepare the learning experience for the learner, to scaffold it (Wood, Bruner & Ross, 1976; Cazden, 1983), checking learning in the process. A second role is to model behavior which the learner might eventually follow, in terms of demonstrating both a critical dimension and a rigor in dealing with sources of knowledge, and also exemplifying a methodical and cautious mode of expressing ideas to others. A final role is that of challenging and contradicting as a means of stimulating the reformulation of a student's ideas, and self-critique. If these roles are crucially important parts of the nondigital educational process, why are they not treated as essential in digital education also?

The value of these educational elements (which I bracket for the sake of convenience under the umbrella of "expert interventions") has, of course, been considered by others (e.g., avowed digital skeptics such as Brabazon, 2002 and Keen, 2007), and indeed by authors in this volume (see e.g., Kop & Bouchard; Pegrum). So I am by no means the first to point out that the mere ability of Web 2.0 technologies to provide access to a cornucopia of information, along with a myriad of resources for participation and interaction, is not enough for education. Students also need some sort of "information literacy" (Pegrum, this volume), including an ability to critique and evaluate. This seems relatively uncontentious.

However, what is often missing in accounts of digital education is any analysis of how exactly students can in practice cultivate this critical faculty and use it consistently. If we recall my third cameo, in which students from a school in Leeds examined three websites, we remember that they at first swallowed completely and uncritically the lies and distortions which those sites pedaled. In other words, even students who are "Digital Natives" in Prensky's view, and use the web every day, do not necessarily have the necessary critical faculties, built in. It is apparent that if students are simply to be left to their own devices, even in interaction with other students, they may not develop an appropriately critical perspective quickly or at all. On the contrary, they seem to see the Web as highly authoritative, a source of unquestioned wisdom and truth. So the question for digital educators must be, if we accept that learners need a far greater criticality, how are they to develop it?

Pegrum suggests one approach reminiscent of the Leeds lesson, in which teachers could highlight the fraudulent nature of "spoof websites," and use that as a basis for showing students how to deal critically with such online material. This is a useful starting point for information literacy. But I would argue that in digital education we need to make the point far more strongly and explicitly that such critical skepticism needs to be developed through extensive human guidance. We then need to discuss in greater detail how precisely students are to learn this criticality.

To put it another way, digital educators need to reassert the importance of their role as experts, and reassert the importance of intervening as appropriate in order to take learning to the next level (Pegrum, 2009).

Web 3.0, the global brain, and the wisdom of crowds

If we share Prensky's optimism about technology, could we perhaps hope that the Web will do the job for us in future? We are told that Web 3.0 will be smarter than Web 2.0, so perhaps it will provide the kind of expert educational interventions I am arguing for?

The jury is still out on what precisely Web 3.0 will be, but here is one definition:

> [Web 3.0 is] a third phase in the evolution of the World Wide Web, based on the idea that the Internet "understands" the pieces of information it stores and is able to make logical connections between them.
> (http://www.macmillandictionary.com)

It is said that Web 3.0 will be, among other things, "The Intelligent Web" (Spivack, 2007), and perhaps the process has already started, since "an essential part of Web 2.0 is harnessing collective intelligence, turning the web into a kind of global brain" (http://oreilly.com). The general idea behind this seems to be that if we can link up millions of ideas and pieces of information from blogs, wikis, and so on, and build connections (such as "tags") between them, then Web 3.0 will become a sort of pulsating global intelligence in itself.

Underlying this thinking is the concept sometimes known as "crowd-sourcing," implying "that a large group of people can create a collective work whose value far exceeds that provided by any of the individual participants" (O'Reilly & Batelle, 2009, p. 2). In turn the assumption here is that—as Surowiecki (2005) suggests in his book *The Wisdom of Crowds*—a larger group will always be more intelligent that an "elite few." Note that traditional expertise, personified as "an elite few," has once again been explicitly demoted, on the assumption that the wisdom of the masses is better than any smaller group of experts. The eventual vision seems to be to replace human expertise (apparently now in the hands of a sinister coterie of "elite" experts) with a "democratic" global digital brain. Human expertise will be dead at last. Long live digital intelligence.

The limits of technology

Before we get too enthusiastic, however, perhaps we need to ask whether, in terms of education, such a brainy digital creature will really be able to do the job we need it to do? Can technology, as well as offering the first two ingredients I set out above, namely access to information and the chance for interaction and participation, also be able fully to provide the other three ingredients, offering the kind of expert interventions I am calling for?

If we need to look beyond the hype of Web 2.0 technologies as a panacea for education, going "beyond the wow factor" (to borrow a phrase from Murray & Barnes, 1998), I suggest we need to be even more cautious with any claims for Web 3.0 in future. In my view, even if "collective intelligence" results in large collections of facts and pieces of information, tagged together at great speed, this is a long way from the kinds of expert scaffolding, modeling, and other interventions I consider important to the educational process. In the first place, collective thinking often leads to enormous stupidity and failure, not intelligence, as the recent global banking crises demonstrates. Furthermore, if we consider the three cameos again, what the teachers offered in those scenarios was not simply a host of information of the kind that a Web 3.0 "global brain" might aspire to, nor mere opportunities for interaction and participation. Those educators offered qualitatively different interventions (scaffolding learning; modeling behavior; challenging and contradicting, among others), of a kind which no technology is yet even close to offering.

In the case of scaffolding, it may be that to some extent technologies can assist in this, but at the moment they are still a long way short of what a sensitive and aware human educator can offer. In terms of modeling behavior, it is difficult to envisage how any technology could offer this type of model in a way which even approximates to human behavior, particularly if we consider the back-and-forth daily modeling which a professional classroom teacher provides. In terms of challenging and contradicting, I suggest that the kind of sensitivity and tact needed for this role, the ability to value a student's opinion and yet sensitively to contradict it, challenge it and take the learner to the next step, is well beyond any technology as currently visualized, and probably always will be. This is in addition to the human, emotional, and social dimensions, and the value of face-to-face human interaction, which are central to many significant educational experiences.

The upshot is that for full educational normalization of Web technologies in the service of learning, we need a carefully planned and structured blending of what Web technologies can do effectively (such as offering access to information and opportunities for interaction) with an equal or greater weight given to areas where human educators can operate better, for example the kinds of expert interventions I have outlined. This means as a first step avoiding simplistic "technicist" notions that the technology can or should do everything without human involvement. There should be no place in education for imprudent exaggerations of what technology can actually achieve, nor for attempts to cut out human elements for reasons of cost or convenience.

Secondly, it requires us to plan and research the ways in which such a mix of roles can best operate in each educational setting and circumstance. Learners must be given both the opportunities for access to ideas and interaction that technology can furnish, and also full access to human experts confident in their role, able to scaffold, assess, model, and challenge or even contradict when appropriate, in a suitably sensitive and timely manner. The technology and the human must work together equally.

This broad perspective on the role of the education as a dialogical process chimes well with how Kop and Bouchard (this volume) describe Freire's perspective on the role of the teacher in education. Importantly, Freire felt that "this capacity for critical engagement is not present if educators are reduced to facilitators" and this is surely true. Although it is now a commonplace, as was noted above, that teachers can usefully act as "facilitators" whose aim is to make learning easier, they should surely also, in their important role of challengers and contradictors, make students' lives more difficult at times, as a means of stimulating them to rethink simplistic or ill-developed views. They might do this by questioning, challenging, and contradicting. This may seem at odds with much of contemporary writing on education, which seems to favor comfort and ease; however, it is surely true that if educators are to lead students beyond their comfort zones, toward truly distinctive and creative areas of thinking and understanding, then this element of challenge must be part of their role. Teachers as facilitators sometimes, but as *difficultators* too, when the need arises.

Let me put it plainly: I consider that those writers who recommend the accommodation approach to digital education, telling educators simply to change our practice to "accommodate" to our students' tastes and habits, fundamentally misunderstand and misrepresent both the aims and processes of effective quality education. I would argue for an education which is not "learner-centered" but "learning-centered." This is because education is not the same thing as entertainment, and nor is it a commodity whose sole criterion and ambition is sales, smiles, and satisfaction. Those who treat it as such, in my view, fail catastrophically to understand even the rudiments of the role of education in human growth and in society at large. As digital educators, we should resist them.

Conclusion: Beyond the "Wow" factor

My aim in this chapter is not to be a luddite, to destroy technology and go back to traditional modes of education. My intention instead is to argue that although technology, in particular the Web, can offer some impressive ingredients for learning, particularly in terms of access to information and to means of interaction, those ingredients in themselves are not enough, despite the apparent hype to the contrary. I would argue that too much attention has been paid to those elements, in the media and also at times in academic and educational research, on the mistaken assumption that they alone will do the job. Educational experts in this vision are thereby demoted, treated as some sort of authoritarian and dictatorial force for repression, to be "bypassed" and sidelined, labeled as simple facilitators, mere waiters at someone else's banquet. This, in my view, is to misrepresent the crucial role of expertise, and the importance of sensitive and appropriate expert human intervention, in the wider educational process.

The Web is crowded with loud voices, many of which are calling in the direction of ease, access, interaction, participation, and fun. But we need to be aware that often, "if you peak behind the Web 2.0 blog and wiki curtain . . . you'll find the man pulling the levers is either an enterprise vendor or an analyst eager to sell to business customers" (Clarke, 2006, n.p.). Such forces tend to make us forget about the more challenging aspects of our role, and the importance of these more challenging behaviors to the endeavor of digital education as a whole. It is too easy to be seduced by apparently more friendly and more popular elements of education, which might be cheaper to provide and may get higher satisfaction ratings and wider smiles in the short term. But I suggest that unless digital educators can resist these blandishments, and keep faithful to the fundamental elements of what makes education different from entertainment, which includes intervention, challenge, and critique even when these are unpopular, we run the risk of failing our own profession, and in the long run of failing our learners too.

References

Allford, D., & N. Pachler (2007). *Language, autonomy and the new learning environments*. Bern: Peter Lang.

Appleyard, B. (2008). Stoooopid . . . why the Google generation isn't as smart as it thinks. *The Sunday Times*, July 20. Retrieved July 10, 2010, from http://technology.timesonline.co.uk/.

Bax, S. (2003). CALL—past, present and future. *System, 31*(1), 13–28.

Bax, S. (2010). Magic wand or museum piece? The future of the interactive whiteboard in education. In M. Thomas & E. Cutrim Schmid (Eds.), *Interactive whiteboards for education: Theory, research and practice* (pp. 264–277). Hershey, PA: Information Science Reference.

Bijker, W. (1997). *Of bicycles, bakelites, and bulbs: Toward a theory of sociotechnical change*. Cambridge, MA: MIT Press.

Cazden, C. B. (1983). Adult assistance to language development: Scaffolds, models, and direct instruction. In R. P. Parker & F. A. Davis (Eds.), *Developing literacy: Young children's use of language* (pp. 3–17). Newark, DE: International Reading Association.

Chambers, A., & Bax, S. (2006). Making CALL work: Towards normalization. *System, 34*, 465–479.

Clarke, G. (2006). Berners-Lee calls for Web 2.0 calm. *The Register*. Retrieved August 10, 2010, from http://www.theregister.co.uk/2006/08/30/web_20_berners_lee/Hansson, T. (Ed.) (2008). Handbook of research on digital information technologies: Innovations, methods and ethical issues. Hershey, PA.: ISR

Keen, A. (2007). *The cult of the amateur: How the democratization of the digital world is assaulting our economy, our culture, and our values*. New York: Doubleday Currency.

Kennedy, G., Dalgarno, B., Gray, K., Judd, T., Waycott, J., Bennett, S., Maton, K., Krause, K. L., Bishop, A., Chang, R., & Churchward A. (2007). The net generation are not big users of Web 2.0 technologies: Preliminary findings. In *ICT: Providing choices for learners and learning. Proceedings Ascilite Singapore 2007.* Retrieved July 10, 2010, from http://www.ascilite.org.au/ conferences/ singapore07/procs/kennedy.pdf

Lorenzo, G., Oblinger, D., & Dziuban, C. (2007). How choice, co-creation, and culture are changing what it means to be net savvy. *Educause Quarterly, 30*(1). Retrieved May 10, 2010, from http://www.educause.edu/ EDUCAUSE+Quarterly/EDUCAUSEQuarterlyMagazineVolum/HowChoice CoCreationandCultureA/157434

Murray, L., & Barnes, A. (1998). Beyond the "wow" factor—evaluating multimedia language learning software from a pedagogical viewpoint. *System, 26*, 249–259.

O'Reilly, T., & Battelle, J. (2009). Web squared: Web 2.0 five years on. Retrieved July 10, 2010, from http://assets.en.oreilly.com/1/event/28/web2009_websquared-whitepaper.pdf

Pegrum, M. (2009). *From blogs to bombs: The future of digital technologies in education.* Crawley, Western Australia: UWA Publishing.

Prensky, M. (2001). Digital natives, digital immigrants. *On the Horizon, 9*(5), 1–6.

Rogers, E. (1995). *Diffusion of innovations* (4th ed.). New York: Free Press.

Spivack, N. (2007). The third-generation web—Web 3.0. Retrieved February 7, 2010, http://www.intentblog.com/archives/2007/02/nova_spivack_th.html

Strickland, J. (2007). How web 2.0 works. Retrieved July 19, 2010, from http:// computer.howstuffworks.com/web-20.htm

Surowiecki, J (2005). *The wisdom of crowds.* New York: Random House.

Teachers TV (2006). Secondary ICT–Web Literacy. Retrieved July 10, 2010, from http://www.teachers.tv/ videos/secondary-ict-web-literacy

Wood, D. J., Bruner, J. S., & Ross, G. (1976). The role of tutoring in problem solving. *Journal of Child Psychiatry and Psychology, 17*(2), 89–100.

Contributors

Philip Banyard is a reader in psychology at Nottingham Trent University, UK, and has recently been involved in a number of national research projects on the impact of technology on learning. Along with his interest in research, he has been influential in the teaching of psychology at a national level in the UK. For twenty years, he was a chief examiner for national examinations in psychology and he has also published several textbooks for psychology students.

Stephen Bax is reader in English language, learning, assessment and technology at CRELLA (Centre for Research in English Language Learning and Assessment) at the University of Bedfordshire, UK. At CRELLA, he is involved in a variety of areas of applied linguistic research, including the use of computers in language learning (CALL), the use of computers in language testing (CALT), and areas of discourse including computer mediated discourse analysis (CMDA). He teaches on the MA in applied linguistics and supervises research students. He previously taught in the Arab world, Latin America, and East Asia. He has recently completed a book entitled *Discourse and Genre* for Palgrave Macmillan.

Thomas Berger has been director of the Institute of interdisciplinary Research (inter.research e.V.) in Fulda, Germany, since 1999. During this time, he has been involved in a number of research and innovation projects in the areas of e-learning and computer-supported cooperative learning. His current research interests include topics such as mobile and game-based learning approaches and their influence on the learning culture of educational organizations. He received his diploma degree in applied computer science in 1999 at the University of Applied Sciences in Fulda and developed his research interest in learning (foreign languages) and training (intercultural competences) with new media in the Department of Social and Cultural Sciences.

Petra Wiyakti Bodrogini is an ICT training manager in the Education Development Center (EDC), Jakarta, working on the USAID-funded Decentralized Basic Education (DBE) 2 project. She received an S-1 (bachelor) degree in psychology from Gadjah Mada University, Indonesia, and an MSc in social psychology from the London School of Economics and Political Science, UK, under the British Chevening Award. Prior to joining EDC, she was a lecturer and program coordinator in the Psychology Department at Universitas Widya Dharma, Central Java, Indonesia. Her research interests are in teaching, learning, community development work, and research in the public, academic, and private sectors. She is now managing Active Learning with ICTs and distance education programs for teacher trainers at primary level, as well as facilitating online professional development programs for lecturers of university partners across seven project provinces.

Paul Bouchard is graduate program director of adult education at Concordia University (Montreal) in Canada. His research interests are self-direction in learning, mediated learning environments, educational policy, and international cooperation. Dr. Bouchard has been president of the Canadian Association for Research in Adult Education (CASAE/ACÉÉA). He has acted as a consultant in the areas of educational curriculum, teacher training, and supervision for the governments of Quebec, Haiti, and Mali. He has also worked on educational projects in Tunisia and Ecuador. He is currently reviewer for CJSAE, SSHRC, FQRSC, and CIRIEC-España. His first undergraduate degree was in music performance.

Kelli S. Burns is an assistant professor in the School of Mass Communications at the University of South Florida. Her research interests include social media use in public relations; the intersection of social media and popular culture; and online and user-generated advertising. She is the author of the 2009 book *Celeb 2.0: How Social Media Foster Our Fascination with Popular Culture*. Her research has been published in the *Journal of Advertising, Journal of New Communications Research, Newspaper Research Journal*, and the *International Journal of Interactive Marketing and Advertising*. Burns received a doctorate in mass communication from the University of Florida where she was a presidential fellow, a master's degree in mass communication from Middle Tennessee State University, and a bachelor's degree in mathematics and business administration from Vanderbilt University.

Mary Burns has been involved in education since 1984 when she first began teaching French in Kingston, Jamaica. In the early 1990s, she used her one Apple IIE to help her 8th grade Latin students better understand content and concluded her teaching career in 2004 in a 1:1 environment at the Tecnológico de Monterrey in México. Since 1997, she has worked to help teachers in the United States, Africa, the Middle East, and México better understand how digital technologies can improve teaching and learning and has helped government agencies plan for and use instructional technology. Since 2007, she has focused on the use of ICT in Asia, primarily in Indonesia. She has conducted research and published widely on instructional technology and teachers' uses of technology.

Chaka Chaka is a senior lecturer and coordinator of the English Unit within the Department of Humanities Education at Walter Sisulu University, South Africa. He previously taught at the University of the Free State (South Africa). His research interests include the following areas: computer-mediated communication (CMC); electronic learning (e-learning); computer-assisted language learning (CALL); mobile learning (m-learning); mobile assisted language learning (MALL); Web 2.0 learning/Mobile Web 2.0 learning; Web 3.0/Mobile Web 3.0 learning; Semantic Web learning/Mobile Semantic Web learning; online genre and discourse analysis; knowledge management (KM); and learning organization (LO). He has published book chapters related to each of these research areas.

Cristina Costa is a member of the central research team at Salford University in the UK. Her role is to champion innovative means of convening and disseminating research activity, and promote collaborative research ventures with the use of new web technologies. Her research focuses on the use of information and communication technologies in a changing environment and she has a particular interested in analyzing the advantages and also the implications of using the social web for teaching, learning and research.

Dafne González has been an EFL/ESP teacher for more than 30 years. She graduated in language teaching, has a masters degree in applied linguistics, and a PhD in education. She has coordinated the Graduate Studies in Education Programs and has been the head of the Specialization in Informatics and Education at Universidad Simón Bolívar in Caracas, Venezuela. A webhead since 2002, she has been the lead coordinator of the TESOL Electronic Village Online (EVO) since 2006, and comoderator of the EVO Becoming a Webhead (BaW) online Workshop since 2004. She has also been teaching the course

"Teaching Vocabulary and Grammar Online" for the TESOL Principles and Practices of Online Teaching Certificate Program since 2004. She was a member of the TESOL Technology Advisory Committee, and is now member of the TESOL CALL-IS Steering Committee. Currently, she is the head of the Spanish Program for Languagelife (a project of Languagelab.com) in Second Life.

Lianne Kerlin has recently completed a degree in psychology and is currently working as a research associate within the psychology department at Nottingham Trent University, UK. The two most recent projects she has worked on while in this position include the "Narrowing the Gap" Becta project alongside Jean Underwood and Phil Banyard, and the "Heart to Heart" Heart Research UK project.

Rita Kop has been a researcher for the National Research Council Canada's Institute for Information Technology since September 2009. She has been involved at all levels of technology integration in adult education from early adoption of e-learning in adult education and university classrooms to advanced technology applications in small and medium enterprises and community education centers. Her current research focuses on human learning in educational networked systems on the NRC Personal Learning Environment Project. Before Dr. Kop joined the NRC she was an assistant professor at Swansea University in the UK after a career as a teacher and headteacher in Dutch primary education. Her research interests are personalized learning, distance education and informal networked learning.

Cristina Palomeque holds a masters degree in Teaching English as a Foreign Language from the Universitat Pompeu Fabra (UPF) in Barcelona. She is currently a doctoral student in the Department of Language and Literature Education at the Universitat de Barcelona (UB) and also works as a lecturer in the Department of Language and Literature Education. Her research is focused on computer-assisted language learning (CALL). She is currently carrying out research in the study of interaction and learning processes which occur in foreign language learning/teaching contexts in 3D virtual worlds as well as through web 2.0 tools.

Mark Pegrum is an assistant professor in the Graduate School of Education at the University of Western Australia, where he teaches mainly in the area of e-learning. His research focuses on the increasing integration of Web 2.0 and mobile technologies into everyday life, and examines the pedagogical, social, and sociopolitical implications of phenomena such as blogs and wikis, podcasts and video mashups, social networking sites, and virtual worlds. His most recent book is *From Blogs to Bombs: The Future of Digital Technologies in Education* (2009). He currently teaches in Perth, Hong Kong, and Singapore and has given presentations on e-learning in Australia and New Zealand, East and Southeast Asia, and the UK and Europe.

Joannah Portman Daley is a doctoral candidate in Writing and Rhetoric at the University of Rhode Island, completing a research study that explores the intersections of digital literacy, social media, and civic engagement. She also serves as associate director of technology for the Writing and Rhetoric Department. Joannah regularly teaches Writing in Electronic Environments, a course dedicated to exploring renewed conceptions of writing inspired by digital technologies, as well as classes in first-year writing and writing for community service. She has presented on the curricular incorporation of Web 2.0 pedagogies at numerous international conferences.

James Stiller is a lecturer in psychology at Nottingham Trent University. His research interests include a broad range of topics, from technology use in the classroom to human–animal interactions. He is an expert on the structure and functions of networks and was responsible for the network analyses on the research project "Narrowing the Gap."

Paul Sweeney is an independent consultant with a strong background in educational technology, language teaching, and virtual worlds. In various guises, he has designed and project-managed global projects in IT teacher training, student communities, and web-based courseware development and learning management system deployment. In his previous role as director of education for Languagelab.com, he oversaw teacher training, content creation for formal and informal learning programs, and all course delivery across English and Spanish programs. He is an influential and sought after speaker at international conferences.

Michael Thomas is director of the MA TESOL by e-learning and lectures in digital business communication and CALL at the University of Central Lancashire, UK. Among his publications are *Handbook of Research on Web 2.0 and Second Language Learning* (2009), *Interactive Whiteboards for Education: Theory, Research and Practice* (with E. C. Schmid) (2010), *Task-Based Language Learning & Teaching with Technology* (with H. Reinders) (2010), and *Online Learning* (2011). He is editor of the *International Journal of Virtual and Personal Learning Environments* and has guest edited special editions of the *Australasian*

Journal of Educational Technology and the *International Journal of Emerging Technologies and Society.*

Jean Underwood, professor of psychology at Nottingham Trent University in the UK, has extensive experience of research and evaluation work in ICT in education and, although well known for her expertise in quantitative methods, has extensive experience in qualitative research techniques. She has lead on a number of national projects involving the implementation and evaluation of e-learning, of which "Narrowing the Gap" is one. Since 1998, she has been editor of the journal *Computers in Education.*

Index